ABRAHAM LINCOLN'S

POLITICAL FAITH

ABRAHAM LINCOLN'S

POLITICAL FAITH

Joseph R. Fornieri

NORTHERN

ILLINOIS

UNIVERSITY

PRESS

DeKalb

Library of Congress Cataloging-in-Publication Data

Fornieri, Joseph R.

Abraham Lincoln's political faith / Joseph R. Fornieri.

p.   cm.

Enlargement of author's thesis (doctoral), 1996.

Includes bibliographical references (p.) and index.

ISBN 10: 0-87580-605-8 (alk. paper) (pbk.)

ISBN 13: 978-0-87580-605-1 (alk. paper) (pbk.)

ISBN 0-87580-315-6 (alk. paper) (cloth)

1. Lincoln, Abraham, 1809–1865—Political and social views. 2. Lincoln, Abraham,

1809–1865—Religion. 3. United States—Politics and government—1861–1865.

4. Political theology—United States—History—19th century. 7. Religion and politics—

United States—History—19th century. 7. Religion and politics—United States—

19th century. I. Title.

E457.2 .F73 2003

973.7'092—dc21

2002040996

To my loving and wise parents, Joseph P. and Beatrice A. Fornieri,

and to my girls, all three of them:

My wife, Pam, and my two daughters, Isabella and Natalie.

CONTENTS

ACKNOWLEDGMENTS

This book began as a doctoral dissertation written in 1996. I would like to express my gratitude to my teachers and friends at the Catholic University of America, David Walsh, Philip G. Henderson, and Claes G. Ryn; to my editor, Martin Johnson, for his outstanding professionalism, guidance, and enthusiasm; and to Kevin Butterfield, Sarah Atkinson, and Susan Bean. It was a pleasure working with Northern Illinois University Press.

Thanks to my wife, Pamela D. Fornieri, for her loving support and patience throughout the years; to my parents, Joseph P. and Beatrice A. Fornieri; to my in-laws, Richard and Alice Hawkins; and to Uncle Carl "Carlo" Silvio, my elder sibling.

Thanks to John Murley, my indefatigable chairman and the Captain of Political Science at the Rochester Institute of Technology; to Dean Andrew Moore; and to my wonderful colleagues and friends in Liberal Arts at RIT, especially Doris Borrelli, *cugina mia,* for reading the manuscript and for her excellent suggestions.

Thanks to Father Ernest Fortin for his support while I was at Boston College from 1989 to 1991, to Father Robert Sokowlowski, to Frank J. Williams, to David E. Long, to David Hein, to William D. Pederson, and to Deborah Evans and Harold Holzer for their assistance with the cover photo.

And a special thanks to Kenneth L. Deutsch for reviewing this work over the summer of 2001, and for his continued guidance and friendship throughout the years—that is, *amicitia,* in St. Thomas's sense of the word.

ABRAHAM LINCOLN'S

POLITICAL FAITH

Taking up the anti-slavery ordinance of 1787, that had been applied to all the North-west Territory, Mr. Lincoln presented that act of the fathers of our republic, the vindicators of our liberty, and the framers of our government, as the *best* exposition of their views of slavery as an institution. It was also a most striking commentary of their political faith, and showed how the views of those political sages, to whom we owe liberty, government, and all, comported with the new-fangled doctrines of popular rights, invented in these degenerate latter days to cloak the spread of slavery.

—Lincoln's Speech at Springfield,

October 4, 1854,

as reported by the *Illinois Journal*

Chapter One

LINCOLN AND
AMERICAN CIVIL THEOLOGY

The Civil War was precipitated by two irreconcilable visions of the American dream vying for the nation's soul. Paradoxically, both North and South claimed to be fighting for liberty, but meant contradictory things by the term. For the South, liberty meant the right of sovereign states to secede in defense of the moral, religious, and constitutional right to slavery. For the North, it meant the God-given right of each to enjoy the fruits of his or her own labor under the auspices of a national Union. Two radically opposed understandings of the people's rights and liberties were proclaimed to be sanctioned by the same God. More profoundly than any of his contemporaries, Abraham Lincoln discerned that the national ordeal stemmed from a fundamental breakdown over the moral grounding of the first principles of American republicanism:

> The world has never had a good definition of the word liberty, and the American people, just now, are much in want of one. We all declare for liberty; but in using the same *word* we do not all mean the same *thing*. With some the word liberty may mean for each man to do as he pleases with himself, and the product of his labor; while with others the same word may mean for some men to do as they please with other men, and the product of other men's labor. Here are two, not only different, but incompatable things, called by the same name—liberty. And it follows that each of the things is, by the respective parties, called by two different and incompatable names—liberty and tyranny.[1]

Lincoln viewed the politics of the Civil War era in terms of civil theology. He interpreted the conflict over slavery as a struggle between rival moral justifications of the American regime competing for public authoritativeness. Northern and southern extremists alike appealed to the absolute claims of religion in their apocalyptic condemnations of one another. The distinguished historian of American religion Sydney E. Ahlstrom explains: "When the cannons roared in Charleston harbor, therefore, two divinely authorized crusades were set in motion, each of them absolutizing a given social and political order. The pulpits resounded with a vehemence and absence of restraint never equaled in American history." To be sure, each side girded itself with the Bible to vindicate its particular vision of American public life.

Lincoln pondered this irony in his Second Inaugural Address at the conclusion of the war:

> Both read the same Bible, and pray to the same God; and each invokes His aid against the other. It may seem strange that any men should dare ask a just God's assistance in wringing their bread from the sweat of other men's faces; but let us judge not that we be not judged. The prayers of both could not be answered; that of neither has been answered fully. The Almighty has His own purposes.[2]

By "invoking the favor and guidance of Almighty God" in their new Confederate Constitution, southerners believed that they had remedied a defect of the Constitution of 1787, whose silence about God, in their view, resulted in the corruption, infidelity, and fanaticism of the North. The southern defense of slave society relied upon a divinely sanctioned right of mastery over others for its legitimacy; and it implied a corresponding critique of northern free society as decadent and heretical. "The motto of the Confederacy, *Deo vindice* (God will avenge), spoke to the South's self-identity as a Christian nation," observes historian Ronald C. White, Jr. While Presbyterian divines of the South like Frederick Ross preached that slavery was "ordained by God" and should be publicly accepted as a divine curse upon the black race, radical abolitionists of the North like William Lloyd Garrison proclaimed that there could be "no Union with slaveholders" and reviled the Constitution as "a covenant with death, and an agreement with hell" for its concessions to the institution. Even the "Little Giant," Stephen A. Douglas, Lincoln's nemesis from Illinois who decried the mixing of religion and politics, toted the weight of the Bible to justify popular sovereignty's ethical neutrality toward slavery. Appealing to Matthew 7:1 ("judge not lest ye be judged"), Douglas urged citizens to refrain from making any judgments about slavery's inherent good or evil. He believed that this ethically neutral approach to conflict resolution would remove the root cause of sectional strife: the divisiveness of moral absolutes in politics. In sum, each of the foregoing alternatives propounded during the Civil War era—the proslavery theology of Ross, the radical abolitionism of Garrison, and the popular sovereignty of Douglas— defended its particular interpretation of American public life through an appeal to religious norms. Each attempted to mold the climate of public opinion consonant with its own conception of the public good. Indeed, each claimed to provide the most authoritative interpretation of American political order.[3]

In response to the rival accounts of American republicanism proffered during the Civil War era, Abraham Lincoln articulated the most compelling justification of popular government ever given to the world. His name has become virtually synonymous with democracy, a form of government he concisely defined as being "of the people, by the people, for the people." Lincoln, however, has been characterized not only as the paragon of democracy but also as the exemplar of American civil theology, because he discerned so profoundly that political order derives its legitimacy from an ultimate, transcendent order. His ability to pursue the logic of public policies to their underlying moral foundations is of enduring significance to American political thought.[4]

The twin characterizations of Lincoln as the preeminent representative of American democracy and of American civil theology are actually correlative. Lincoln's reflections on democracy implied a wider theological reflection on the moral grounding and destiny of American self-government. He understood that claims for and against slavery and the Union were themselves predicated upon a more comprehensive vision of God, history, human nature, and society. His defense of democracy was informed by a transcendent standard. In his view, a legitimate republican government was bound to and limited by the universal moral law revealed by God in the Bible, known through human reason, and promulgated by the Declaration.

Lincoln's articulation of American republicanism was profoundly imbued by a biblical ethos. He maintained that "the good old maxims of the Bible are applicable, and truly applicable to human affairs." He thus spoke of the nation's "political faith" and "the sacred history of republican America." As a young man, he extolled a "political religion" that would elicit reverence for the laws. Defending "the early faith of the republic" against the heresy of popular sovereignty, he upheld "those sacred principles enunciated by our fathers." Repudiating the Kansas-Nebraska Act of 1854, he proclaimed, "my ancient faith teaches me that 'all men are created equal.'" And at Peoria, he called for a restoration of "the national faith." Lamenting the transformation of public opinion on slavery from the initial toleration of the institution as a necessary evil, to its subsequent justification as a social and political blessing, he warned, "Little by little, but steadily as man's march to the grave, we have been giving up the OLD for the NEW faith." In effect, Lincoln characterized the struggle over slavery as one between competing political faiths.[5]

Lincoln envisioned the Declaration of Independence as a moral covenant that promulgated the first principles of the nation's political faith. The principles of the Declaration were sacred and therefore worthy of reverence because they constituted a rational expression of humankind's participation in the divine law that governs the universe. Slavery was wrong because it was "universally granted to be, in the abstract, a gross outrage of the law of nature." In sum, Lincoln interpreted the Declaration of Independence as a declaration of the precepts of natural law. The authority of the people was not self-legitimating but was derived from the supreme authority of God: clearly, the will of the people could be right or wrong depending on whether it corresponded to an ultimate standard of right and justice. Without the foundation of transcendence to provide a stable rule and measure for judging and guiding public life, democracy was morally indistinguishable from despotism and "the will of the stronger." Natural rights were antecedent to government because they came from the hand of the Creator as their unshakable foundation. They were not the gift of government but of God. Human beings were entitled to such rights by virtue of their very humanity, not by an act of their state. Indeed, this natural-law understanding of rights and correlative duties was clearly articulated by John Dickinson, one of the founders at the Constitutional Convention from Pennsylvania, who stated during the Revolution: "Our liberties do not come from charters; for these are only the declarations of preexisting rights. They do not depend on parchments or seals; but come from the King of Kings and the Lord of all the earth."[6]

Because he understood the Declaration as the regime's political Decalogue, Lincoln regarded the moral approbation of slavery as comparable to infidelity, and he likened it metaphorically to the Jews' breaking their covenant with God and embracing the idolatry of the golden calf. By attempting to justify slavery as consistent with the principles of democratic government, Americans were guilty of a spurious and base "moral equivalency" that failed to discriminate between a popular government bound by legitimate moral ends and a popular government that merely substituted the despotism of the king with the despotism of the white majority. Thus, Lincoln reminded his generation that they were "descending from the high republican faith of our ancestors, to repudiate that principle and to declare by the highest act of our government that we have no longer a choice between freedom and slavery—that both are equal with us."[7]

It must be emphasized that Lincoln's account of American political order was formulated not as an abstract doctrine but as a concrete historical response to the rival civil theologies or "political faiths" of proslavery theology, popular sovereignty, and radical abolitionism that competed to shape the public mind during the Civil War era. Because his political thought combined the biblical tradition of Judeo-Christianity and the American republican tradition of self-government, it may be described as biblical republicanism. It is the purpose of this book to analyze Lincoln's biblical republicanism as constituted by the mutual and complementary influence of reason and revelation. The term "biblical republicanism" is my characterization of Lincoln's civil theological interpretation of American public life. It denotes his irreducible combination of the biblical and republican traditions as a symbolic form of political order that is sui generis. Though Lincoln himself never used the term, I believe it accurately describes the religious and moral outlook that informed his political thinking.[8]

A familiarity with the concept of civil theology will enhance an understanding of Lincoln's biblical republicanism. Civil theology—those deep-seated beliefs, norms, and practices that constitute a regime's political culture—is tantamount to the supreme moral justification that guides public life.[9] Scholars of American civil theology agree that Abraham Lincoln is its preeminent exemplar. Indeed, for a statesman whose life was devoted primarily to political action, Lincoln's reflections on politics were both philosophical and theological.[10]

The concept of civil theology has been described in related, though not identical, terms as a "civil religion," "political creed," "political religion," "moral consensus," "public philosophy," and "political theology." Common among all these descriptions is the view that civil theology represents some binding, all-encompassing moral vision of public life affirmed by the regime. The etymology of the term is instructive; it originates from the Latin words *"civilis"* (an adjective denoting citizens, civilian or political) and *"theologia"* (a noun meaning theology). Taken together, these words denote a theology that pertains to public life. The adjective *"civilis"* specifies a certain kind of theology, one that is proper to the citizen and civic life; and the union of *"civilis"* with *"theologia"* implies a coincidence between religion and politics.[11]

Civil theology situates public life within a wider horizon that includes God, history, humanity, and society. It undertstands political order to be derived from a divine order that constitutes the supreme basis of moral obligation: political norms and aspirations are thus sanctioned by a religiously grounded faith. Christopher Lasch evokes the concept of civil theology when he states, "A people's way of life has to be embedded in 'sacred order'—that is, in a conception of the universe, ultimately a religious conception, that tells us 'what is not to be done.'" Dedication to this "sacred order" not only constitutes the shared basis of civility but also invests public life with meaning, purpose, and direction.[12]

Civil theology conveys a shared notion of public life by affirming and defending the fundamental political norms of the regime. It defines a people's collective identity by providing a sense of historical continuity that links the deeds of the past, the circumstances of the present, and the aspirations of the future. By so doing, it mirrors and sanctions the collective memories, loves, and hopes that bind *(religare)* citizens together to some shared public good. Indeed, civil theology reflects the very ethos of a nation. Whether implicitly or explicitly, it answers the "why?" of public life and expresses the crowning purpose or goal of political existence. It is, in fact, tantamount to society's self-interpretation. Because political institutions alone do not fully manifest the spirit of a people, the character of a regime is best revealed in light of its end (telos), the conception of justice affirmed by its civil theology.[13]

Civil theology seems to involve a dangerous fusion of religion and politics that should give pause to citizens in a free republic. If unbalanced, the interaction between religion and politics implicit to the concept of civil theology may corrupt the integrity of both spiritual and temporal realms.[14] Historically, the confounding of these realms has either sanctified politics or politicized religion, resulting in sectarian intolerance, millenarian crusades, and secular messiahs. Thus, civil theology presents a dilemma: on the one hand, it views the public appeal to religious norms as inevitable, since the morality that steers politics must rely upon some ultimate foundation for its legitimacy; on the other, its combination of religion and politics appears to be highly combustible, like mixing gasoline and fire. For this reason, the dynamic tension between religion and politics has posed an enduring question to Western political thinkers who have sought a proper balance between the two realms of temporal and transcendent authority. Indeed, the historical lineage of civil theology in the West can be traced from antiquity (Plato, Cicero, Varro) through the Middle Ages (Augustine, Aquinas) and into the modern era (Machiavelli, Hobbes, Spinoza, Rousseau).[15]

Despite more recent developments that have led to the strong secularization of American culture, a number of important scholars continue to recognize the influential role of religion in American public life.[16] In his renowned work *Civil Religion in America,* Robert N. Bellah maintains that "the separation of church and state has not denied the political realm a religious dimension. . . . This public religious dimension is expressed in a set of beliefs, symbols, and rituals that I am calling the American civil religion." Bellah observes that the notion of sovereignty in American politics is derived ultimately from God:

> In American political theory, sovereignty rests, of course with the people, but implicitly, and often explicitly, the ultimate sovereignty has been attributed to God. This is the meaning of the motto, "In God we trust," as well as the inclusion of the phrase "under God" in the pledge of the flag. What difference does it make that sovereignty belongs to God? Though the will of the people as expressed in majority vote is carefully institutionalized as the operative source of political authority, it is deprived of an ultimate significance. The will of the people is not itself the criterion of right and wrong. There is a higher criterion in terms of which this will can be judged; it is possible that the people may be wrong.[17]

And in a seminal work, *The Naked Public Square,* Richard John Neuhaus explains that the public appeal to religious norms is inevitable. Because man is a *homo religiosus* in search of ultimate meaning, the public evocation of religion occurs willy-nilly. Whether or not it is acknowledged explicitly, an underlying, supreme justification tacitly guides public life. Neuhaus contends further that the denial of transcendent authority opens a spiritual vacuum that is filled by an ersatz or pseudo–civil theology. For example, it may be argued that the ethical relativism of contemporary liberal democracy nonetheless presumes an absolute moral justification that affirms the norms of individual autonomy and radical egalitarianism as preeminent values that supersede all other obligations. Thus, even when absolute moral claims are explicitly denied in public life, they are nevertheless affirmed tacitly. As will be seen, Lincoln's characterization of popular sovereignty as a pseudophilosophy coincides with Neuhaus's description of "ersatz religion." Although popular sovereignty sought to banish moral absolutes from public life, according to Lincoln it nevertheless sanctioned an ethical relativism that tacitly encouraged the perpetuation and nationalization of slavery.[18]

As a genus of theology, civil theology may be subdivided into three classes depending upon its articulation of the religious dimension in public life: explicit civil theology, ersatz religion, and implicit civil theology. In the first case, the civil theology is articulated within the context of a "Holy Commonwealth" where the religious dimension in public life is explicitly sectarian. Ancient Israel, the aspiration of a Holy Roman Empire in the Middle Ages *(sacrum imperium)*, and Puritan New England provide examples of this explicit civil theology, though a functional division between the sacred and spiritual realms existed in each case.[19]

In the second type of civil theology, ersatz religion, a temporal power seeks to deny or arrogate divine sovereignty. The totalitarian regimes of the twentieth century are examples of ersatz religion. The ideologies of communism and fascism both sought to murder the Judeo-Christian God and to replace him with a human power that was beyond good and evil and freed from any higher moral obligation. This glorification of secular power has led to the divinization of the state or the leader as an object of sacred veneration. Totalitarian tyrants sought to wield both the sacred and the secular swords with absolute power, becoming a law unto themselves of which there could be no higher appeal in either principle or practice.[20]

To the extent that it denies or ignores the religious grounding of the political norms it purports to uphold, liberal democracy is also prone to the danger of ersatz religion. The coherence and meaning of liberal virtues like equality, liberty, and tolerance are, in fact, undermined by removing their transcendent foundation. For instance, if there are no fixed standards to guide public life, then why should tolerance be preferred to intolerance? As Leo Strauss warned the postwar generation of social scientists, the celebration of tolerance as a supreme political value per se without any reference to universal truth and a hierarchy of moral ends requires us to tolerate intolerance, thereby putting an end to tolerance altogether. As Neuhaus contends, the denial of moral absolutes cannot be sustained, since the public square abhors a vacuum. Inevitably, the vacuum will be filled by some tacit justification to give meaning and purpose to politics. The practical result of ersatz religion is the same: the spiritual void is filled by a pseudo–civil theology that nevertheless affirms (whether explicitly or inadvertently) some apparent good it regards as preeminent. The "good" of ersatz religion is spurious because it substitutes a true and authentic moral good for the regime with one that is actually harmful to the regime. Since there is no higher authority to bind the actions of the state, politics ultimately becomes an exercise of personal will and may even be regarded as a vehicle for secular salvation.[21]

Finally, the affirmation of civil theology may be implicit to public life. That is to say, the invocation of religious norms may occur within the confines of a separation of church and state that prohibits an explicit sectarian establishment. Indeed, American civil theology is an example of this type of civil theology. Justice Douglas provided a compelling statement of this implicit civil theology that so characterizes American public life in *Zorach v. Clauson* (1952):

We are a religious people whose institutions presuppose a Supreme Being. We guarantee the freedom to worship as one chooses. We make room for as wide a variety of beliefs and creeds as the spiritual needs of man deem necessary. We sponsor an attitude on the part of government that shows no partiality to any one group and lets each flourish according to the adherents and the appeal of its dogma. When the state encourages religious instruction or cooperates with religious authorities by adjusting the schedule of public events to sectarian needs, it follows the best of our traditions. For then it respects the religious nature of our people and accommodates the public service to their spiritual needs. To hold that it may not would be to find in the Constitution a requirement that the government show a callous indifference to religious groups. That would be preferring those who believe in no religion over those who do believe.[22]

It may be alleged that the cherished doctrine of "separation of church and state" forbids religion from playing any role in American public life. Does not the First Amendment's prohibition of "an establishment of religion" preclude religion from American public life? On the contrary, a presentation of Lincoln's biblical republicanism will show that a nonsectarian interpretation of the Bible, one concordant with unassisted human reason, may be viewed as publicly authoritative within the context of the separation of church and state. In fact, the founders never intended an absolute separation of church and state. Significantly, the phrase is nowhere to be found in the Constitution. The metaphor of a "wall of separation" between church and state was coined by Thomas Jefferson in a personal letter more than ten years after the approval of the First Amendment and was misconstrued subsequently as a legal doctrine in *Everson v. Board of Education* (1947) by the Supreme Court in its interpretation of the establishment clause of the First Amendment. As originally conceived by the founders, the prohibition against a sectarian establishment was not intended to banish religion entirely from public life, but to prevent the creation of a national church that would corrupt the integrity of both the secular and sacred spheres. Indeed, the First Amendment could not have been intended to prohibit absolutely any cooperation or interaction between religion and politics in American public life since it was approved by representatives who supported religious establishments in their own states. These men supported an establishment at the state level, but not at the national level. Furthermore, the same Congress that enacted the First Amendment also readopted the Northwest Ordinance of 1787 that explicitly promoted religion as beneficial to the republic: "Religion, morality, and knowledge, being necessary to good government and the happiness of mankind, schools and the means of learning shall forever be encouraged." If the members of the First Congress who drafted the First Amendment intended to forbid any cooperation between religion and public life, it is highly unlikely that they also would have sought to promote religion in the only territory under their guiding authority.

The Constitution's ban of a national establishment and its injunction against religious tests were a necessary condition of political equality and the consent of the governed in the United States. These clauses intended to prevent the national government from promoting the rights of one sect at the expense of another group. Indeed, Charles Carroll, a signer of the Declaration and a Roman Catholic, was one of the most determined advocates of the Constitution's ban on religious tests, not because he was hostile to religion, but because he had been barred from public life on account of his beliefs. The ban on religious tests was thus supported by those who sought a sacred sphere beyond the reach of government power to exercise freely their religion in the regime without fear of persecution or "second-class citizenship." The prolonged and bloody wars of religion that ravaged Europe in the sixteenth and seventeenth centuries taught the founders that to confer special privileges to members of a particular religious sect was incompatible with republican government and equal rights. Given the religious diversity of the United States, the founders believed that a national church would jeopardize the natural right to religious liberty and endanger the safety and happiness of society. As a means to prevent this, the Constitution's prohibition against an establishment of religion and its guarantee of free exercise may be viewed in positive terms as a necessary condition for the general vitality of religion within society. In *Religion in American Public Life,* A. James Reichley concisely describes the intentions of the founders on the First Amendment:

> Some ambiguity was no doubt present in the meaning of the establishment clause from the start. But there is nothing in it inconsistent with the virtually unanimous view among the founders that functional separation between church and state should be maintained without threatening the support and guidance received by republican government from religion.[23]

Indeed, the founders' view of separation of church and state never prevented them from recognizing the centrality of religion to the maintenance of the regime's republican institutions. Reichley states, "As the leaders of the generation of the Revolution passed gradually from the scene, they left a nation that saw no contradiction between the concept of separation of church and state and the concept that the legitimacy of republican government must be ultimately rooted in religion." The following observation by Benjamin Rush, among the most revered and learned of the founders, verifies Reichley's interpretation: "The only foundation for a useful education in a republic is to be laid in religion. Without it there can be no virtue, and without virtue there can be no liberty, and liberty is the object and life of all republican governments." For Rush, republican liberty depended upon virtue, which in turn depended upon a religious education to reinforce the core moral teachings and practices of American republicanism. Similarly, John Adams once explained: "We have no government armed with power capable of contending with human passions unbridled by morality and religion. Our constitution was made only for a moral and a religious people. It is wholly inadequate for the government of any other." According to Adams, "religion and virtue are the only foundations, not only of republicanism and of all free government, but of social felicity under all government and in all combinations of human society." Indeed, the centrality of religion to American public life was confirmed by Alexis de Tocqueville in the nineteenth century when he remarked, "I do not know whether all Americans have a sincere faith in their religion—for who can search the human heart?—but I am certain that they hold it to be indispensable to the maintenance of republican institutions."[24]

Following George Washington's precedent, Lincoln proclaimed various national days of religious thanksgiving and fasting as chief executive during the Civil War. The nondenominational character of these executive proclamations affirmed the sacred sphere of religion in the American regime within the constitutional confines of the nonestablishment clause and the ban on religious tests. In the first of many such proclamations throughout the war, Lincoln announced a "'day of public humiliation, prayer and fasting, to be observed by the people of the United States with religious solemnities, and the offering of fervent supplications to Almighty God for the safety and welfare of these States, His blessings on their arms, and a speedy restoration of peace.'" The language of this ordinance was taken verbatim from a precedent established by the First Congress of the United States. Moreover, it should not be forgotten that Lincoln's annual Thanksgiving Day Proclamation of 1863 established the customary date of our national holiday: "I do, therefore, invite my fellow citizens in every part of the United States, and also those who are at sea and those who are sojourning in foreign lands, to set apart and observe the last Thursday of November next as a day of Thanksgiving and Praise to our beneficent Father who dwelleth in the Heavens." Paying tribute to Lincoln's important role as the steward of the nation's political faith, Schuyler Colfax, speaker of the House, in his eulogy to the slain president, reminded his fellow countrymen "that the last Act of Congress signed by [Lincoln] was one requiring that the motto, in which he sincerely believed, 'In God we trust' should hereafter be inscribed upon all our national coins." Indeed, Lincoln's myriad executive proclamations upheld the supreme claim that religion had on the lives of the American people and acknowledged the dependence of the state and human institutions upon God. The state should play a supporting, but limited, role in publicly affirming religion without favoring a particular sect, coercing beliefs repugnant to conscience, or regulating actions that pose no substantial threat to the public interest.[25]

The public invocation of religion by the chief executive of the United States was forthrightly established through the precedent of George Washington, whose Farewell Address of 1796 contained one of the most celebrated and enduring appeals to religion in American public life:

Of all the dispositions and habits, which lead to political prosperity, religion and morality are indispensable supports. In vain would that man claim the tribute of patriotism, who should labor to subvert these great pillars of human happiness, these firmest props of the destinies of men and citizens. The mere politician, equally with the pious man, ought to respect and to cherish them. A volume could not trace all their connection with private and public felicity. Let it simply be asked, where is the security for property, for reputation, for life, if the sense of religious obligation desert the oaths, which are the instruments of investigation in courts of justice? And let us with caution indulge the supposition that morality can be maintained without religion. Whatever may be conceded to the influence of refined education on minds of peculiar structure, reason and experience both forbid us to expect, that national morality can prevail in exclusion of religious principles. It is substantially true, that virtue or morality is a necessary spring of popular government.[26]

In his last public address to the nation as president—a speech he knew would be scrutinized by succeeding generations as the final admonition of a sagacious father to his children—Washington clearly emphasized the indispensability of religion to republican government. Indeed, the Farewell Address would inspire the young Abraham Lincoln a generation later, and the ecumenical character of Washington's religious speech would influence him as president. Both Washington and Lincoln refused to identify the civil theology of the American regime with a particular church or sectarian denomination.[27]

Lincoln's biblical republicanism can be analyzed further in terms of four related dimensions: its substance (public opinion); its agent (the cultural elite); its form (biblical republicanism); and its end (liberty and Union). A four-dimensional approach helps to identify the constituent parts of his civil theology. Each part or dimension plays an important role in providing a comprehensive moral justification for public life.

Public opinion is the substance of biblical republicanism. The relationship between civil theology and public opinion is twofold: on the one hand, civil theology is itself *constituted by* shared opinions about politics, justice, and the common good; on the other, civil theology *acts upon* public opinion by disposing it toward an overarching conception of the public good. Accordingly, public opinion may be viewed respectively as either the *subject* matter of biblical republicanism (a nexus of opinions that constitute a creed of public life) or as the *object* of civil theology (the prevailing climate of public opinion or public policy that biblical republicanism attempts to guide).

Civil theology presumes a distinction between public opinion, which is transitory, and that which is more abiding. The ephemeral and fleeting character of the former cannot be considered properly as civil theological, for it does not substantively influence the public ethos. It would be absurd to characterize all public opinion as civil theological. To do so would confound the deeper, more abiding ethos of a people with a passing trend or fad. Public opinion becomes civil theological only when it begins to influence practically the habits and self-understanding of the citizenry. It becomes civil theological when it is able to compete with established opinions for public authoritativeness. What truly distinguishes Lincoln's view of public opinion as civil theological was his profound recognition that public policy, laws, and legal institutions relied upon a deeper, philosophical view of human nature: "Public opinion settles every question here—any policy to be permanent must have public opinion at the bottom—something in accordance with the philosophy of the human mind as it is." According to Lincoln, public policy must take its normative bearings from a sound philosophical anthropology that accounts for the various dimensions of human experience, the spiritual as well as the material.[28]

Throughout his struggle against the extension of slavery, Lincoln consistently pointed out the crucial role of public opinion in a republican form of government: "In this age, and this country, public sentiment is every thing. *With* it, nothing can fail; *against* it, nothing can succeed." Indeed, public opinion supplies the motives or springs to political action. It disposes citizens to the rule of law and their political institutions. Unlike despotisms and tyrannies that restrict public opinion, a democratic republic purports to be based upon consent and civic involvement. In theory, public policies in a free society should reflect the will of the people. The will of the people, however, can be unjust if it is unbounded by legitimate moral standards. The very essence of Lincoln's leadership thus involved a moral stewardship that sought to guide public opinion toward just policies and ends. As Lincoln well knew, the freedom implicit to a popular form of government entailed the possibility of either ennobling or "debauching" public opinion. By fostering a climate of opinion that debased the humanity of the African American, Douglas disposed the public mind toward accepting the principle of racial superiority as the legitimate interpretation of American public life. This view, coupled with the logic of the *Dred Scott* decision, made it possible to divest even free blacks of all constitutional protections, privileges, and immunities.[29]

Lincoln's biblical republicanism emphasized the reciprocity between public policy and public opinion. The two were inseparably linked. Public opinion disposed either the enactment or rejection of public policy, and, conversely, the enactment or rejection of public policy influenced the climate of public opinion—that is, the ethos of the citizenry. The legal sanctioning of a policy tended to convey the impression of a moral sanctioning. The enactment of a policy and its corresponding modification of public opinion may even transform society's ethos, modifying its civil theology and therefore altering the letter and spirit of its political institutions. Lincoln explained that the ethical neutrality implicit to popular sovereignty dehumanized the African American as an article of property and that this perception would result in policies that would tolerate the indefinite perpetuation of the institution:

> Now let me call your attention to one thing that has really happened, which shows this gradual and steady debauching of public opinion. . . . [T]here has

been a change wrought in you, and a very significant change it is, being no less than changing the negro, in your estimation, from the rank of a man to that of a brute. . . . Is not this change wrought in your minds a very important change? Public opinion in this country is everything. In a nation like ours this popular sovereignty and squatter sovereignty have already wrought a change in the public mind to the extent I have stated.

Lincoln's reference to the "gradual and steady debauching" of public opinion made it clear that he was not speaking of a fleeting belief but of a more abiding phenomenon.[30]

Metaphorically, public opinion is related to public policy in the same way that fire is related to heat. Fire produces heat, just as public opinion produces public policy. Likewise, the existence of heat presumes fire, just as public policy presumes public opinion. To carry the analogy further, the intensity of fire determines the intensity of heat, just as the intensity or saliency of public opinion determines whether it is eventually adopted as a public policy.

In his speech at New Haven, which deserves more scholarly attention than it has received, Lincoln elucidated the role of "philosophical public opinion" in American public life:

Whenever this question [of slavery] shall be settled, it must be settled on some philosophical basis. No policy that does not rest upon some philosophical public opinion can be permanently maintained. And hence, there are but two policies in regard to Slavery that can be at all maintained. The first, based on the property view that Slavery is right, conforms to that idea throughout, and demands that we shall do everything for it that we ought to do if it were right. We must sweep away all opposition, for opposition to the right is wrong; we must agree that Slavery is right, and we must adopt the idea that property has persuaded the owner to believe—that Slavery is morally right and socially elevating. This gives a philosophical basis for a permanent policy of encouragement.

The other policy is one that squares with the idea that Slavery is wrong, and it consists in doing everything that we ought to do if it is wrong.

At New Haven, Lincoln spoke of a permanent "philosophical basis" that guided public opinion and that necessarily disposed the enactment or rejection of public policy. This "philosophical public opinion" and its "philosophical basis" is tantamount to civil theology.[31]

Since public opinion is the very substance of civil theology, a permanent change in the climate of public opinion will necessarily result in a transformation of the moral character—the ethos—of the regime itself. Popular sovereignty and proslavery theology were particularly insidious because they promoted opinions that were inimical to the maintenance of self-government. Criticizing the debauched climate of public opinion of his time, Lincoln rhetorically asked "in all soberness, if all these things [that promote slavery], if indulged in, if ratified, if confirmed and endorsed, if taught to our children, and repeated to them, do not tend to rub out the sentiment of liberty in the country, and to transform this Government into a government of some other form?" The embrace of such opinions would "subvert, in the public mind, and in practical administration, our old and only standard of free government, that 'all men are created equal,' and . . . substitute for it some different standard" that affirmed "the natural, moral, and religious right to enslave another."[32]

Lincoln shared Plato's recognition that the climate of public opinion reflects the mores and manners of society. This insight led Plato to describe the republic as "the soul of man writ large." In a similar manner, Lincoln identified the climate of public opinion as the "public mind," stating that slavery's advocates "will endeavor to impress upon the public mind that the negro is not human." Like Plato, he well understood the connection between law and morality and how the people could be either corrupted or ennobled by their laws. In sum, Lincoln's various references to a "standard of free government," the "public mind," "philosophical public opinion," and the "philosophical basis" of public policy are corresponding ways for expressing public opinion as the substance of his civil theology.[33]

Public opinion, though, may be either true or false. Lincoln emphasized that it must correspond to the truth of reality, that it must be "in accordance with a philosophy of the human mind as it is." That is to say, normative standards must take their bearings from experiences that have an empirical basis in reality. Political prescriptions must seek to preserve a balance of consciousness by accounting for the various dimensions of human experience. Political ideology, as opposed to political philosophy, falsifies reality by reducing the richness and complexity of human experience and history to the determinations of a single cause: class, gender, race. Lincoln relied upon the mutual influence of the standards of human reason and divine revelation to distinguish between just and unjust accounts of public life.

The second dimension of biblical republicanism refers to the political agents or actors who actually affirm, articulate, and defend a civil theological vision of public life. Lincoln clearly understood the powerful role of leaders in shaping public opinion: "Whoever moulds public sentiment, goes deeper than he who enacts statutes, or pronounces judicial decisions. He makes possible the inforcement of these. . . ." The public acceptance of a leader's vision reveals not only the inner life of its author but also the character of the people who are willing to embrace, reject, or tolerate it. In effect, the agents of a civil theology are the nation's cultural elite, those individuals who possess the requisite abilities and influence to articulate a compelling vision of political order. For better or for worse, the influence of these individuals provides policies with an impression of moral legitimacy.[34]

Here, the word "leader" is applied broadly to include various members of the cultural elite, not only elected officials but anyone who may pervasively influence the climate of public opinion: poets, heroes, the clergy, scholars,

teachers, authors, and, perhaps most unfortunately, in recent times, enter-
tainers, athletes, and the mass media. To borrow a memorable phrase from
the John Adams–Thomas Jefferson correspondence, the cultural elite represents "the natural aristocracy" of the nation. Adams defined this natural aristocracy as "all those men who can command, influence, or procure more
than an average of votes; by an aristocrat every man who can and will influence one man to vote besides himself. Few men will deny that there is a natural aristocracy of virtues and talents in every nation and in every party, in
every city and village." The natural aristocracy are the leaders of public opinion. Indeed, their role in shaping the moral climate of public opinion was
acknowledged by the founders as essential to the perpetuation of republican
government. Washington himself emphasized that "it is essential that public
opinion should be enlightened."[35]

A sociopolitical vision of order may be presented in different symbolic
forms. The truth of reality is by no means exhausted by discursive reason
and propositional logic. The aspirations, hopes, and obligations that bind a
people together may be communicated to the public in different ways.
Whether they are expressed in a historical, mythical, or philosophical
form, these sociopolitical visions may profoundly influence the climate of
public opinion.[36]

The Gettysburg Address was a timeless expression that distilled the
essence of the American creed, and it is a perfect example of Lincoln's crucial role as a member of the cultural elite in defining an ultimate vision of
public life. The momentous speech—and the Declaration of Independence,
for that matter—could not have been written by anyone at anytime.
Notwithstanding their universal import, each was the work of a particular
individual who possessed extraordinary intellectual gifts and confronted particular historical circumstances. The talents of these individuals enabled
them to capture the national spirit of their people. The historical milieu in
which Lincoln's biblical republicanism emerged was likewise shaped by the
opinions of other natural aristocrats who defined the political landscape of
the Civil War era.[37]

Because the common good does not emerge spontaneously, it is an essential task of political leadership to guide public opinion toward a legitimate
moral end. Without this authoritative guidance, it is unlikely that the public
good will prevail against competing opinions based on the particular interests
of a group or individual. In *A General Theory of Authority,* Yves Simon explains
that "the ability of truth 'to get itself accepted in the competition of the market' must have a cause antecedent to the set of random events made of man's
opinions, inclinations, traditions and prejudices, objections and replies, occasional pieces of valid information and occasional errors." By "an antecedent cause" Simon refers to the crucial function of moral authority in
directing the regime toward the common good. True statesmanship must
evoke what John Courtney Murray has described as "a moral consensus."
A leader's success in guiding public opinion toward just ends, however,

depends on two related factors: the leader's ability to communicate a vision that will inspire citizens to follow, and virtuous citizens who are capable of responding to the leader's call.[38]

In recognition of the pervasive influence and grave responsibility that leaders possessed as agents of public opinion, Lincoln often reserved his most biting criticism for members of the cultural elite. Clearly, for Lincoln, not all opinions were "created equal." He distinguished between noble opinions that corresponded to the truth of reality and base opinions that implied a distorted account of human nature and society. In his struggle against secession, Lincoln argued that the southern public mind had been debased by the spurious doctrine of states' rights propounded by John C. Calhoun and others whose "insidious" teachings gradually disposed the people of the South to break up their government. In his "4th of July Speech 1861 to a Special Session of Congress," Lincoln characterized the leaders of public opinion in the South as the "movers" of secession and rebellion who subtly manipulated public opinion to serve and protect their own self-interest:

> It might seem, at first thought, to be of little difference whether the present movement at the South be called "secession" or "rebellion." The movers, however, well understand the difference. . . . Accordingly they commenced an insidious debauching of the public mind. They invented an ingenious sophism, which, if conceded, was followed by perfectly logical steps, through all the incidents, to the complete destruction of the Union. The sophism itself is, that any state of the Union may, *consistently* with the national Constitution, and therefore *lawfully,* and *peacefully,* withdraw from the Union, without the consent of the Union, or of any other state. The little disguise that the supposed right is to be exercised only for just cause, themselves to be the sole judge of its justice, is too thin to merit any notice.
>
> With rebellion thus sugar-coated, they have been drugging the public mind of their section for more than thirty years. . . .[39]

The distinction between a statesmanship that serves the public good and a sophistry that seeks the private interest of a particular group, section, or race was crucial to Lincoln's civil theological outlook. He consistently applied this distinction to northern and southern political leaders alike. Accusing Douglas, a northerner, of political irresponsibility in light of his sway over national affairs, Lincoln described him as "a man of vast influence, so great that it is enough for many men to profess to believe anything, when they once find out that Judge Douglas professes to believe it." It is noteworthy that Lincoln described the Little Giant and his followers as "teachers of this insidious popular sovereignty." On another occasion, he explained: "Judge Douglas, and whoever like him teaches that the negro has no share, humble though it may be, in the Declaration of Independence . . . is in every possible way preparing the public mind, by his vast influence, for making the institution of slavery perpetual and national." By characterizing Douglas and other members of the cultural elite as "teachers" of public opinion, Lincoln recognized that statecraft is, in fact, soul craft—inevitably, government shapes the moral character of its citizens. By portraying the leaders of public opinion as teachers, Lincoln challenged the cultural elite of his time to take responsibility for the moral consequences of their actions. He consistently linked the "ignoble teaching" to its teacher, the sophistry to its sophist.[40]

Ideas have consequences. The opinions of a few gifted individuals may have an enormous impact on public opinion and corresponding public policies. Among the South's cultural elite, John C. Calhoun was perhaps most instrumental in transforming public opinion on slavery from that of a necessary evil to that of a social and political blessing. Attempting to exonerate himself from a heavy burden of guilt at the end of his life, Calhoun disclaimed any responsibility for the impending crisis in his final speech to Congress: "Having faithfully done my duty to the best of my ability, both to the Union and to my section, throughout the whole of this agitation [over slavery], I shall have the consolation, let what will come, that I am free from all responsibility." Lincoln, however, was unwilling to absolve Calhoun. In fact, he held him and other members of the cultural elite to more exacting standards of accountability given their pervasive public influence. This explains Lincoln's particular vehemence toward the teachers of proslavery theology, described in chapter 3. Secession and slavery would never have acquired such legitimacy without Calhoun's prominent influence on southern public opinion. In Lincoln's view, Calhoun's legacy was particularly detrimental since it led to a public disavowal of the Declaration, the moral beacon of American popular government:

> I know that Mr. Calhoun and all the politicians of his school denied the truth of the Declaration. I know that it ran along in the mouths of some Southern men for a period of years, ending at last in that shameful though rather forcible declaration of [Senator John] Pettit of Indiana, upon the floor of the United States Senate, that the Declaration of Independence was in that respect "a self evident lie," rather than a self-evident truth.[41]

If the first dimension of biblical republicanism is public opinion and the second is leadership, the third dimension is its form—its defining essence and its specific substance that distinguishes it from all other accounts of public life. The form of Lincoln's civil theology is constituted by his integration of the biblical and republican traditions of order. My general use of the term "biblical republicanism" to characterize Lincoln's ultimate moral justification for American public life is aptly named after the specific form of his civil theological outlook. An analysis of the formal dimension of biblical republicanism requires an examination of its constituent parts and their ethical arrangement.

Although public opinion is the substance of civil theology, it is not static; it may take on different shapes at different times. The peculiar form or shape of public opinion corresponds to a particular civil theological outlook. This form supplies the ruling principle that directs the climate of public opinion. The relationship between formal cause and civil theology is analogous to the relationship between soul and body. As the soul is the ruling principle of the body, so biblical republicanism is the guiding principle, the spirit that animates Lincoln's civil theological outlook.

By providing an ultimate moral justification for free labor that combines the biblical teaching of Genesis 3:19 with the republican principle of equal consent, the following passage clearly manifests the form of Lincoln's biblical republicanism:

> In the early days of the world, the Almighty said to the first of our race "In the sweat of thy face shalt thou eat bread"; and since then, if we except the *light* and the *air* of heaven, no good thing has been, or can be enjoyed by us, without having first cost labour. And, inasmuch [as] most good things are produced by labour, it follows that [all] such things of right belong to those whose labour has produced them. But it has so happened in all ages of the world, that *some* have laboured, and *others* have, without labour, enjoyed a large proportion of the fruits. This is wrong, and should not continue. To [secure] to each labourer the whole product of his labour or as nearly as possible, is a most worthy object of any good government.[42]

Because God has obliged the entire human race to labor as a condition of its existence, no human being is exempt from laboring. Such an exemption constitutes a transgression of cosmic justice because it attempts to elevate one above the human condition at the expense of his fellow human beings. In sum, Lincoln's defense of free labor combined the biblical precept of Genesis 3:19, the principle of equal consent in the Declaration, and the Enlightenment liberal teaching of John Locke that each person has a right to property in himself. Biblical republicanism thus vindicated each human being's God-given right to enjoy the fruits of his or her labor. In Lincoln's civil theology, the political teachings of American republicanism are revealed in the Bible and reinforced through natural reason.[43]

The fourth dimension of Lincoln's biblical republicanism is its end, the overarching public good affirmed by his civil theology. Lincoln maintained that the Declaration of Independence promulgated the moral ends of the American regime, that its teaching on legitimate government meant that a just regime must be dedicated to protecting the natural rights of life, liberty, and pursuit of happiness. Expressed another way, the goal of government was to secure the "safety and happiness" of the people. Though the Declaration articulated the ends of a legitimate government, it did not establish a concrete, institutional framework whereby those goals could be realized. Like Publius who warned against disunion and who revealed the inadequacies of the Articles of Confederation, Lincoln believed that a weak government that could not control domestic faction jeopardized the people's safety and happiness. For Lincoln and Publius, the ends of government promulgated by the Declaration were best secured under the Constitution of 1787, which possessed sufficient energy to safeguard liberty and to maintain a Union dedicated to the principles of the revolution. In sum, the end of Lincoln's biblical republicanism may be summarized by Daniel Webster's motto of the inseparability of liberty and Union: "Liberty *and* Union, now and for ever, one and inseparable."

According to Lincoln, preserving the Union meant preserving the moral principles and ideas that the Union stood for. It meant upholding the aspirations of civil and religious freedom in the Declaration and perpetuating the established rule of law and legal process in the Constitution. Under the shadow of secession, en route to his inauguration, Lincoln delivered a speech in Trenton, New Jersey, that clearly defined the end, the telos, of his leadership as perpetuating a Union dedicated to the founding ideals of the regime: "I am exceedingly anxious that this Union, the Constitution and the liberties of the people shall be perpetuated in accordance with the original idea for which that struggle was made. . . ." Of course, the "original idea" of the American Revolution meant the principles of liberty and equality in the Declaration. Lincoln saw his struggle against the South's secession in defense of slavery as an attempt to extend and apply more consistently the principles of the American Revolution. The appropriateness for distinguishing between civil theologies in terms of their ends becomes quite vivid when contrasting the exclusivity of Adolf Hitler's twisted vision of a *volksgemeinschaft* (racially united community) to the inclusiveness of Lincoln's moral vision of a Union dedicated to the promise of liberty and equality for all human beings.[44]

Lincoln's conception of liberty and Union combined a moral obligation to the Declaration with a legal obligation to the Constitution. Under the established rule of law, the moral ends promulgated by the Declaration must be legally determined within the institutional framework provided by the Constitution. Lincoln saw these two documents as complementary charters of American republicanism. The unwavering devotion to the inseparability of liberty and national Union has constituted an important tradition in American republicanism that can be traced from the first generation of founders (Washington, Adams, and Publius) to the second generation of Whig nationalists (Webster and Clay) to the third generation of Republicans (Lincoln and Seward). Proponents of this view held that the blessings of liberty were "intimately connected to the Union as a national, not a federal, republic." The overriding principle or end to which Lincoln was dedicated as a leader, outweighing all other goals, was preserving the moral and legal integrity of both liberty and Union.[45]

Although Lincoln's biblical republicanism is sui generis in its combination of reason and revelation, important antecedents within the Judeo-Christian and republican traditions of American order nonetheless influenced it. Regardless of sectarian differences, the Bible was authoritative to Americans during the Civil War era who turned to it not only as a source of spiritual solace but also as a practical guide to everyday life. In his insightful analysis of the Second Inaugural Address, Ronald White places Lincoln's observation in the speech that "Both read the same Bible, and pray to the same God" within its wider historical context: "The centrality of the Bible in nineteenth-century America cannot be overemphasized. The publication of the Bible soared above all other books. . . . [I]n the nineteenth [century] the Bible was fundamentally a personal resource in life and in death." White points out that the soldiers of the Civil War were "products of the Second Great Awakening," a spiritual revival that swept the nation in the mid-nineteenth century. James McPherson goes so far as to describe these soldiers as "the most religious in history." Given the preeminence of a biblical ethos in America, revivalists of the Second Great Awakening like Robert Baird concluded, "The impression prevails among our statesmen that the Bible is emphatically the foundation of our hopes as a people."[46]

The use of the adjective "biblical" is wholly appropriate to the unmediated and nondenominational character of Lincoln's public and private faith, which was based primarily on his own interpretation of the Bible. The religious environment of Lincoln's youth left a lasting impression on his mature religious outlook: his parents were members of the Separate Baptist church that "accepted no creed but the Bible." The primacy of this personal encounter with the Bible remained a common denominator of Lincoln's faith throughout his life. While many of Lincoln's beliefs seem to resonate with a particular theological system—especially that of Calvinism—and, even though he attended church services in both Springfield and in Washington, D.C., as president, it is historically well documented that he eschewed official church membership. His own conscientious reservations about accepting fully the doctrines of a particular creed may have prevented him from identifying with any specific church or denomination.[47]

The term "republicanism" constitutes the political self-understanding of the founders. In framing their particular version of republican government, the founders prudently integrated various elements of the classical, Christian, and modern liberal traditions of political thought. Their interpretation of popular rule drew from the collective wisdom found in the writings of ancient, medieval, and modern political historians and political thinkers. British constitutionalism, classical and modern republicanism, Reformed Christianity, the Scottish Enlightenment, and Lockean liberalism all played a role in the shaping of American republicanism.[48] Indeed, a continuous republican tradition of American political thought can be traced from the Revolutionary period to the formation of the Republican Party in Lincoln's own time. The Thomas Jefferson who penned the Declaration, the founders at the Constitutional Convention, Publius in the *Federalist,* and Daniel Webster in his struggle against nullification provide some of the more notable expressions of this tradition whose common denominator may be defined in terms of its commitment to popular government and ordered liberty under the auspices of a national Union. Following Publius, Lincoln viewed republican government as a specific form of self-government that balanced the necessary political goods of both power and liberty, thereby striking a prudent mean between the extreme potentialities of either tyranny or anarchy into which majority rule was liable to degenerate. The crisis of secession prompted Lincoln to reconsider the dilemma faced by Publius in attempting to balance an energetic government that could protect the people's liberties with a limited government that would not encroach upon their liberties, "'Is there, in all republics, this inherent, and fatal weakness?' 'Must a government, of necessity, be too strong for the liberties of its own people, or too weak to maintain its own existence?'"[49]

In *Federalist 9,* Publius explained that the republican government established by the founders intended to remedy the defects implicit to self-government:

> A FIRM Union will be of the utmost moment to the peace and liberty of the States as a barrier against domestic faction and insurrection. It is impossible to read the history of the petty republics of Greece and Italy, without feeling sensations of horror and disgust at the distractions with which they were continually agitated, and at which they were kept in a state of perpetual vibration, between the extremes of tyranny and anarchy.[50]

According to Publius, not any Union; but a "FIRM Union" was the best safeguard of the people's liberties. Consonant with Publius's description of the tendency of republican government to degenerate into the extremes of tyranny and anarchy, Lincoln warned that insurrection and disunion would subvert the delicate balance of power and liberty established by the Constitution of 1787:

> Plainly, the central idea of secession, is the essence of anarchy. A majority, held in restraint by constitutional checks, and limitations, and always changing easily, with deliberate changes of popular opinions and sentiments, is the only true sovereign of a free people. Whoever rejects it, does, of necessity, fly to anarchy or despotism. Unanimity is impossible; the rule of a minority, as a permanent arrangement, is wholly inadmissable; so that, rejecting the majority principle, anarchy, or despotism in some form, is all that is left."[51]

The two cultural forces of republicanism and Judeo-Christianity represent important currents in the mainstream of American political order. Lincoln drew upon both and integrated them in his moral justification of American self-government. To be sure, the founders saw the compatibility of these two traditions.[52] For instance, Benjamin Rush conveyed the harmony between republicanism and revelation in these terms: "A Christian, I say again, cannot fail of being a republican, for every precept of the Gospel inculcates those degrees of humility, self-denial, and brotherly kindness, which are directly opposed to the pride of monarchy and the pageantry of a court." In a letter to Rush, John Adams concurred: "The Bible contains the most profound philosophy, the most perfect morality, and the most refined policy, that ever was conceived upon the earth. It is the most republican book in the world." Adams thereby distinguished the religious grounding of natural rights in the American Revolution from the more secular basis of human rights in the French Revolution:

> If [the] empire of superstition and hypocrisy should be overthrown, happy indeed will it be for the world; but if all religion and morality should be overthrown with it, what advantage will be gained? The doctrine of human equality is founded entirely in the Christian doctrine that we are all children of the same Father, all accountable to Him for our conduct to one another, all equally bound to respect each other's self love.

Indeed, the great commentator of American political culture, Alexis de Tocqueville, observed: "In France I had seen the spirits of religion and of freedom almost always marching in opposite directions. In America I found them intimately linked together in joint reign over the same land." By combining these two traditions of American order—the biblical faith of Judeo-Christianity and the republicanism of the founders—so deeply and coherently, Lincoln represents the fullest expression of the American political mind.[53]

The general contours of Lincoln's biblical republicanism may be revealed further by associating each tradition with a historical representative. For purposes of conceptual clarity, John Winthrop and Thomas Jefferson are appropriate models of the biblical and republican traditions in America, respectively. Lincoln's thought, of course, cannot be reduced to either Winthrop or Jefferson, but each man and his philosophy dramatically affected America's wider political culture in which Lincoln's biblical republicanism took shape.

Lincoln's belief that America had a divine mission or calling to serve as an exemplar of democracy to the world was influenced by the cultural force of New England Puritanism as represented by John Winthrop.[54] While aboard the ship *Arabella* en route to the New World, John Winthrop, the first governor of the Massachusetts Bay Community, delivered a sermon entitled a *Modell of Christian Charity* in which he envisioned the Puritan community as a "City upon a Hill." The biblical metaphor, taken from Matthew 5:14, suggested a mission or special calling of the Puritans to manifest God's providential order. Their "Holy Commonwealth" was established to provide an inspiration to the world, a beacon for other nation's to fix their gaze upon:

> The God of Israel . . . shall make us a praise and glory, that men shall say of succeeding plantations: the lord make it like that of New England; for we must Consider that we shall be as a City upon a Hill, the eyes of all people are upon us; so that if we shall deal falsely with our god in this work we have undertaken and so cause him to withdraw his present help from us, we shall be made a story and a by-word through the world. . . .

The "biblical archetypes" of "Exodus, Chosen People, Promised Land, New Jerusalem, Sacrificial Death and Rebirth" expressed by Winthrop have exerted an enduring influence on American civil theology.[55]

The Puritan idea of mission implied a relationship of corresponding rights and responsibilities. On the one hand, the notion obliged them to act in accordance with the demands of a model community. On the other, it entitled them to a chosen status, one denoting a unique relationship with the Creator. Nevertheless, as Winthrop sternly warned, divine favor could be withdrawn if the Puritans failed to live up to their moral responsibilities. Their success as a model Christian community was by no means inevitable, since it depended upon an unwavering fidelity to their divine calling. Failure would make them a "by-word," a disgrace, to the rest of the world; it would discredit their mission. Winthrop believed that success or failure of the Puritan spiritual experiment in America would reverberate throughout the entire world and throughout all times as either a model worthy of praise and imitation or a "by-word" of contempt and avoidance.

The biblical self-interpretation of the Puritans continued to influence the nation during the founding period, but with a more secular meaning. During this time, the idea of mission was increasingly applied to America's national destiny and its political institutions. Parallel to Winthrop's interpretation of the city on a hill, Publius explained the global and philanthropic implications of the Constitution's ratification in *Federalist 1*:

> It has been frequently remarked that it seems to have been reserved to the people of this country, by their conduct and example, to decide the important question, whether societies of men are really capable or not, of establishing good government from reflection and choice, or whether they are forever destined to depend for their constitutions on accident and force. If there be any truth in the remark, the crisis at which we are arrived, may with propriety be regarded as the era in which that decision is to be made; and a wrong election of the part we shall act, may, in this view, deserve to be considered as the general misfortune of mankind.[56]

And in *Federalist 11*, Publius noted that it was the unique calling of the American people to prove to Europe and the rest of the world that it was indeed possible for people to govern themselves:

> Facts have too long supported these arrogant pretensions of the European. It belongs to us to vindicate the honor of the human race, and to teach that assuming brother moderation. Union will enable us to do it. Disunion will add another victim to his triumphs. Let Americans disdain to be the instruments of European Greatness! Let the thirteen States, bound together in a strict and indissoluble union, concur in erecting one great American system, superior to control of all trans-atlantic force or influence, and able to dictate the terms of the connection between the old and the new world![57]

Like Winthrop, Publius affirmed a mission, a unique calling, for the American people: "It belongs to us to vindicate the honor of the human race." But Winthrop stressed the universal import of the Puritan *spiritual endeavor* while Publius emphasized the worldwide significance of the American *political experiment*. Furthermore, the belief in an "indissoluble Union" as a necessary safeguard to preserving the American experiment from the threat of domestic anarchy and foreign invasion is a common republican theme raised by Publius, Webster, and Lincoln.[58]

At the dawn of the nineteenth century, Thomas Jefferson spoke of the United States as an "Empire for liberty" and "the world's best hope." In his First Inaugural Address, Jefferson noted the global significance of the election of 1800 in demonstrating to the world the viability of republican government. This was the first election in history to result in the peaceful transition of power between partisan rivals who had charged each other with espousing principles that were antithetical to the regime. The success of this transition of power would establish an important precedent throughout the world of resolving partisan differences through the electoral process rather than through a revolution—that is, through an appeal to "ballots" rather than "bayonets," as Lincoln would remind the nation six decades later in the election of 1860.[59]

In 1833, Daniel Webster opposed nullification because it threatened to extinguish the American experiment, thereby depriving the world of any hope for democratic government:

> [I]f the friends of nullification should be able to propagate their opinions, and give them practical effect, they would, in my judgment, prove themselves the most skilful "architects of ruin," the most effectual extinguishers of high-raised expectation, the greatest blasters of human hopes, that any age has produced. They would stand up to proclaim, in tones which would pierce the ears of half the human race, that the last great experiment of representative government had failed. They would send forth sounds, at the hearing of which the doctrine of the divine right of kings would feel, even in its grave, a returning sensation of vitality and resuscitation. Millions of eyes, of those who now feed their inherent love of liberty on the success of the American example, would turn away from beholding our dismemberment, and find no place on earth whereupon to rest their gratified sight. Amidst the incantations and orgies of nullification, secession, disunion, and revolution, would be celebrated the funeral rites of constitutional and republican liberty.

Webster's defense of the Union in 1832 against nullification anticipated Lincoln's similar defense a generation later in 1861 against secession. Indeed, Webster's speeches were one of the few sources that Lincoln consulted when he prepared his First Inaugural Address. These Whig nationalists held that America's mission to serve as an exemplar of republican government to the world was best secured through an inviolable Union that was dedicated to the principles of liberty and equality in the Declaration.[60]

Of all American leaders, Abraham Lincoln has provided the most enduring vision of America as an exemplar of democracy to the world. Consistent with the idea of mission found in the writings of Winthrop, Publius, Jefferson, and Webster, Lincoln repeatedly emphasized that the destiny of democratic government throughout the world depended upon the fate of the American experiment during the Civil War. He defined the struggle as one that

> embraces more than the fate of these United States. It presents to the whole family of man, the question, whether a constitutional republic, or a democracy—a government of the people, by the same people—can, or cannot, maintain its territorial integrity, against its own domestic foes. . . . Our popular government has often been called an experiment. . . . It is now for [us] to demonstrate to the world that those who can fairly carry an election, can also suppress a rebellion—that ballots are the rightful, and peaceful, successors of bullets; and that when ballots have fairly, and constitutionally, decided, there can be no successful appeal, back to bullets; that there can be no successful appeal, except to ballots themselves, at succeeding elections.[61]

Unlike the despotisms of the Old World that were based on the accidents of force or birth, the American regime was based on a universal creed of civil and religious liberty. Indeed, the Declaration, the nation's moral covenant, promised something "more than National Independence." It "held out a great promise to all the people of the world to all time to come." Lincoln defined the promise of America in this way:

> *Most governments* have been based, practically, on the denial of equal rights of men . . . ours began, by *affirming* those rights. *They* said, some men are too ignorant, and vicious, to share in self-government. Possibly so, said we; and, by your system, you would always keep them ignorant, and vicious. We proposed to give all a chance; and we expected the weak to grow stronger, the ignorant, wiser; and all better, and happier together.
>
> We made the experiment; and the fruit is before us.

Lincoln saw America as the custodian and standard-bearer of democratic government to the world. The stain of slavery undermined America's moral credibility in the eyes of the world. It was intolerable for a nation that purported to stand for the idea of freedom and equality to embrace slavery as a "positive good." In effect, argued Lincoln, "We were proclaiming ourselves political hypocrites before the world, by thus fostering Human Slavery and proclaiming ourselves, at the same time the sole friends of Human Freedom."[62]

America's mission also consisted of providing hope and inspiration to other peoples and nations. The failure to preserve democratic government during the Civil War would discredit democracy throughout the world as a legitimate form of governance. Like Jefferson, and like his Whig predecessors,

Daniel Webster and Henry Clay, Lincoln described the United States as the "last best hope of earth." In his "Annual Message to Congress on Dec. 1, 1862," delivered a year into the war, he explained the worldwide significance of the conflict:

> Fellow-citizens, *we* cannot escape history. . . . The fiery trial through which we pass, will light us down, in honor or dishonor, to the latest generation. . . . We know how to save the Union. The world knows we do know how to save it. . . . In *giving* freedom to the *slave,* we *assure* freedom to the *free*—honorable alike in what we give, and what we preserve. We shall nobly save, or meanly lose, the last best, hope of earth. Other means may succeed; this could not fail. The way is plain, peaceful, generous, just—a way which, if followed, the world will forever applaud, and God must forever bless.[63]

Using a biblical metaphor from 1 Peter 4:12, Lincoln viewed the Civil War as a "fiery trial." The original context of the metaphor describes the martyrdom of the early Christian community. The term "martyr" is derived from the Greek word *"martyros,"* meaning witness. Martyrdom was a test or a trial of the early Christians who bore witness to their faith. Similarly, Lincoln viewed the Civil War as a national trial that tested the American people's willingness to bear witness to their political faith. Like Winthrop, who warned the Puritan community that the failure of their mission would make them a "by-word" of disgrace to the rest of the world, Lincoln explained that the failure to preserve the Union and its promise of equality would incur dishonor to the latest generation.[64]

And like Winthrop, who envisioned the "Holy Commonwealth" of New England to represent a Second Israel, Lincoln similarly described the American people as having a unique mission or national destiny under God's providence. Reflecting upon his providential role in guiding the national destiny of the American people shortly before the outbreak of the Civil War, Lincoln observed, "I shall be most happy indeed if I shall be an humble instrument in the hands of the Almighty, and of this, his almost chosen people, for perpetuating the object of that great struggle." This ironic reference to Americans as an "almost chosen people" provided an important qualification of the nation's mission; it introduced an ambiguity consistent with Lincoln's ironic sense of the distance between human intention and divine providence. His qualification seemed to distinguish between the "almost chosen" status of the American people and the actual chosen status of the Jews. While the mission of the Jews as a chosen people was spiritual, the mission of Americans as an "almost chosen people" was political. Though the nation's commitment to the principles of freedom and self-government had entitled it to a chosen status, its failure to live up to these principles had justified the use of the qualifier "almost." Therefore, according to Lincoln, America's status as a chosen people was not inevitable, but conditional; it was dependent upon the nation's fidelity to its political creed. In sum, the

designation "almost chosen people" challenged Americans to fulfill their responsibilities in a time of national trial while subtly reminding them of their
flaws and shortcomings. It inspired action without arrogance and promoted
duty coupled with humility.[65]

While there are many representatives of the American republican tradition, Thomas Jefferson, who penned the Declaration and who warned of a
divine judgment upon the sin of slavery, is most appropriate to an analysis
of Lincoln's biblical republicanism. Robert Bellah observes, "The phrases of
Jefferson constantly echo in Lincoln's speeches." In his magisterial work, *A
New Birth of Freedom*, Harry V. Jaffa traces the influence of Jefferson's republicanism on Lincoln. By his own account, Lincoln understood Jefferson's
principles to be "the definitions and axioms of free society." Paying tribute
to the republican legacy of the author of the Declaration of Independence,
Lincoln remarked:

> All honor to Jefferson—to the man who, in the concrete pressure of a struggle
> for national independence by a single people, had the coolness, forecast, and ca-
> pacity to introduce into a merely revolutionary doctrine, an abstract truth, ap-
> plicable to all men and at all times, and so embalm it there, that to-day, and in
> all coming days, it shall be a rebuke and a stumbling-block to the very harbin-
> gers of re-appearing tyranny and oppression.

Most notably, Lincoln's republicanism was influenced by Jefferson's interpretation of the Declaration as "an expression of the American mind" and as
the "genuine effusion of the soul of the country." Indeed, Lincoln once
stated that he "did not have a feeling politically that did not spring from the
sentiments embodied in the Declaration"[66]

Jefferson's speech prepared for the fiftieth anniversary of the Declaration's signing confirms Lincoln's view of the document's centrality to American republicanism:

> May it be to the world, what I believe it will be (to some parts sooner, to others
> later, but finally to all), the signal of arousing men to burst the chains under
> which monkish ignorance and superstition had persuaded them to bind them-
> selves, and to assume the blessings and security of self-government. That for
> which we have substituted, restores the free right to the unbounded exercise of
> reason and freedom of opinion. . . . [T]he mass of mankind has not been born
> with saddles on their backs, nor a favored few booted and spurred, ready to ride
> them legitimately, by the grace of God. These are the grounds of hope for oth-
> ers. For ourselves, let the annual return of this day [the Fourth of July] forever
> refresh our recollections of these rights, and an undiminished devotion to
> them.

The republican character of the speech is appreciated further in dialectical
juxtaposition to the views of George Fitzhugh, a contemporary of Lincoln's

and a southern apologist for universal slavery who explicitly repudiated Jefferson's interpretation of equality: "Men are not born entitled to equal rights. It would be far nearer the truth to say that some were born with saddles on their backs, and others booted and spurred to ride them; and the riding does them good. They need the reins, the bit and the spur." Lincoln's biblical republicanism sought to vindicate Jefferson against Fitzhugh's critique of the Declaration and free society. Diagnosing the tragic breakdown of moral consensus that erupted in Civil War, Lincoln observed, "But soberly, it is now no child's play to save the principles of Jefferson from total overthrow in this nation." Despite southern protests to the contrary, Lincoln interpreted the secessionist movement as a repudiation of American republicanism: "It continues to develop that the insurrection is largely, if not exclusively, a war upon the first principles of popular government—the rights of the people."[67]

Lincoln and Jefferson alike saw equality as the quintessence of self-government. "The first principle of republicanism," according to Jefferson, "is, that the *lex majoris partis* is the fundamental law of every society of individuals of equal rights." During the secession crisis, Lincoln reminded the nation that the South had established its government upon a new foundation by abandoning the fundamental principle of equality in their Confederate Declarations of Independence from the Union: "unlike the good old one, penned by Jefferson, they omit the words 'all men are created equal.'"[68]

Despite his well-known aversion to sectarianism, Jefferson was characteristically republican in his recognition of the role that religion played in preserving the manners and mores of democratic society. In his First Inaugural Address, he envisioned an American civil theology that would be "enlightened by a benign religion, professed, indeed, and practiced in various forms, yet all of them including honesty, truth, temperance, gratitude, and the love of man; acknowledging and adoring an overruling providence, which by all its dispensations proves that it delights in the happiness of man here and his greater happiness hereafter." Here Jefferson acknowledged not only the utility of religion in providing political happiness in this life but also its ultimate, transpolitical end in providing greater happiness in the hereafter.[69]

Both Jefferson and Lincoln maintained that the principles of the Declaration formed the creed of America's "political faith." In the First Inaugural, Jefferson described the "essential principles of our government" in civil theological terms as "the creed of our political faith—the text of civil instruction—the touchstone by which to try the services of those we trust." It is noteworthy that, in his original draft of the Declaration, Jefferson initially referred to the truths of the Declaration as "sacred and undeniable." And in a personal letter at the end of his life he described the Declaration in religious terms as "the genuine effusion of the soul of our country at that time" and applauded the "sacred attachments of our fellow citizens to the event" of July 4, 1776. He hoped that such an attachment "may, perhaps, like relics of saints, help to nourish our devotion to this holy bond of Union, and keep it longer alive and warm in our affections." In a like manner, Lincoln compared the Union to a sacramental marital bond and distinguished it from a "free love" arrangement that could be dissolved at will.[70]

Jefferson's correspondence with John Adams on the natural aristocracy vividly manifested the very spirit of republicanism that would influence Lincoln's articulation of the American dream—one in which citizens were entitled to equal rights and equality before the law but were rewarded on the basis of merit rather than the accidents of birth:

> . . . I agree with you that there is a natural aristocracy among men. The grounds of this are virtue and talents. . . . There is also an artificial aristocracy, founded on wealth and birth, without either virtue or talents. . . . The natural aristocracy I consider as the most precious gift of nature, for the instruction, the trusts, and government of society. And indeed, it would have been inconsistent in creation to have formed man for the social state, and not to have provided virtue and wisdom enough to manage the concerns of the society. May we not even say, that that form of government is the best, which provides the most effectually for a pure selection of these natural aristoi into the offices of government? The artificial aristocracy is a mischievous ingredient in government, and provision should be made to prevent its ascendancy. . . . With respect to aristocracy, we should further consider, that before the establishment of the American States, nothing was known to history but the man of the old world, crowded within limits either small or overcharged, and steeped in the vices which that situation generates. A government adapted to such men would be one thing; but a very different one, that for the man of these States. Here every one may have land to labor for himself, if he chooses; or, preferring the exercise of any other industry, may exact for it such compensation as not only to afford a comfortable subsistence, but wherewith to provide for a cessation from labor in old age. Every one, by his property, or by his satisfactory situation, is interested in the support of law and order.[71]

Jefferson's discussion of the natural aristocracy contains numerous references to republican political norms including ordered liberty, self-government, equality, civic virtue, the right to enjoy the fruits of one's labor, Locke's view of the individual's right of property in himself, and the promise of material and moral improvement for the meritorious. In characteristic republican fashion, Jefferson provided a vivid contrast between the liberty of the New World and the despotism of the Old World. For both Jefferson and Lincoln, the American experiment in self-government was dedicated to the elevation of the human spirit while the despotisms of the Old World were committed to its debasement.

Jefferson's contrast between old and new borrowed the same biblical metaphors used by the Puritans to describe their mission in America. According to Winthrop, New England represented a "Second Israel." The Puritans, like the Hebrews of old, were a "chosen people." By analogy, the

Hebrews' exodus from Egypt into the Promised Land prefigured the Puritans' exodus from the Old World into the New World. In each case, God's chosen people fled from the corruption of the old order to experience a spiritual transformation. In each case, the mission held universal significance. The chosen people were an example to the entire world. Their success or failure implied monumental consequences for all people throughout all times. In each case, the chosen people were tested by a spiritual trial that prepared them for their new relationship with God. Just as the Israelites had to wander throughout the desert wilderness before they entered the Promised Land, so the Puritans had to sail across the Atlantic Ocean and endure the "howling wilderness."

The biblical distinction between old and new was applied to the nation's political institutions as well. The Old World governments of Europe that were predicated on the principle of divine right were analogous to the idolatry of Pharaoh's rule in Egypt. The New World of America represented a second Israel in its promise of equality for all mankind and in its commitment to the moral covenant of the Declaration of Independence. To carry the analogy further, the symbols of old and new represented the unredeemed rule of divine right and the newly redeemed popular government in the United States whose national motto promised a *novus ordo seclorum* (a new order for the ages) based on the principles of civil and religious liberty. In sum, the apostle Paul's spiritual contrast between the old and the new order in 2 Corinthians 5:17 was applied by Winthrop, Jefferson, and Lincoln to describe the unique calling of the American people in establishing a *novus ordo seclorum* that would supersede the despotism, corruption, and vice of Europe.

Yet Jefferson was a slaveholder. Does this not exclude him from consideration as an important source of American republicanism? While Lincoln made no excuses for Jefferson's moral weakness in this regard, he consistently pointed out that Jefferson, unlike the southern elite of his own time, was deeply ashamed of slavery and considered it to be a social and political evil anathema to American republicanism and repugnant to natural law and right. His condemnations of slavery and his early efforts to abolish it peacefully were cited by Lincoln as evidence that he intended to place the institution on a path of ultimate extinction.[72]

In particular, Lincoln appealed to Jefferson's memorable warning of a divine judgment for the national sin of slavery in *Notes on the State of Virginia:*

> And can the liberties of a nation be thought secure when we have removed their only firm basis, a conviction in the minds of the people that these liberties are of the gift of God? That they are not to be violated but with His wrath? Indeed I tremble for my country when I reflect that God is just; that his justice cannot sleep forever: that considering numbers, nature and natural means only, a revolution in the wheel of fortune, an exchange of situation, is among possible events; that it may become probable by supernatural interference! The Almighty has no attribute which can take side with us in such a contest.[73]

In his debates with Stephen Douglas, Lincoln once again appealed to the authority of Thomas Jefferson in conveying the moral gravity of slavery:

> Judge Douglas ought to remember when he is endeavoring to force this policy upon the American people that while he is put up in that way a good many are not. He ought to remember that there was once in this country a man by the name of Thomas Jefferson, supposed to be a Democrat—a man whose principles and policy are not very prevalent amongst Democrats to-day, it is true; but that man did not take exactly this view of the insignificance of the element of slavery which our friend Judge Douglas does. In contemplation of this thing, we all know he was led to exclaim, "I tremble for my country when I remember that God is just!" We know how he looked upon it when he thus expressed himself. There was danger to this country—danger of the avenging justice of God in that little unimportant popular sovereignty question of Judge Douglas. He [Jefferson] supposed there was a question of God's eternal justice wrapped up in the enslaving of any race of men, or any man, and that those who did so braved the arm of Jehovah—that when a nation thus dared the Almighty every friend of that nation had cause to dread His wrath. Choose ye between Jefferson and Douglas as to what is the true view of this element among us.[74]

By invoking Jefferson's authority, Lincoln chastised Douglas for trivializing the moral gravity of slavery. The appeal to Jefferson also shielded Lincoln from Douglas's allegation that he was an extremist, an abolitionist. Politically speaking, it thwarted Douglas's non sequitur that the appeal to moral absolutes necessarily translated into the immoderate policy of abolitionism; for, as the entire nation knew, Jefferson, who was both a southerner and a slaveholder, nevertheless opposed slavery in principle and looked forward to its eventual extinction.[75]

Lincoln's appeal to filial piety—ancestral reverence for the founders—was yet another characteristic of American republicanism in the nineteenth century. While his appeal to the founders reminded the nation of its moral obligations, it also constituted a prudent political maneuver. As a defensive move, it exonerated Lincoln from the damaging charge of abolitionism. As an offensive maneuver, it waged a poignant counterargument by undermining Douglas's purported fidelity to the founders. Lincoln cleverly used the testimony of the father of the Democratic Party against Douglas. According to Lincoln, the Democrat Party had forfeited the inheritance of its founder through its moral indifference to slavery. The Republican Party was in fact the legitimate heir to Jefferson's legacy, since it sought to contain the evil of slavery. Thus, the Republican Party, not the Democrats, represented the authentic version of American republicanism. Indeed, Lincoln considered the founders worthy of reverence not simply because they were ancestral but because of what they accomplished and represented: despite imperfections, most notably the blight of slavery, they had wisely framed a political edifice that sought conformity with the natural rights enshrined in the Declaration.

Lincoln's biblical republicanism represents a civil theological interpretation of American public life that combines the Judeo-Christian tradition of biblical faith and the founders' republican tradition of self-government. Despite the voluminous literature on Lincoln, few works have offered a sustained exploration of the philosophical coherence of his combination of reason and revelation. Although Lincoln has been consistently recognized as an exemplar of American civil theology, most studies have discussed him incidentally as part of the broader context of religion in the American regime. Rather, the essence of Lincoln's political thought is constituted by the mutual influence of the biblical and republican traditions, which he envisioned as both complementary and philosophically compatible. To Lincoln, the republican principles of America's founding were sacred insofar as the nation's political order participated in God's divine order.[76]

Chapter Two

BIBLICAL REPUBLICANISM

The cogency of Lincoln's civil theology can be attributed to the depth of his thought, to his command of the English language, and, perhaps most important, to his profound understanding of the Bible. If public opinion is the subject matter of civil theology, then persuasion is its means. Lincoln's success as a leader depended upon his ability to persuade the American people that slavery was evil and to induce them to sacrifice for the common cause of liberty and Union. Lincoln viewed Scripture as an authoritative, normative standard to be approximated both personally, in his own life, and politically, in the life of the nation. Expressing gratitude to an African American ministry group who had given him a Bible as a gesture of their support, Lincoln praised Scripture in these powerful terms:

> In regard to this Great Book, I have but to say, it is the best gift God has given to man.
>
> All the good the Saviour gave to the world was communicated through this book. But for it we could not know right from wrong. All things most desirable for man's welfare, here and hereafter, are to be found portrayed in it.[1]

Ronald C. White, Jr., points out that Lincoln's reply could have been "the gracious words by a wise politician to a group who made the Bible their best gift to the President." But perhaps, he notes, the reply contained "the heartfelt words from one who was discovering more of the wisdom of the Bible for himself as he sought to understand the whirlwind of the war." Whatever his motive, Lincoln's impromptu response seems to have exaggerated the role of the "Great Book" as the sole arbiter of moral judgment. To avoid possible distortions of his civil theological intention, an analysis of Lincoln's use of biblical language should begin with a consideration of his view of the danger and limits of applying the precepts of the Bible literally to politics without prudential deliberation. While Lincoln may have viewed the Bible as the preeminent source of wisdom (if judged from the statement above), he clearly did not view it as *the sole and exclusive* source of moral guidance in politics. Rather, he recognized that a literal appeal to the Bible did not always clearly point out one's specific duty or course of action. Because God's revealed word could be misinterpreted and perverted by human beings (as it was when used to justify proslavery and disunionist policies), Lincoln was critical of both northern abolitionists and southern proslavery theologians for exploiting Scripture to justify policies that led to disastrous moral consequences. Furthermore, in addition to revelation, Lincoln believed that human reason was able to discern good from evil: "I think that if anything can be proved by natural theology, it is that slavery is morally wrong."[2]

Thus, Lincoln envisioned a harmony between faith and reason that mutually confirmed the authoritativeness of the nation's founding creed. While president, the mature Lincoln reputedly conveyed the relationship between reason and revelation to his old friend Joshua Speed by telling him to "take all of this book [the Bible] upon reason that you can, and the balance on faith, and you will live and die a happier and better man." Though these words were not written by Lincoln himself (they were reported by Speed after his conversation with the president), I believe that they nevertheless accurately describe his view of a complementary relationship between faith and reason. Lincoln's teaching on reason and revelation eschews the contemporary extremes of a purely secular political rationalism that rejects the authority of revelation and a fideism that rejects the authority of reason. Contrary to either extreme, he envisioned the participation of human reason in accordance with divine reason, and he believed that human reason was illuminated through its openness to God's grace. Both reason and revelation cooperate in the determination of prudent judgments. Because reason is the common language of public discourse in a nonsectarian society, leaders who invoke religion should explore Lincoln's example in translating the basic moral precepts of the Bible into rational terms.[3]

In responding to a group of abolitionist ministers who urged immediate emancipation regardless of the consequences, Lincoln emphasized that the precepts of the gospel could not be applied directly and literally to politics without prudential mediation:

> The subject presented in the memorial is one upon which I have thought much for weeks past, and I may even say for months. I am approached with the most opposite opinions and advice, and that by religious men, who are equally certain that they represent the Divine will. I am sure either the one or the other class is mistaken in that belief, and perhaps in some respect both. I hope it will not be irreverent for me to say that if it is probable that God would reveal his will to others, on a point so connected with my duty, it might be supposed he would reveal it directly to me; for, unless I am more deceived in myself than I often am, it is my earnest desire to know the will of Providence in this matter. *And if I can learn what it is I will do it!* These are not, however, the days of miracles, and I suppose it will be granted that I am not to expect a direct revelation. I must study the plain physical facts of the case, ascertain what is possible and learn what appears to be wise and right. The subject is difficult, and good men do not agree.

Lincoln's acknowledgment that "good men do not agree" on difficult moral questions reflects a humility that is directly opposed to the dogmatism and dualism indicative of contemporary ideological thinking that seeks to demonize political opponents.[4]

Biblical republicanism eschewed a rationally uninformed faith that diminished the need for human discernment and prudential judgment. The Bible did not abolish the need for rational inquiry; it perfected it. A literal appeal to the Bible said nothing in regard to the concrete determination of public policy. It did not take into account the various contingencies that must be weighed and balanced when applying the moral claim. Lincoln's response to the moral idealists of his own time should serve as a warning to contemporaries who likewise rely upon a literal interpretation of the Bible to decide public policy:

> The "Free Soil" men . . . [i]n declaring that they would "do their duty and leave their consequences to God," merely gave an excuse for taking a course that they were not able to maintain by a fair and full argument. To make this declaration did not show what their duty was. If it did we should have no use for judgment, we might as well be made without intelligence, and when divine or human law does not clearly point out what is our duty, we have no means of finding out what it is by using our most intelligent judgment of the consequences.[5]

Indeed, Lincoln recognized fully that the most godly intentions could lead to the most ungodly consequences. Roughly a decade after criticizing the Free-Soil Party for its imprudence, Lincoln would similarly criticize radical abolitionists like John Brown who believed that they had direct access to God's will: "An enthusiast broods over the oppression of a people till he fancies himself commissioned by heaven to liberate them." Given the variability of time and circumstance, it is quite conceivable that divine law may be ambiguous, that is, not immediately manifest, on particular questions. For this reason Thomas Aquinas explains that the precepts of the natural law are to be applied under various circumstances: "the general principles of the natural law cannot be applied to all men in the same way on account of the great variety of human affairs: and hence arises the diversity of positive laws among various people."[6]

In Lincoln's civil theology, the moral legitimacy of a political teaching or public policy depended upon its congruence with the precepts of the Bible, the principles of republicanism, and the conclusions of unassisted reason. One may thus speak of the "three R's of biblical republicanism" as complementary guides to American public life: reason, revelation, and republicanism. As related ways of knowing, the "three R's" reinforced one another in illuminating the same moral and political truths.

An appreciation of biblical republicanism must now consider the various ways that Lincoln invoked the Bible as a source of moral authority and "pertinent quotations" relevant to the politics of the Civil War era. In sum, Lincoln used biblical language in at least five different ways: (1) theologically, to ponder God's providential role in order and history; (2) civil theologically, as a transcendent rule and measure to judge public life; (3) evocatively, for stylistic purposes and rhetorical emphasis; (4) allegorically, to clarify or didactically to convey a respective political teaching by means of a biblical illustration; (5) and existentially, as a meditative unfolding of his personal experience of biblical faith. These five uses of Scripture are not mutually exclusive. They are interrelated elements that reflect the richness of Lincoln's civil theological outlook, and, as Lincoln often showed, the same speech may use biblical symbolism in different senses.

The failure to appreciate Lincoln's multifaceted approach to the Bible will inevitably result in distorted interpretations of his civil theology. For example, an interpretation of his biblical language as purely rhetorical and stylistic leads to the cynical conclusion that he invoked religion exclusively for its political utility, that his use of religious language was merely a political expedient to accommodate the prejudices of a Bible-reading nation. Such a view overlooks the core experiences of biblical faith sincerely conveyed in Lincoln's private and public speeches, the congruence between those utterances, and the testimony of those who corroborated his faith. It fails to take into account the consistent manifestation of Lincoln's faith in private writings from his youthful correspondence with Joshua Speed in 1842 to his mature correspondence with a Quaker woman two decades later. On the other hand, a purely literal interpretation of Lincoln's rhetorical flourishes taken from the Bible will lead to the drastic conclusion that he was messianic, even fanatical, in his expectations of politics and that he confounded spiritual and secular authority. This literal interpretation overlooks Lincoln's humble submission to the mystery of divine providence as expressed in both his public and private speeches. It also fails to recognize his prudence in pursuing a course of moral action between the extremism of the northern abolitionists and southern fire-eaters. In sum, both the instrumental and literal interpretation of Lincoln's religious language reduce the complexity and richness of his biblical expression to the narrow confines of one level of communication. Rather, Lincoln appealed to the Bible in various ways for different purposes depending on the context of his speech.[7]

Each instance of Lincoln's biblical language may be classified as either essential or incidental depending upon whether the teaching of the Bible corresponded directly or indirectly to his life and political teaching. When Lincoln used biblical symbolism allegorically, didactically, or evocatively, the precepts of the Bible applied only indirectly to his overall political teaching as a means to enhance pedagogy or style. As a rhetorical device, his appeal to the Bible was ancillary to the political point he was making; therefore, it was not intended to be interpreted literally. When used existentially, theologically, or civil theologically, however, Lincoln applied the teachings of the Bible directly to his own life and to the nation. His use of biblical symbolism thus involved an essential moral and religious correspondence between the precepts of the Bible and personal and political order. When used in this sense, Lincoln turned to the Bible in search of existential meaning and theological insight to bring himself and the nation in closer communion with God.

Lincoln used biblical language in a theological sense to ponder God's role in order and history. His theological language contemplates ultimate questions about the nature of God, providence, grace, creation, and cosmic justice. Divinity itself is clearly identifiable as the subject of theological language. Consider how Lincoln's plea for peace during his First Inaugural Address invoked the transcendent judgment of the Judeo-Christian God, whose attributes include truth and justice: "If the Almighty Ruler of nations, with his eternal justice, be on your side of the North, or on yours of the South, that truth, and that justice, will surely prevail, by the judgment of this great tribunal, the American people." Here, Lincoln portrayed God in theological terms as the Supreme Ruler and Judge of the American people who must nevertheless play their part as actors upon a cosmic stage without knowing how the drama will unfold.[8]

Lincoln's Second Inaugural Address is perhaps one of the most notable expressions of his theological approach to biblical language:

> The Almighty has His own purposes. "Woe unto the world because of offences! for it must needs be that offences come; but woe to that man by whom the offence cometh!" If we shall suppose that American Slavery is one of those offences which, in the providence of God, must needs come, but which, having continued through His appointed time, He now wills to remove, and that He gives to both North and South, this terrible war, as the woe due to those by whom the offence came, shall we discern therein any departure from those divine attributes which the believers in a Living God always ascribe to Him? Fondly do we hope—fervently do we pray—that this mighty scourge of war may speedily pass away. Yet, if God wills that it continue, until all the wealth piled by the bond-man's two hundred and fifty years of unrequited toil shall be sunk, and until every drop of blood drawn with the lash, shall be paid by another drawn with the sword, as was said three thousand years ago, so still it must be said "the judgments of the Lord, are true and righteous altogether."[9]

The Second Inaugural pondered the ultimate theological significance of the Civil War and the role of providence in guiding the destiny of the nation through its "fiery trial." Indeed, Mark A. Noll and Reinhold Niebuhr both agree that Lincoln far exceeded the theological depth of the religious thinkers of his own time. At the moment of final victory, when the North demanded a triumphalist assertion of its rectitude, Lincoln assigned culpability to both sides and affirmed the inscrutability of providence, nevertheless trusting that God would bring about some ultimate good from the national ordeal.[10]

The public expression of Lincoln's theology in the Second Inaugural corresponds remarkably with an earlier private reflection he wrote around the time of the Emancipation Proclamation that was discovered subsequently in his personal notebook by his secretaries, John Nicolay and John Hay, shortly after his death. Lincoln's secretaries appropriately entitled this reflection, "Meditation on the Divine Will:"

> The will of God prevails. In great contests each party claims to act in accordance with the will of God. Both *may* be, and one *must* be wrong. God can not be *for,* and *against* the same thing at the same time. In the present civil war it is quite possible that God's purpose is something different from the purpose of either party—and yet the human instrumentalities, working just as they do, are of the best adaptation to affect His purpose. I am almost ready to say this is probably true—that God wills this contest, and wills that it shall not end yet. By his mere quiet power, on the minds of the now contestants, He could have either *saved* or *destroyed* the Union without a human contest. Yet the contest began. And having begun He could give the final victory to either side any day. Yet the contest proceeds.[11]

The biblical symbolism of Lincoln's utterance is theological insofar as it raises questions about the divine nature and God's providence. It is also existential, springing from a personal quest for meaning and order. The meditation is not the utterance of a disinterested spectator removed from events but the work of an anguished participant searching for ultimate meaning. Confronting the mystery of existence, Lincoln tried to make sense of the vast suffering around him. In doing so, his soul was poised within the dynamic yearnings of faith by acknowledging the vast distance between human pretensions and God's providential design while nevertheless humbly trusting in God's benevolence.

Significantly, the meditation takes as its starting point trust in a God who is free from contradictions: "God can not be *for* and *against* the same thing at the same time." It presumes the ability of reason to grasp something about the nature of the divine. Although human reason is limited, it does have access to some parts of God's providential order: it can affirm justice, benevolence, and truth as attributes of the divine will. Nevertheless, God's overall design was ultimately mysterious and unfathomable to both sides of the conflict. Neither side could claim perfect certitude; neither could claim perfect rectitude. Both were culpable before God; both were mistaken in their pretensions of righteousness. In sum, Lincoln's meditation evinces a private search for order that is informed by a genuine biblical faith. Avoiding the extremes of moral apathy or self-righteousness, he strove to attune himself to the divine measure without confounding his own will with God's.

Because it has been identified as an authentic private reflection, the "Meditation on the Divine Will" is particularly relevant to an analysis of

Lincoln's biblical faith. Nicolay and Hay published it in response to allegations by William Herndon, Lincoln's law partner from Springfield, that the
president was an infidel. By providing the motivational context of Lincoln's
religious experience, their testimony corroborates the common sense interpretation of the speech as a sincere expression of biblical faith:

> But if it may be said that [Lincoln's faith] was, after all, an exoteric utterance
> springing from those relations of religion and good government which the wis-
> est rulers have always recognized in their intercourse with people, we will give
> one document which Mr. Lincoln wrote in September 1862, while his mind was
> burdened with the weightiest questions of his life, the weightiest with which
> this century has had to grapple. Wearied with all the considerations with law
> and expediency which he had been struggling for two years, he retired himself
> and tried to bring some order in his thoughts by rising above the wrangling of
> men and parties, and pondering the relations of human government to the Di-
> vine. In this frame of mind, absolutely detached from earthly considerations,
> he wrote this meditation. It has never been published. It was not written to be
> seen of men. It was penned in the awful sincerity of a perfectly honest soul try-
> ing to bring itself in closer communion with its maker.

Indeed, Nicolay and Hay clearly appreciated Lincoln's multifaceted approach
to the Bible. Though they candidly acknowledged the important role of religion in supporting republican government, they also appreciated the sacred,
mysterious, and binding character of religion for Lincoln apart from its political utility.[12]

In his intellectual biography *Abraham Lincoln: Redeemer President,* Allen C.
Guelzo concurs with the assessment of Nicolay and Hay. Guelzo, who argues
that Lincoln was inclined toward the rational religion of Thomas Paine in
his youthful days, sees the Meditation as a sincere and mature expression of
Lincoln's biblical faith, which was implicit from his youth but which deepened and developed throughout the experience of personal suffering during
the war:

> The memorandum . . . contains the most radically metaphysical question ever
> posed by an American President. Lincoln had come, by the circle of a lifetime
> and the disasters of the war, to confront once again the Calvinist God who
> could not be captured or domesticated into Tom Paine's Almighty Architect,
> who possessed a conscious will to intervene, challenge, and reshape human
> destinies without regard for historical process, the voice out of the whirlwind
> speaking to the American Job.[13]

Lincoln used biblical language in a civil theological sense as a normative standard to judge public life. When used civil theologically, the precepts of the Bible constituted a source of moral obligation that bound the
nation. If the emphasis of theological language was metaphysical, the

emphasis of civil theological language was moral. Nonetheless, the two were intimately related in Lincoln's civil theology, since the moral participated in the metaphysical. The justice of human institutions, policies, and enactments were adjudicated in terms of their conformity with a divine standard revealed in the Bible and confirmed through right reason *(recta ratio)*. When used in a civil theological sense, Lincoln invoked biblical precepts as a rule and measure to validate the principles of American republicanism and to gauge the moral progress or decline of the regime. In his speech at New Haven, Connecticut, on March 6, 1860, Lincoln employed civil theological language when he contended that a respect for God's justice required that slavery should be publicly stigmatized as "a great moral, social and political evil":

> To us [northerners] it appears natural to think that slaves are human beings; *men, not property*; that some of the things, at least, stated about men in the Declaration of Independence apply to them as well as to us. I say, we think, most of us, that this Charter of Freedom applies to the slave as well as to ourselves, that the class of arguments put forward to batter down that idea, are also calculated to break down the very idea of a free government, even for white men, and to undermine the very foundations of free society. We think Slavery a great moral wrong, and while we do not claim the right to touch it where it exists, we wish to treat it as a wrong in the Territories, where our votes will reach it. We think that a respect for ourselves, a regard for future generations and for the God that made us, require that we put down this wrong where our votes will properly reach it. We think that species of labor an injury to free white men—in short, we think Slavery a great moral, social and political evil, tolerable only because, and so far as its actual existence makes it necessary to tolerate it, and that beyond that, it ought to be treated as a wrong.

Lincoln's speech at New Haven can be seen as a reply to proslavery theologians, who attempted to justify the institution as a social and political blessing. On the contrary, Lincoln argued that to characterize slavery as anything other than "a great moral, social and political evil" was to disrespect God's created order by denying the unique dignity of each individual created in the image of God. It was to degrade an entire class of people from the level of human beings to the rank of beasts. Lincoln thus assigned preeminence to the initial resolution of the moral question of slavery's inherent good or evil as essential in guiding subsequent public policy decisions about its extension or restriction. His defense of the "foundations of free society" constituted a reply to George Fitzhugh's "mud-sill" critique of free labor in *Sociology for the South; or, The Failure of Free Society.*[14]

One of Lincoln's tersest arguments against slavery linked Jesus' Golden Rule in Matthew 7:12 with the republican principle of consent of the governed: "This is a world of compensations; and he who would *be* no slave, must consent to *have* no slave. Those who deny freedom to others, deserve it not for themselves; and, under a just God, can not long retain it." Lincoln viewed the biblical injunction of the Golden Rule and the republican principle of equal consent as correlative. The principle of mastery behind slavery thus violated both the teachings of the Bible and American republicanism. Because no one would himself consent to be governed as a slave, no one is justified in enslaving another without that person's consent. To do so is unfair, since the master exempts himself from a standard that should apply equally to all human beings. In Lincoln's words, "The master not only governs the slave without his consent; but he governs him by a set of rules altogether different from those which he prescribes for himself." By claiming to be entitled to special treatment and therefore exempt from the same norms that govern others, the master, in effect, pridefully attempts to elevate himself to a superhuman status above his fellow human beings.[15]

Lincoln used biblical language in an allegorical and didactic sense to expound a political teaching with an illustration from the Bible. When used didactically, the biblical symbolism was obviously pedagogical. Lincoln's appeal to the Bible was incidental and ancillary to the main point or subject under discussion. The prevailing biblical ethos of the times explains why Lincoln was able to express biblical teachings allegorically and didactically in a manner that would be taken for granted by his audience. Indeed, the Bible once served as a common reference point for civil discourse. It was regarded as an authoritative standard to human life, both temporal and spiritual. For this reason George Anastaplo characterizes the King James Bible as a constitution in the broad sense of the term, a moral guide that "defines a community and regulates its conduct."[16]

Perhaps the most celebrated example of Lincoln's allegorical use of the Bible is his House Divided speech:

> *"A house divided against itself cannot stand."*
> I believe this government cannot endure, permanently half *slave* and half *free*.
> I do not expect the Union to be *dissolved*—I do not expect the house to *fall*—but I *do* expect it will cease to be divided.
> It will become *all* one thing, or *all* the other.
> Either the *opponents* of slavery, will arrest the further spread of it, and place it where the public mind shall rest in the belief that it is in the course of ultimate extinction; or its *advocates* will push it forward, till it shall become alike lawful in *all* the States, old as well as *new—North* as well as *South*.[17]

The immediate political motive of the House Divided speech was to maintain solidarity within the Republican Party, preventing its members from forming an "unholy alliance" with Stephen A. Douglas, who had recently broken with the Buchanan administration over the proslavery Lecompton Constitution in Kansas. Douglas opposed the proposed constitution on purely pragmatic grounds, not because he thought slavery was wrong in principle. In his view, the Lecompton Constitution did not reflect true popular sovereignty because the vote that led to its adoption was blatantly fraudulent: antislavery forces refused to participate in the election. The Little Giant's break with Buchanan tempted notable Republicans like William Seward and Horace Greeley to embrace him as a leader of the antislavery forces. Lincoln, however, argued that Douglas was unfit as a standard-bearer of the Republican Party, since he rejected its core principle: the recognition of slavery's inherent moral evil and its threat to the Union. It was in an attempt to uphold the core principles of his party that Lincoln appealed to the house divided metaphor from Matthew 12, which accentuated the importance of an underlying moral consensus that would understand slavery as evil to the American regime. In its original biblical context, the metaphor intended to reveal the spiritual authority of Christ. In response to the Pharisees, who attempted to portray him as a sorcerer who invoked evil to cure others, Christ explained that evil could not be used to exorcise evil: "Every kingdom divided against itself is brought to desolation; and every city or house divided against itself shall not stand." In sum, Jesus revealed that his healing was done not through evil or black magic but through divine love (agape) in the name of the Father.[18]

The failure to appreciate the allegorical character of Lincoln's use of the house divided metaphor and the interrelated historical, social, and political context in which it was delivered inevitably leads to perverse conclusions. For example, the psychohistorian Dwight G. Anderson insists that the metaphor must be interpreted literally as a self-referential statement by Lincoln to persuade the American public of his own divinity. In order to establish his credentials as a secular messiah, Lincoln appropriated the very metaphor used by Christ to reveal his own spiritual authority. Offering a more plausible interpretation, Charles B. Strozier contends that Lincoln's use of the house divided metaphor was self-referential: the metaphor refers to the division in Lincoln's psyche and domestic life at the time of the speech. But Lincoln did not intend the metaphor as a revelation of his personal divinity, nor was it a psychological confession. Rather, it primarily conveyed the importance of an underlying moral consensus to American public life, one that understood slavery as anathema to republican government and a danger to the Union. Just as Christ referred to the unity of kingdoms and houses, so Lincoln referred to the moral integrity of the Union. If a moral consensus could not be reached concerning the public recognition of slavery's inherent evil and its threat to the Union, Lincoln warned of a transformation in the national ethos that would prepare the way for the indefinite perpetuation of the institution and the eventual corruption of the regime.[19]

The interpretation of the house divided metaphor as a simplistic representation of geographic division between the existence of slavery in the South and its absence in the North is likewise inadequate. The geographic division was incidental to Lincoln's more profound teaching concerning the moral climate of public opinion. He consistently stated that the U.S. Constitution prohibited the national government from interfering with slavery where it already existed in the states. In other words, without an explicit legal authorization to abolish slavery, he was willing to tolerate a division of the house along geographic lines as a necessary evil provided slavery be placed on a path of ultimate extinction when circumstances permitted. Furthermore, the historical context reveals that the House Divided speech was addressed primarily to the antislavery forces from the North who were contemplating an "unholy alliance" with Stephen Douglas. The metaphor impressed upon the Republican Party the need for moral unity in its resistance to slavery. The Republican Party could not claim to embody the regime's founding principles by embracing the leadership of Stephen Douglas, who was indifferent to the moral gravity of slavery. An alliance with Douglas endangered the moral integrity of the antislavery coalition and would undermine its mission to vindicate the natural rights teaching of the Declaration of Independence. Thus, in Lincoln's view at the time of the speech in 1858, the geographic division between North and South was derivative of the more fundamental division over the ultimate meaning of slavery and its relationship to American republicanism. The lack of moral clarity among Republicans who contemplated an alliance with Douglas after he had repudiated the proslavery Lecompton Constitution merely on procedural grounds amply demonstrated that the northern public mind was itself divided.

Although popular sovereignty attempted to provide an alternative between the free soil and proslavery positions, its moral indifference practically amounted to the perpetuation and extension of the institution. Lincoln maintained that the slavery question could be resolved in the long term on the basis of only two realistic possibilities: the institution could be treated either as a positive good to be extended or as a necessary evil to be contained and, eventually, abolished. In practice, Lincoln explained that the doctrines of popular sovereignty and proslavery theology had the same debasing effect on the public mind. By permitting the institution to spread into the virgin territories under federal control, both policies granted slavery a national imprimatur that radically contradicted the spirit of the nation's founding principles and the intention of the founders, who hoped to place slavery on a path of extinction.

Lincoln's house divided metaphor profoundly emphasized the correspondence between public opinion and policy. More precisely, the house divided represented a permanent and abiding chasm in the moral climate of public opinion—"the public mind." A policy that tolerated slavery as either a positive good or as something devoid of intrinsic moral significance would have dulled the nation's moral conscience and corrupted its public ethos. The insidious debauching of the public mind had to be courageously faced before the extension of slavery in the federal territories became a settled policy. Thus, a decisive moral resolution of slavery's relationship to the Union had to be reached: "I do not expect the Union to be *dissolved*—I do not expect the house to *fall*—but I *do* expect it will cease to be divided. It will become *all* one thing, or *all* the other." Lincoln's interpretation of popular sovereignty as providing a tacit moral sanction to slavery is confirmed by his explicit reference to "the public mind" in the next sentence of the House Divided speech: "Either the *opponents* of slavery, will arrest the further spread of it, and place it where the public mind shall rest in the belief that it is in the course of ultimate extinction; or its *advocates* will push it forward, till it shall become alike lawful in *all* the States, *old* as well as *new*—North as well as *South*." The failure to reach a moral resolution upon the inherent evil of slavery would have allowed the continuation of a policy contrary to the principles of the Declaration, debased the nation's public mind, and corrupted its ethos, thereby preparing the way for the indefinite perpetuation of the institution.

Lincoln's didactic use of biblical language occurred not only in public addresses but also in his private utterances. The correspondence between his public and private religious utterances reveals the extent to which the Bible genuinely imbued his thinking on all levels. For example, in a private letter, he explained to a colleague: "By the fruit the tree is to be known. An evil tree can not bring forth good fruit. If the fruit of electing Mr. Clay would have been to prevent the extension of slavery, could the act of electing have been evil?" Lincoln's passage referred to Matthew 12:33, where Jesus states: "Either make the tree good, and his fruit good; or else make the tree corrupt, and his fruit corrupt: for the tree is known by his fruit." Teaching the importance of solidarity within the Republican Party, Lincoln applied another biblical analogy from Matthew 12:30: "And as to men, for leaders, we must remember that 'He that is not for us, is against us; and he that gathereth not with us scattereth.'"[20]

Lincoln used biblical language in an evocative sense for rhetorical and stylistic purposes. His evocative appeal to the Bible stirred the "religious imagination" of his audience through emotion and rhetorical flourish. When used evocatively, the biblical symbolism was directed primarily at the passions (the heart) rather than at reason (the head). To be sure, public speakers must necessarily avail themselves to rhetoric as a necessary means of persuasion, especially when addressing large audiences. Assemblies and congregations will not be persuaded by means of logical demonstration alone. Evocative biblical language seized upon the listener's attention, providing needed emphasis to an argument. Lincoln often cited the Bible to exaggerate the gravity of a point, thereby heightening his audience's awareness of the moral issue involved. His evocative use of biblical language mimicked the fire-and-brimstone oratory of the frontier preachers during the Second Great Awakening who Lincoln encountered in his youthful days in New Salem.[21]

The opening lines of the Gettysburg Address are perhaps the best example of Lincoln's evocative use of biblical rhetoric. The speech is utterly suffused with the style, cadence, and archetypes of the King James Bible. To commemorate the solemnity of the event, the opening "Four score and seven years" of the speech evoked the passage of time in the same manner as the King James Bible. For instance, it recalled the language of the Book of Esther 1:4 ("an hundred and fourscore days") and Psalm 90 ("The days of our years are three score years and ten"). Even the repetition of monosyllabic words paralleled the style of the King James Bible. The religious imagery of "dedicate," "consecrate," and "hallow" was used evocatively throughout the speech to reinforce the supreme sacrifice made by those who gave their lives for duty. In his eulogy, Lincoln did not distinguish specifically between soldiers of the North and South. He spoke of the "dead" in general, recognizing the sacrifice of each side in terms of a wider, national suffering and meaning. The Gettysburg Address also combined evocative language with allegorical and theological symbolism. It portrayed the history of the nation in the allegorical terms of birth, consecration, trial, sacrificial suffering, death, redemption, and rebirth. Significantly, the four score and seven years places the nation's founding at 1776, the year of the Declaration, the creed of the regime's political faith. Although conceived and baptized in liberty, the life of the nation was stained by the original sin of slavery. Its fidelity to the proposition that all men are created equal would be tested through the "fiery trial" of Civil War. Soldiers on the battlefield had not died in vain. Their death was sacrificial, for they had "consecrated" and "hallowed" the ground for future generations. The national ordeal was not meaningless; it would lead to a future transfiguration. Rebirth would occur through death and suffering. The nation could be redeemed from the sin of slavery through a new birth of freedom symbolized by a Union freed from the shackles of slavery. The allegory distilled the essence of the American creed. It affirmed equality as the "central idea" of the regime and taught that the national sacrifice was for a noble cause: to vindicate republican government "of the people, by the people, for the people" by preserving the Union and its promise of equality to all human beings. Nonetheless, the stirring language of the Gettysburg Address should not obscure its immediate political motive: in November 1863, Lincoln asked the nation to confirm the Emancipation Proclamation, which he had decreed in January of the same year. His reference to "this nation under God" at the end of the speech used biblical language theologically to remind the nation of the omnipresence of divine judgment and providence. In effect, Lincoln asked his audience to consider events from a standpoint that was *sub species aeternitatis* (under the aspect of eternity).[22]

Another example of how Lincoln employed biblical symbolism evocatively may be found in an early speech that he delivered during the 1839 debate over the subtreasury system:

> I know that the great volcano at Washington, aroused and directed by the evil spirit that reigns there, is belching forth the lava of political corruption, in a current broad and deep, which is sweeping with frightful velocity over the whole length and breadth of the land, bidding fair to leave unscathed no green spot or living thing, while on its bosom are riding like demons on the waves of Hell, the imps of that evil spirit, and fiendishly taunting all those who resist its destroying course, with the hopelessness of their effort; and knowing this, I cannot deny that all may be swept away. Broken by it, I too, may be; bow to it I never will.

Indeed, Lincoln's language more closely resembles the sermon of a frontier preacher or a canto from Dante's *Inferno* than a discussion of national economic policy. One might speculate that the youthful politician was practicing his rhetoric and oratory.[23]

Lincoln's condemnation of James Polk and the Mexican War provides an early example of his multifaceted use of the Bible. This youthful articulation of biblical republicanism, whereby Lincoln anticipated his biblical case against slavery two decades later, sought to remind Polk that "the Almighty will not, be evaded." If Polk would not clarify the cause and justification of the war, "I shall be fully convinced, of what I more than suspect already, that he is deeply conscious of being in the wrong—that he feels the blood of this war, like the blood of Abel, is crying to Heaven against him." Lincoln's appeal to the story of Cain and Abel in Genesis illustrated the importance of a leader's accountability to God and the people. Cain's evasion of fraternal responsibility ("Am I my brother's keeper?") parallels Polk's evasion of political responsibility. In addition to allegorical symbolism, Lincoln used biblical language in an evocative sense to persuade his listeners of Polk's guilt. His evocation of Cain's ruthless fratricide of Abel pricked the moral conscience of the nation. The images of "the blood of this war, like the blood of Abel," were intended to capture the religious imagination of his listeners and to arouse righteous indignation against Polk. By means of this biblical association, Lincoln attempted to convince his listeners that, like Caine, President Polk could not evade responsibility for the slaughter of innocent blood. A day of reckoning was at hand. A genuine biblical ethos informed Lincoln's politics, not merely incidentally, as a didactic or evocative means to teach or persuade his listeners, but essentially, as a teaching that conveyed a profound truth revealed by the Bible and applicable to public life. Lincoln's condemnation of Polk relied upon the biblical notions of guilt and sin. It appealed to an implicit moral awareness that God had implanted in the hearts of mankind and to a higher justice that regulates human conduct. Polk could not evade the promptings of the human heart no matter how much he attempted to delude himself. Because the basic moral injunctions of this divine order are known through common experience, Polk "is deeply conscious of being in the wrong." Lincoln's interpretation of moral experience presumed the workings of an inner voice or conscience whose murmurings were derived ultimately from God and were rationally accessible. In sum, his view of moral awareness relied upon the biblical understanding of conscience as a rational law inscribed by God upon the human heart and mind.[24]

Lincoln's response to the Reverend John Mason Peck, "a prominent Baptist" minister in Illinois who, according to David Donald, informed Lincoln "the Government of the United States committed no aggression on Mexico" provides another early example of his biblical republicanism. Lincoln's reply to Peck, like his challenge to Polk, is significant because it also anticipates important elements of his mature civil theology:

> If you *admit* that they are facts [that demonstrate Polk's aggression] then I shall be obliged for a reference to any law of language, law of states, law of nations, law of morals, law of religion—any law human or divine, in which an authority can be found for saying those facts constitute *"no aggression."* . . . Possibly you consider those acts too small for notice. Would you venture to so consider them, had they been committed by any nation on earth, against the humblest of our people? I know you would not. Then I ask, is the precept "Whatsover ye would that men should do to you, do ye even so to them" obsolete?—of no force?—of no application?

Two decades later, Lincoln would likewise invoke the Golden Rule against slavery. He consistently appealed to this biblical precept over two decades, first to oppose American aggression against Mexico and subsequently to oppose proslavery theology. Furthermore, the strong tone of Lincoln's reply to Peck is consistent with the subsequent glimpses of righteous indignation that he would direct against proslavery theology. When he witnessed the exploitation of the Bible to justify either the Mexican War or slavery's extension, Lincoln's criticism of the clergy was vehement.[25]

Lincoln's attention to the different but complementary kinds of law based on discrete jurisdictions and spheres of authority may be attributed to the influence of the legal environment that he occupied as a lawyer, the profession to which he devoted most of his adult life. His reply to Peck presumes the harmony between human law and divine law. According to Lincoln, the application of the general precepts of the various kinds of laws to the specific circumstances of the Mexican War all lead to the same moral conclusion—the war was unjust. Throughout his public life, Lincoln maintained a natural law understanding of moral right: the justice of human laws was judged by their conformity to a transcendent rule and measure revealed in Scripture and confirmed by human reason. This natural law understanding was conveyed by Sir William Blackstone in his *Commentaries on the Laws of England,* which Lincoln had read while studying to become a lawyer: "Upon these two foundations, the law of nature and the law of revelation, depend all human laws; that is to say, no human law should be suffered to contradict these." Indeed, the compatibility between the law of reason and revelation was an important element of the founders' republicanism as well. James Wilson, a member of the Constitutional Convention, a strong devotee of a national Union, and a subsequent Supreme Court justice, conveyed this understanding of the natural law in *The Laws of Nature* in 1790:

> How shall we, in particular cases, discover the will of God? We discover it by our conscience, our reason, and by the Holy Scriptures. The law of nature and the law of revelation are both divine; they flow, though in different channels, from the same adorable source. It is, indeed, preposterous to separate them from each other. The object of both is—to discover the will of God—and both are necessary for the accomplishment of that end.

Though it cannot be proved with certainty that Lincoln read the legal writings of Wilson, he nonetheless shared this conception of the relationship between reason and revelation. The natural law understanding articulated by Blackstone and Wilson permeated both Lincoln's legal environment and America's political culture.[26]

Lincoln used biblical language in an existential sense to convey the core religious experiences of his inner life. Existential language manifested his personal response to the divine. Whereas Lincoln invoked biblical language theologically to reflect upon the divine action in order and history, he used it existentially to express his personal relationship to God and his response to God's calling. Existential language was both self-referential and self-reflective. It conveyed, as much as is possible within the limits of language, its author's response to those interior experiences—pathos—that touch one's very core: faith, hope, love, mystery, awe, grace, conversion, suffering, despair, fear, providence, and fate.[27]

LINCOLN'S BIBLICAL FAITH

An analysis of Lincoln's existential use of biblical language necessarily leads to a consideration of his personal faith. The precise character of Lincoln's religious belief has been the subject of controversy given the conflicting testimony of those who knew him, his reticence in sharing matters of conscience with others, his unwillingness to join a church, and the apotheosis of Lincoln by those who have sought to baptize him as a member of their own congregation. The fundamental question of whether Lincoln sincerely believed in a living God who guided the destinies of both nations and human beings is important in ascertaining the character and development of the faith that imbued his biblical republicanism.[28] Was Lincoln's use of biblical language merely a rhetorical convention, part of the cultural currency of the time? Was it the product of an agnostic metaphysician who invoked the Bible for its social and political utility as Straussian scholars contend?[29] On the contrary, Lincoln's civil theology was rooted in a profound religious belief. Historians David Randall and Richard Current conclude quite rightly that Lincoln "was a man of more intense religiosity than any other President the United States has ever had." Based upon the primary sources documented in Lincoln's own speeches and writings and corroborated by the testimony of others who knew him, it can be shown that Lincoln sincerely believed in what may be described as a biblical faith. The core elements of his faith included a belief in the Judeo-Christian God of righteousness who is the Supreme Judge of individuals and nations; an abiding trust in God's providence and the benevolence of his Grand Design; a belief in a personal calling to serve others and the nation as an "instrument of God"; a reliance upon the supernatural force of God's grace, which assists those who are willing to respond; a belief in the efficacy of prayer to establish a closer union between God and his creatures; and the humble recognition of divine mystery. While reason and revelation cooperated as sources of moral guidance in biblical republicanism, revelation provided Lincoln with teachings about providence and grace that transcended the limits of his unassisted human reason. In an Augustinian sense, faith even preceded reason for Lincoln. His faith in a living God whose providence continued to guide the destinies of individuals and nations and whose benevolence would ultimately bring good out of suffering was in itself a crucial presupposition—a leap of faith into the light—that sustained his trust in the intelligibility of the seemingly chaotic world around him in which so much darkness and death had descended. Believing in the efficacy of prayer, Lincoln once poignantly confessed, "I have been driven many times to my knees by the overwhelming conviction that I had nowhere else to go. My own wisdom and that of all about me seemed insufficient for that day."[30]

The controversy surrounding Lincoln's religious views began shortly after the president's death when William Herndon, his former law partner in Springfield, announced that he was an "infidel." Herndon's testimony is important, although some scholars have placed far too much emphasis upon it to support their allegations that Lincoln was a skeptic. Yet these allegations rest upon only a partial interpretation of Herndon's testimony. At other times, Herndon argued that Lincoln was, in fact, a believer. A consideration of the reliability of Herndon's testimony requires that his remarks about Lincoln's religion be placed in context. Herndon was responding to what he considered to be the hagiographic qualities of J. G. Holland's biography, *The Life of Abraham Lincoln,* published in 1865. In particular, he was outraged by a personal testimony in Holland's biography by Newton Bateman, superintendent of Illinois schools, who claimed that Lincoln had made a profession of the Christian faith to him during the 1860 presidential election. According to Herndon, Bateman's account was inconsistent not only with Lincoln's personal views but with the president's personal character, since he was extremely reticent when it came to matters of the heart: "He was the most secretive, reticent, shut-mouthed man that ever existed." If taken seriously and consistently, Herndon's observation seems to raise doubts about his own reliability concerning matters of Lincoln's personal faith. Lincoln would have been reticent in sharing matters of faith with his law partner as well. In his biography of Herndon, David Donald explains that the former was "[d]ecidedly unorthodox in his own view [and] was not willing to have his law partner canonized as a Protestant saint." Donald further claims that "Herndon had little personal knowledge of his law partner's religious beliefs."[31]

Though Herndon alleged that Lincoln was an infidel at times, on other occasions he made conflicting statements that supported the case for the sincerity of Lincoln's biblical faith. For instance, he once observed that, "whether orthodox or not, he [Lincoln] believed in God and immortality; and even if he questioned the existence of future eternal punishment he hoped to find a rest from trouble and a heaven beyond the grave." Herndon's remarks about Lincoln's letter to his dying father was yet another instance where he seemed to provide support for Lincoln's faith in a living God and in an afterlife. In a letter addressed to his stepbrother, John D. Johnston, on January 12, 1851, Lincoln offered the following consolation to his dying father:

> I sincerely hope Father may yet recover his health; but at all events tell him to remember to call upon, and confide in, our great, and good, and merciful Maker; who will not turn away from him in any extremity. He notes the fall of a sparrow, and numbers the hairs of our heads [Matthew 10:30–31]; and He will not forget the dying man who puts his trust in Him. Say to him that if we could meet now, it is doubtful whether it would not be more painful than pleasant; but that if it be his lot to go now, he will soon have a joyous [meeting] with many loved ones gone before; and where [the rest] of us, through the help of God, hope ere-long [to join] them.[32]

As a testimony of Lincoln's personal faith, perhaps not too much emphasis should be placed upon these final words of consolation to a dying father. What is most illuminating, however, is Herndon's insistence in his letter to a Mr. Abbott dated February 18, 1870, that Lincoln was sincere:

> It has been said to me that Mr. Lincoln wrote the above letter to an old man simply to cheer him up in his last moments, and that the writer did not believe what he said. The question is, Was Mr. Lincoln an honest and truthful man? If he was, he wrote that letter honestly, believing it. It has to me the sound, the ring, of an honest utterance. I admit that Mr. Lincoln, in his moments of melancholy and terrible gloom, was living on the border land between theism and atheism, sometimes quite wholly dwelling in atheism. In his happier moments he would swing back to theism, and dwell lovingly there. . . . So it seems to me that Mr. Lincoln believed in God and immortality as well as heaven—a place.[33]

What accounts for Herndon's inconsistency? In sum, Herndon "was driven to overstatement" by the apotheosis of Lincoln and by hagiographers who sought to baptize the president as a member of their congregation.[34] Regardless of the conclusion one draws from Lincoln's letter of consolation to his father, Herndon's statement shows that he himself entertained conflicting, if not contradictory, opinions of his law partner's faith and therefore cannot be accepted as the sole and final authority on the subject. David Donald's work *Lincoln's Herndon* helps to place Herndon's testimony on Lincoln's religion in its proper context:

> The furious bickering over Lincoln's religious views was mostly a matter of muddled thinking and inadequate definition of terms. For example, Herndon asserted that Lincoln *"was in short an infidel*—was a Universalist—was a Unitarian—a Theist"—four distinct propositions in the same sentence. Herndon correctly observed that his partner never joined any Christian church. He was probably warranted in asserting that Lincoln disliked the fundamentalist theology prevalent in his day. But so anxious was Herndon to prevent his partner's becoming a Calvinistic demigod that he overstated his case.[35]

The character of Lincoln's biblical faith may be illuminated further through a consideration of the various religious environments that influenced his belief. Lincoln's childhood reading included the religious classics of the Bible and John Bunyan's *Pilgrim's Progress*. The Calvinism of his parents, who were members of the Separate Baptist church, was an important influence during his youthful days in Kentucky and Indiana. In contradistinction to the Regular Baptists, the Separate Baptists viewed the Bible as their sole creed, and the early influence of an unmediated faith that emphasized one's personal encounter with the Bible persisted throughout his adult life. Though Lincoln never joined a Baptist church and may have even rebelled against his father's faith and the emotionalism of frontier religion, Guelzo states that Calvinism "was ingrained so deeply into him that his mental instincts would always yield easily to any argument in favor of determinism or predestination, in favor of the helplessness of humanity to please God, in favor of melancholy as the proper estimate of the human condition." William E. Barton, author of *The Soul of Abraham Lincoln,* a book Guelzo describes as "the most serious and balanced investigation of Lincoln's religion," states: "The rock-bottom foundation of Abraham Lincoln's faith was the ultra-Calvinism of his boyhood. He was reared a Predestinarian. To this he added a strong rationalistic tendency, inherent in his nature, and strengthened by his study of Paine and Volney. . . . He profoundly believed himself an instrument of the divine will, believing that will to be right, and creation's final law."[36]

When he moved to New Salem, Illinois, Lincoln was exposed to a group of liberal thinkers who introduced him to Thomas Paine's *Age of Reason* and C. F. Volney's *Ruins*. These Enlightenment works provided a critique of orthodox Christianity and offered a rational religion purged of superstition and intolerance in its place. Allegedly, during this period Lincoln composed "a book of infidelity" that presented arguments against Christianity. Herndon reported that the book was snatched from Lincoln's hands by his employer at the time, Samuel Hill, who then threw it into the fire lest it should ruin the aspiring young man's political future. Lincoln's alleged book of infidelity and his reading of Paine have been adduced as proof that he was an atheist. Yet the reliability of Herndon's testimony is dubious. Roughly thirty years after the president's death, Herndon visited New Salem for only one day to collect information about Lincoln's relationship with Ann Rutledge. By the time Herndon conducted his visit, New Salem had long ceased to remain an actual town, since most everyone who lived there thirty years earlier had moved away from the remote village. Indeed, Herndon himself never saw Lincoln's alleged book of infidelity but relied upon hearsay that was itself highly dubious. The reliability of Herndon's account is even less credible given the subsequent, conflicting testimony of Mentor Graham, the schoolmaster of New Salem who taught Lincoln surveying, introduced him to Samuel Kirkham's *English Grammar,* lodged him in his home, and, in the words of Barton, "knew more about Lincoln's religious views during his years at New Salem than any other man." Graham explained that Lincoln had shown him a book he had written on the subject of universal salvation, the belief that divine punishment is not indefinite and that through the infinite mercy of God all of his creatures will eventually be saved from eternal damnation. Graham explained that the alleged book of infidelity was actually

> a defense of universal salvation. The commencement of it was something about the God of the universe never being excited, mad, or angry. I had the manuscript in my possession some week or ten days. I have read many books on the subject, and I don't think in point of perspicacity and plainness of reasoning I ever read one to surpass it. I remember well his argument. He took the passage, "As in Adam all die, even so in Christ shall all be made alive," and followed with the proposition that whatever the breach or injury of Adam's transgression to the human race was, which no doubt was very great, was made right by the atonement of Christ.[37]

Graham's testimony is consistent with the accounts of others who claimed to have heard Lincoln defend universal salvation. The strong predestinarian tenor of Lincoln's belief also supports Graham's assessment, as does his rationalist frame of mind in which he relentlessly pursued the logic of fundamental propositions to their ultimate conclusion. Graham also provided an alternative account of the book burning. Though he was not present himself, Graham reported that the episode Herndon referred to actually described a letter written by Hill to his friend John McNamur concerning their mutual affection for Ann Rutledge. Apparently, there was a love quadrangle between Ann Rutledge and the three bachelor friends of New Salem:

Hill, McNamur, and Lincoln. Hill's lost letter to McNamur was discovered by some schoolchildren who presented it to Lincoln, the postmaster of New Salem at this time. Fearful that his personal affections would be revealed, Hill snatched the letter from Lincoln's hands and consigned it to the flames. The scant and unreliable evidence of primary witnesses coupled with the credible testimony of Mentor Graham, who actually saw Lincoln's book on universal salvation and who provided an alternative account of the allegedly burned book, suggests that Herndon confounded the stories of Hill's letter with Lincoln's work on universal salvation.[38]

It is not claimed that Herndon was a liar. In fact, Herndon's testimony is extremely valuable in revealing the unorthodox elements of Lincoln's belief. Undoubtedly, Lincoln must have had reservations about evangelical Christianity that prevented him from formally joining a church. In an early letter to Mary Owen, the youthful Lincoln candidly admitted his lack of church attendance: "I've never been to church yet, nor probably shall not soon. I stay away because I am conscious I should not know how to behave myself." Lincoln was known to have parodied the mannerisms and oratory style of the frontier preachers. Even Lincoln's wife admitted that his views were unorthodox. When interviewed by Herndon, Mary Todd Lincoln attempted to express her husband's belief in these terms: "Mr. Lincoln had no faith and no hope in the usual acceptation of those words. He never joined a Church; but still, as I believe, he was a religious man by nature. . . . [I]t was a kind of poetry in his nature, and he was never a technical Christian."[39] Mary Todd's statement that her husband was "never a technical Christian" may have meant nothing more than a recognition that Lincoln never officially joined a church, or it could have meant that he had more serious reservations about Christian orthodoxy. In any event, she seems to have identified two important elements of her husband's faith that existed alongside one another: a religious nonconformity and a religious inclination deeply embedded in the man's character. Because it reflects only a portion of the truth— namely, that Lincoln's views deviated from established orthodoxy on certain articles of faith—Herndon's testimony about Lincoln's religion requires serious qualification and clearer examination. It does not follow that because Lincoln could not assent to all of the theological dogmas of orthodox and evangelical Christianity that he was in fact a skeptic, atheist, or infidel. Moreover, the term "infidel" is itself misleading, since it was used so broadly in the nineteenth century by Herndon and others to characterize those who did not subscribe to orthodox, evangelical Christianity. If true, Lincoln's belief in universal salvation would have earned him the title of infidel. William E. Barton, who as a frontier preacher had a firsthand knowledge of religious environments similar to those of Lincoln's youth, remarked that one could be branded an infidel for believing that the earth was round. This context should be kept in mind when examining Lincoln's reply to the charges of infidelity leveled against him by Peter Cartwright, a frontier preacher, who was competing against him for a congressional seat in the election of 1846:

> A charge having got into circulation in some of the neighborhoods of this District, in substance that I am an open scoffer at Christianity, I have by the advice of some friends concluded to notice the subject in this form. That I am not a member of any Christian Church is true; but I have never denied the truth of Scriptures; and I have never spoken with intentional disrespect of religion in general, or of any denomination of Christians in particular. It is true that in early life I was inclined to believe in what I understand is called the "Doctrine of Necessity"—that is, that the human mind is impelled to action by some power, over which the mind itself has no control; and I have sometimes (with one, two or three, but never publicly) tried to maintain this opinion in argument. The habit of arguing thus however, I have, entirely left off for more than five years. And I add here, I have always understood this same opinion to be held by several of the Christian denominations.[40]

In this public handbill, addressed to the voters of the Seventh Congressional District, Lincoln flatly denied having ever intended to insult anyone's religion. Neither Herndon nor Ward Hill Lamon, who wrote an unflattering 1872 biography of the president based on some material gathered by Herndon, mentioned the handbill. Though Lincoln claimed never to have denied the truth of Scriptures, he was unwilling to reveal his personal beliefs. The only positive affirmation he offered was an explanation of his belief in the "Doctrine of Necessity," which resembled the predestinarian teaching of his youthful religious environment. In response to Cartwright's allegations, it was wholly appropriate for Lincoln to refuse to provide a profession of faith beyond what was publicly relevant. To capitulate to a political opponent who compels one to proclaim publicly the private matters of his own heart would be to surrender the most sacred right of conscience. The logic of Cartwright's charges would compel all candidates to reveal their personal creed as a criterion of their suitability to office, in effect violating the Constitution's prohibition against religious tests, pressuring them to violate the integrity of their conscience if they deviated from strict orthodoxy. It would force candidates to proclaim self-righteously their doctrinal purity before the public. Though private matters of the heart were not publicly relevant to the campaign, Lincoln believed some religious actions and beliefs nevertheless were. "I do not think I could myself," wrote Lincoln, "be brought to support a man for office, whom I knew to be an open enemy of, and scoffer at, religion. Leaving the higher matter of eternal consequences, between him and his Maker. I still do not think any man has the right thus to insult the feelings, and injure the morals of the community in which he may live. . . ."[41]

In addition to the Calvinism of his youthful days, a second important influence on Lincoln's religious outlook was the teaching of the Reverend James Smith, minister of the First Presbyterian Church in Springfield. The Lincolns became acquainted with Smith after he conducted the funeral service for their second son, Eddie, who died in 1850. Smith, a Scotsman from

Glasgow, was a deist in his youth. His subsequent conversion experience led him to take up the cause of demonstrating the compatibility between reason and revelation. Smith gained a reputation throughout the West for debating with skeptics and deists and converting them to the reasonableness of Christianity. In a legendary showdown against the widely known infidel author C. G. Olmstead, Smith triumphed after three weeks of debate. During the debate, Smith crafted a book that demonstrated the harmony between faith and reason entitled *The Christian's Defence, Containing a Fair Statement and Impartial Examination of the Leading Objections Urged by Infidels, against the Antiquity, Genuineness, Credibility, and Inspiration of the Holy Scripture.* The book included a reply to the rational religion of both Paine and Volney. While providing spiritual consolation to Lincoln after the death of his little boy, Smith gave him a copy of this book to provide reflection as well. Allegedly, Lincoln remarked that Smith's arguments in defense of revelation were "unanswerable." Ninian Edwards, Mary Todd's brother-in-law, revealed that after studying Smith's work Lincoln became "convinced of the truth of the Christian religion." Guelzo describes Smith's role in Lincoln's religious as "intellectual, since Smith had thoroughly assimilated the Old School preference for religious argumentation based on reasonableness and probability rather than religious passions or affections." In sum, Smith provided Lincoln an intellectual alternative to the crude emotionalism of frontier religion.[42]

Another work that may have influenced Lincoln's views on the compatibility between faith and reason was Robert Chambers's *Vestiges of the Natural History of Creation.* Herndon reported in his biography of the sixteenth president that the "treatise interested him greatly, and he was deeply impressed with the notion of the so-called 'universal law' evolution." The book attempted to reconcile the new scientific discoveries of the nineteenth century with the teachings of the Bible. In the words of its own author, it was "the first attempt to connect the natural sciences with the history of creation."

In addition to James Smith, a second Presbyterian minister influenced the development of Lincoln's religious belief: the Reverend Phineas Densmore Gurely. Ronald C. White, Jr., explains that it was no coincidence that Lincoln was attracted to these two ministers of the same religious denomination: "I believe he sought and found two Presbyterian preachers who were thoughtful and reasonable in their approach to faith. Both pastors embodied the constellation of ideas and practices that came to be identified with the Old School Presbyterianism." Gurley presided over the Presbyterian church on New York Avenue in Washington, D.C. Of this minister, Lincoln reputedly said, "I like Gurley. He don't preach politics. I get enough of that through the week, and when I go to church, I like to hear the gospel." White documents Lincoln's church attendance at New York Avenue and demonstrates the influence of Gurley's "American Old School Presbyterianism understanding of Reformed theology"

upon Lincoln's Second Inaugural Address. The unwavering belief that human beings were instruments of divine providence was "central to this
American Reformed tradition."[43]

Though Lincoln's faith deepened with maturity—especially after the
death of his son Willie and during the war years—his articulation and interpretation of this faith remained fairly consistent throughout his life. His
spiritual dialogue with Gurley, his more regular attendance at Gurley's New
York Avenue church, the testimony of those who knew him, and his more
frequent references to the divine in his speeches and writings have been
adduced by scholars to show that his religiosity deepened during the war
years. Noah Brooks, a friend of Lincoln's, reported that after the president
"went to the White House he kept up the habit of daily prayer. Sometimes
it was only ten words, but those ten words he had." Julia Taft Bayne, a
sixteen-year-old friend of Lincoln's sons who attended the Fourth Presbyterian Church on New York Avenue with the Lincoln family recollected
that the president would read the Bible after lunch each day, sprawling out
on a chair with his shoes off. Rebecca R. Pomoroy, a nurse who provided
comfort to the Lincoln family after the death of their son Willie in 1862,
corroborated the report. Pomoroy remembered Lincoln telling her, "I am
fond of the Psalms. Yes, they are the best, for I find in them something for
every day of the week." Even though Lincoln's faith may have deepened
during the war, the core elements of his faith were nonetheless present in
his youth, as is vividly manifested in his early correspondence with his
Springfield friend Joshua F. Speed.[44]

The biographers Randall and Current note the consistency and depth of
Lincoln's faith, using the term "fatalism" to describe it. Other historians,
too, have adopted the term. "Biblical faith," however, more accurately describes Lincoln's religious experience. "Fatalism" is accurate in its recognition of the Calvinist tenor of Lincoln's faith and the subordination of his
will to a higher power, but it is misleading and inaccurate insofar as it implies that events in his life were governed by blind chance devoid of any
transcendent meaning, and insofar as it seems to deny the possibility of the
human will to cooperate freely with the Divine Will. As White has shown in
his analysis of the president's mature religious belief, "Historians and Lincoln biographers have too often equated fatalism and providence. . . . In fatalism, events unfold accoding to certain laws of nature. In Christian theology, God's divine power is able to embrace human freedom and
responsibility." The belief in the sovereignty of God's providence was perfectly consistent with the theology of the Reformed tradition. Lincoln's belief that he played some part in God's grand design involved much more
than a passive resignation to an unknown force of "necessity"; rather, it involved an active resolution to subordinate himself to the will of a living God
and an abiding trust that, despite suffering, God was directing human agents
toward some benevolent end.[45]

The core elements of Lincoln's biblical faith are revealed in two early letters he wrote to his friend Joshua Speed in 1842. In each case, the religious language occurs in the context of Lincoln providing advice about Speed's beloved Fanny. In his letter of February 3, 1842, Lincoln consoled Speed, who worried that Fanny's illness would result in death:

> I hope and believe, that your present anxiety and distress about *her* health and *her* life, must and will forever banish those horrid doubts, which I know you sometimes felt, as to the truth of your affection for her. If they can be once and forever removed, (and I almost feel a presentiment that the Almighty has sent your present affliction expressly for that object) surely, nothing can come in their stead, to fill their immeasurable measure of misery. The death scenes of those we love, are surely painful enough; but these we are prepared to, and expect to see. They happen to all, and all know they must happen. Painful as they are, they are not an unlooked-for-sorrow. Should she, as you fear, be destined to an early grave, it is indeed, a great consolation to know that she is so well prepared to meet it. Her religion, which you once disliked so much, I will venture you now prize most highly.

Testifying to the beneficence of providence, Lincoln assured his friend that there was a divine purpose behind the "present affliction." Though he could not claim to be certain, Lincoln admitted to having a "presentiment of the Almighty" that Speed's suffering served some greater design, that perhaps it would in some way confirm his friend's love for Fanny. Lincoln then asked Speed to acknowledge the power of religion in preparing one for a life beyond the grave. Perhaps alluding to the youthful reservations he and Speed shared about frontier religion, Lincoln exhorted his friend to "prize most highly" the faith manifested by his beloved Fanny. At the end of the Civil War, Speed and Lincoln would be reunited, and Speed would testify to the deepening of Lincoln's faith.[46]

In a subsequent letter the same year dated July 4, 1842, Lincoln told Speed: "I believe God made me one of the instruments in bringing your Fanny and you together, which union, I have no doubt He had foreordained. Whatever he designs, he will do for me yet. 'Stand still and see the salvation of the Lord' is my text just now." Lincoln repeated his assurance to Speed that his destiny was guided by a providential design; that things happened for a reason; that life was not a series of unconnected, random events, but that it unfolded according to a divine plan.[47]

The early, private letters to Joshua Speed show that a core of biblical faith coexisted with Lincoln's reservations about the frontier religion of his youthful days. In each case, Lincoln interpreted the events of his own life in reference to the unfolding of God's providential design. Manifesting an openness toward the promptings of grace, he conveyed his personal experience of the divine at work in his life. His articulation of biblical faith reveals a trust *(fiducia)* in the graciousness of a personal God whose mercy and benevolence guides individuals and nations toward some ultimate good. As faithful servant *(fidelitas)*, Lincoln bore witness to God's providential design. God had made him an "instrument" in bringing about good in someone else's life. Humbly submitting to God's will, he confessed, "whatever he designs he will do for me yet." In view of these sincere, private expressions of biblical faith and their consistency with Lincoln's subsequent public and private religious utterances, it is improper to reduce wholesale the youthful Lincoln's religious experience to a mere fatalistic surrender to an impersonal force of destiny. And it is also wrong to conclude that the mature Lincoln shrewdly or "prudently" cloaked his infidelity in the more respectable garb of traditional religion for the sake of political expediency.

Transcending a mere belief in an impersonal force of destiny, the biblical faith animating Lincoln's letters to Joshua Speed testifies to the goodness and power of the living God of Abraham, Isaac, and Jacob. Lincoln writes, "Stand still and see the salvation of the Lord," a direct quotation of Moses found in Exodus 14:13. The original scriptural context is revealing. After wandering through the desert, the Israelites found themselves trapped between Pharaoh's army and the Red Sea. While on the verge of destruction, they fell into anxiety and despair. They began to question God's design. Anticipating Pharaoh's wrath, they reflected upon the ultimate significance of their struggle and journey. Their suffering and exile seemed meaningless. Had they been led out of Egypt only to be forsaken in the barren desert? In their despair, they even considered returning to Egypt: "And they said unto Moses, Because there were no graves in Egypt, hast thou taken us away to die in the wilderness? . . . For it had been better for us to serve the Egyptians, than that we should die in the wilderness" (Exodus 14:11–12). At this climactic point, Moses assured his people that God had not abandoned them. Despite their adversity and fears, God was overseeing events. The story of Moses assuring the Hebrew people of God's providence reveals one of the most fundamental elements of biblical faith: the trust in the graciousness of God's design despite the painful reality of suffering, hardship, and adversity.

The scriptural teaching of Exodus 14 provided Lincoln with transcendent meaning for his own life. It furnished him with an inner strength to overcome his anxieties, trials, and tribulations. Even though he had experienced adversity, like the children of Israel, he continued to trust in God's ultimate deliverance and redemption. Despite the ultimate inscrutability of God's will, Lincoln nonetheless believed that temporal events in his own life and in the world were moving toward some benevolent end, since the universe God created was inclined to the good. Paul's exhortation in Romans 8:28 provides a parallel expression of the biblical faith found in Lincoln's early letters to Joshua Speed: "And we know that all things work together for good to them that love God, to them who are the called according to *his* purpose." Paul describes more than a fatalistic submission to an impersonal destiny. His articulation of biblical faith conveys a trust in the benevolence of a living God who will bring good out of suffering.

Lincoln's subsequent writings during the war reaffirmed the biblical faith manifested in his early letters to Joshua Speed. In his Address at Sanitary Fair, Baltimore, Maryland, on April 18, 1864, Lincoln stated:

> When the war began, three years ago, neither party, nor any man, expected it would last till now. Each looked for the end, in some way, long ere to-day. Neither did any anticipate that domestic slavery would be much affected by the war. But here we are; the war has not ended, and slavery has been much more affected—how much needs not now be recounted. So true it is that man proposes and God proposes.
>
> But we can see the past, though not claim to have directed it; and seeing it, in this case, we feel more hopeful and confident in the future. . . .[48]

In his remarks to a Baltimore Presbyterian synod in late 1863, Lincoln provided an articulation and a personal testimony of biblical faith that parallels Paul's exhortation in Romans 8:28 that "all things work together for good to them that love God," which coheres with his youthful expression of faith in his correspondence with Joshua Speed: "I have often wished that I was a more devout man than I am. Nevertheless amid the greatest difficulties of my Administration, when I could not see any other resort, I would place my whole reliance in God, knowing that all would go well, and that He would decide for the right." The biblical faith described in Romans 8:28 and affirmed by Lincoln throughout his life placed trust in a living God who would bring good out of suffering. This biblical faith transcended the limits of human reason, which, by itself, could not explain suffering. Confined to its own limits, unassisted reason must admit that suffering is either meaningless or random. For Lincoln, the answer to suffering could only be found in reference to some Grand Design, which, in turn, depended upon his faith in a living God. Consequently, he turned to revelation to sustain him as a humble servant who bore witness to God's justice. The biblical teaching on providence provided him with "hope" that things would eventually "turn out right."[49]

As seen in his private letter to Joshua Speed in 1842 and in his subsequent public writings, Lincoln understood himself to be an "instrument" of God. En route to his inauguration in 1861, he stated, "[If] we have patience; if we restrain ourselves; if we allow ourselves not to run off in a passion, I still have confidence that the Almighty, the Maker of the Universe will, through the instrumentality of this great and intelligent people, bring us through this as He has through all the other difficulties of our country." This self-interpretation of a divine calling parallels Paul's reference to "them who are the called according to *his* purpose." Does being an instrument of God suggest the simple identification of one's own will with that of God's? History tells us that fanatics like John Brown also understood themselves as instruments of God. Indeed, Brown believed that he was divinely inspired to punish the sins of the slaveholder and to execute God's judgment on earth: "Without the shedding of blood," went

Brown's chilling motto, "there is no remission of sins." This triumphalist fanaticism is consistent neither with a true understanding of faith nor with Lincoln's understanding of what it meant to be an "instrument of God." Rather, Lincoln's self-understanding reflects what Reinhold Niebuhr and Martin Marty have referred to as an "ironic perspective," an existential and theological outlook that avoids self-righteousness by humbly affirming the ultimate mystery of God's providential design.[50]

Lincoln's interpretation of his own divine calling reveals a humble submission to God's will. He is an instrument of God insofar as he bears witness to God's goodness in the face of trials and tribulations. As David Hein notes, the "instrument of God" may also be understood as a "witness to God" and a "suffering servant." Despite personal sacrifice, the witness to God, like the prophets of old, remains loyal and faithful to the divine voice within. Regardless of how events transpire, the instrument of God continues to bear witness to God's splendor and justice. He seeks to attune himself to the divine measure.

An expression of biblical faith parallel to Lincoln's youthful correspondence with Speed appears in his more mature correspondence with Mrs. Gurney, a Quaker woman who came to the White House to provide "spiritual guidance" during the war. Lincoln corresponded with Gurney on two occasions in 1862 and 1864. The rare personal tone of this correspondence suggests that Lincoln was sincerely moved by Gurney. Perhaps it was the nondoctrinal character of her Quaker faith, or perhaps it was her humble effort to serve the president in his time of anguish. Many of the religious figures in Lincoln's time came to the White House not for spiritual consolation, as did Gurney, but to further their own political agenda. Since the Quakers were conscientious objectors, Gurney could make no partisan demands on Lincoln as a member of the war coalition. After his first encounter with Gurney on October 26, 1862, Lincoln was moved to make a spontaneous testimony of faith in response to her prayer for him:

> I am glad of this interview, and glad to know that I have your sympathy and prayers. We are indeed going through a great trial—a fiery trial. In the very responsible position in which I happen to be placed, being a humble instrument in the hands of our Heavenly Father, as I am, and as we all are, to work out his great purposes, I have desired that all my works and acts may be according to his will, and that it might be so, I have sought his aid—but if after endeavoring to do my best in the light which he affords me, I find my efforts fail, I must believe that for some purpose unknown to me, He wills it otherwise. If I had my way this war would never have commenced; If I had been allowed my way this war would have been ended before this, but we find it still continues; and we must believe that He permits it for some wise purpose of his own, mysterious and unknown to us; and though with our limited understandings we may not be able to comprehend it, yet we cannot but believe, that he who made the world still governs it.[51]

Consistent with his earlier articulation of biblical faith in the letters to Speed, Lincoln referred to himself as a "humble instrument" of God. As he had in his "Annual Message to Congress on Dec. 1, 1862," Lincoln described the Civil War as a "fiery trial." The original context of the metaphor, found in 1 Peter 4:12, described the experience of Christian martyrs who bore witness to their faith. The suffering of the early Christians was meaningful and purposeful as a testimony of their faith. Lincoln thus saw the suffering of the Civil War as a kind of martyrdom that tested himself and the nation to bear witness to God's Grand Design. To be an instrument of God was to be a witness to God's will, which entailed not only self-assertion but also self-effacement, a willingness to serve others for some higher purpose. Indeed, Lincoln's moral commitment to preserve both liberty and Union involved great personal sacrifice and suffering. He well recognized that worldly success was not necessarily a sign of divine favor. Enduring his own "fiery trial" and sacrifice, Lincoln poignantly confided to his friend Owen Lovejoy, "This war is eating my life out, I have strong impression that I shall not live to see the end of it."[52]

Lincoln's correspondence with Gurney reveals him reaching out to divine grace for assistance through his terrible time of trial. Rather than attempting to rely upon his own resources to overcome adversity, Lincoln acknowledged his reliance upon God. His biblical faith manifests not a prideful self-sufficiency but a humble dependence upon God. It is diametrically opposed to the hubris of those leaders like Napoleon who became so intoxicated with their own power that they saw themselves as infallible and invincible. On the contrary, Lincoln confessed that he had "sought" God's "aid" and that he had attempted to bring himself in conformity with the divine will: "I have desired that all my works and acts may be according to his will." He sought a divine illumination that would guide his judgment. He had endeavored to do his best "in the light which he affords me." In a subsequent utterance, Lincoln stated, "amid the greatest difficulties of my Administration, when I could not see any other resort, I would place my whole reliance in God, knowing that all would go well, and that He would decide for the right." Though he could not predict the outcome of events, and though no personal revelation was vouchsafed to him as president, he nonetheless trusted that there was a deeper meaning beyond the suffering. God would ultimately bring good out of the conflict. He thus hoped that "for some wise purpose of his own," mysterious and unknown to mortals, God "permits" such suffering. Rather than becoming a metaphysical rebel like Ivan Karamazov who rejected God's order of creation because he could not comprehend the meaning of innocent suffering, Lincoln affirmed the graciousness of divine being and faithfully bore witness to the truth "that he who made the world still governs it." By his own poignant account, Lincoln confessed to Mrs. Gurney that he was sustained by a biblical faith that was the ground of his hope. He trusted that events in his own life and that of the nation were working toward some ultimate good despite the inability of human reason to comprehend "the problem of pain."[53]

Two years later, Lincoln responded to Gurney in a private letter. This rare personal response may be contrasted to his more general approach during the war of answering letters as a means of communicating his public policy views to a wider audience, knowing full well that the public would scrutinize his reply. The fact that Lincoln remembered events from two years earlier and that his reply was strictly private testifies to the great power and sincerity of his spiritual yearnings. As with his "Meditation on the Divine Will" from September 30, 1862, Lincoln's letter to Gurney on September 4, 1864, seemed to represent a spiritual catharsis for the president during a time of existential anguish:

> I have not forgotten—probably never shall forget—the very impressive occasion when yourself and friends visited me on a Sabbath forenoon two years ago. Nor has your kind letter, written nearly a year later, ever been forgotten. In all, it has been your purpose to strengthen my reliance on God. I am much indebted to the good Christian people of the country for their constant prayers and consolations; and to none of them more than to yourself. The purposes of the Almighty are perfect, and must prevail, though we erring mortals may fail to accurately perceive them in advance. We hoped for a happy termination of this terrible war long before this; but God knows best, and has ruled otherwise. We shall yet acknowledge His wisdom and our own error therein. Meanwhile we must work earnestly in the best light He gives us, trusting that so working conduces to the great ends He ordains. Surely He intends some great good to follow this mighty convulsion, which no mortal could make, and no mortal could stay.

In both of his replies to Gurney, Lincoln contrasted God's perfection to human imperfection and humbly submitted himself to the divine will. Man must not stand in judgment of God. Throughout the chaos of the Civil War, Lincoln continued to affirm God's benevolence.[54]

Lincoln acknowledged the efficacy of Gurney's prayer and the prayers of the American people in strengthening his "reliance on God." His conception of a divinity that could be reached through prayer demonstrates his belief in a living God who cares for his creatures and seeks to guide them through the supernatural power of his grace. The experience of prayer conveyed by Lincoln in the letter to Gurney is exemplary of his biblical faith. In accordance with true piety, Lincoln saw prayer not as a quid pro quo to bribe or bargain with God, but as a means to achieve greater communion with and wisdom from him. Neither the prayers of Gurney nor those of the American people would necessarily guarantee that the war would end soon or that the national suffering would abate. Nevertheless, the power of prayer served to strengthen Lincoln's faith as a witness to God. It helped him to rely upon

God's grace, rather than his own resources, in bearing the awful weight of re-sponsibility during the war. It confirmed his trust in God's providence in guiding the nation toward some grand design that differed from the preten-sions of mere mortals.

The biblical faith manifested in Lincoln's owns speeches and writings cor-responded further with the personal testimonies of those who heard him speak of God's will during the war. On two separate occasions that were at-tested by various eyewitnesses, Lincoln used similar language about a solemn vow he made to God. The first occasion was on Monday, September 22, 1862, when Lincoln presented a draft of the Emancipation Proclamation to his cabinet after the Union's victory at the battle of Antietam. Gideon Welles, the secretary of the navy, reported in his diary that Lincoln called to-gether the cabinet and that his decision to issue the proclamation was part of a "solemn vow" made before God:

> he remarked that he had made a vow, a covenant, that if God gave us the vic-tory in the approaching battle, he would consider it an indication of Divine will, and that it was his duty to move forward in the cause of emancipation. It might be thought strange, he said, that he had in this way submitted the dis-posal of matters when the way was not clear to his mind what he should do. God had decided this question in favor of the slaves. He was satisfied it was right, was confirmed and strengthened in his action by the vow and the results.[55]

Two other eyewitnesses, the secretary of the Treasury, Salmon P. Chase, and the artist Frank B. Carpenter, corroborate Welles's testimony. Chase like-wise recorded an account of the event in his diary on September 22:

> The President then took a graver tone, and said, "Gentlemen: I have, as you are aware, thought a great deal about the relation of this war to slavery. . . . When the Rebel Army was at Frederick, I determined, as soon as it should be driven out of Maryland, to issue a Proclamation of Emancipation, such as I thought most likely to be useful. I said nothing to anyone, but I made the promise to myself and [hesitating a little] to my Maker."

Frank Carpenter, who painted the famous picture of Lincoln signing the Emancipation Proclamation with his cabinet gathered around him, re-ported that while present he heard Lincoln state, "I made a solemn vow before God, that if General Lee was driven back from Pennsylvania, I would crown the result by the declaration of freedom for the slaves." Three eyewitness accounts corroborate Lincoln's fidelity to a personal God who was overseeing events. Though there are some discrepancies concerning what Lincoln actually said, the personal testimony of each supports the claim that Lincoln's decision on the crucial issue of the

Emancipation Proclamation was made in consideration of his ultimate obligation and accountability to a living God.[56]

Lincoln's unwillingness to retract the emancipation to gain public support during the early summer in the election year of 1864 further confirms that his ethical and political decisions were made in reference to a transcendent standard of divine judgment. In 1864, the Democratic Party nominated George B. McClellan for president, who repudiated the Emancipation Proclamation and probably would have revoked it had he been elected. In the early stages of the campaign it looked as though Lincoln was sure to lose. There was a great deal of pressure to renounce the Emancipation Proclamation during the summer months of 1864. The Union was exhausted by war: the death toll of American soldiers killed on both sides reached about half a million. The existence and growth of a substantial peace movement tenaciously voiced opposition to Lincoln's war policies. A miscegenation hoax perpetrated by the *New York World* newspaper attempted to exploit racism against the Republican Party by claiming that emancipation was done to promote interbreeding among blacks and whites. Lincoln was under great pressure to reverse the strides toward black freedom in order to appease the pragmatists of his own party and the War Democrats whose support for the Union was needed to maintain a broad northern coalition to defeat the Confederacy. In his reply to Charles D. Robinson, a War Democrat who expressed concerns about the president's emancipation policy, Lincoln made clear in no uncertain terms that revoking the order would have constituted a treacherous act of infidelity against both God and African Americans: "I am sure you would not desire me to say, or to leave an inference, that I am ready, whenever convenient, to join in re-enslaving those who shall have served us in consideration of our promise. As matter of morals, could such treachery by any possibility, escape the curses of Heaven, or of any good man?" Two days later, Lincoln uttered another statement that seemed to confirm the fact that he had made an earlier "solemn vow" to God: "There have been men who have proposed to me to return to slavery the black warriors . . . to their masters to conciliate the South. I should be damned in time & in eternity for so doing. The world shall know that I will keep my faith to friends & enemies, come what will." After hearing a report of the Fort Pillow massacre, where black soldiers were slaughtered after they had surrendered, Lincoln reaffirmed his commitment to sustain the Emancipation Proclamation and its provision authorizing the use of African American troops for the Union army: "At the beginning of the war, and for some time, the use of colored troops was not contemplated; and how the change of purpose was wrought, I will not now take time to explain. Upon a clear conviction of duty I resolved to turn that element of strength to account; and I am responsible for it to the American people, to the christian world, to history, and on my final account to God." In sum, Lincoln's moral perseverance in both issuing and upholding the Emancipation was informed by his pious commitment to God and decided in consideration of the ultimate tribunal of divine judgment. His "clear conviction of duty" proceeded from a higher moral obligation to the Supreme Judge of individuals and nations.[57]

Lincoln's Judeo-Christian belief in a God of righteousness is further consistent with the accounts of two eyewitnesses who on an entirely different occasion heard the president invoke similar language of a "solemn vow" made before God. Shortly after the battle of Gettysburg, Lincoln met with Union generals D. E. Sickles and James F. Rusling. Sickles, who had a leg amputated at Gettysburg, asked the president whether he had been anxious about the recently fought battle. Rusling recorded Lincoln's response:

> "No, I was not; some of my Cabinet and many others in Washington were, but I had no fears." General Sickles inquired how this was, and seemed curious about it. Mr. Lincoln hesitated, but finally replied: "Well, I will tell you how it was. In the pinch of your campaign there, when everybody seemed panic stricken, and nobody could tell what was going to happen, oppressed by the gravity of our affairs, I went to my room one day, and I locked the door, and got down on my knees before Almighty God, and prayed to Him mightily for victory at Gettysburg. I told him that this was His war, and our cause His cause, but we couldn't stand another Fredericksburg or Chancellorsville. And I then and there made a solemn vow to Almighty God, that if He would stand by our boys at Gettysburg, I would stand by Him. And He *did* stand by you boys, and I *will* stand by Him. And after that (I don't know how it was, and I can't explain it), soon a sweet comfort crept into my soul that God Almighty had taken the whole business into his own hands and that things would go all right at Gettysburg. And that is why I had no fears about you."

Both Rusling and Sickles signed affidavits avowing the truth of their testimony. Sickles stated, "I hereby certify that the foregoing statement by General Rusling is true in substance." Though Rusling's account may be true in substance, more specific elements of it seem discordant with the biblical faith expressed in Lincoln's own speeches and writings. In particular, Lincoln's alleged statement that "our cause is His cause" seems inconsistent with his usual reticence about identifying human pretensions so closely with God's will. Nevertheless, the testimony is clearly consistent with Lincoln's many utterances in which he claimed to rely upon providence in guiding him through the "fiery trial" of the Civil War.[58]

A final poignant testimony of Lincoln's faith is provided by Elizabeth Keckley, who was Mary Todd Lincoln's seamstress and who lived with the Lincolns in the White House during the war years. Keckley wrote a book,

Behind the Scenes, published in 1868, that chronicled her experience. In her memoirs, she recorded a touching episode of Lincoln turning to the Bible for spiritual consolation:

> One day he came into the room where I was fitting a dress for Mrs. Lincoln. His step was slow and heavy, and his face sad. Like a tired child he threw himself upon the sofa, and shaded his eyes with his hands. He was a complete picture of dejection. Mrs. Lincoln, observing his troubled look, asked:
> "Where have you been?"
> "To the War Department," was the brief, almost sullen answer.
> "Any news?"
> "Yes, plenty of news, but no good news. It is dark, dark everywhere."
> He reached forth one of his long arms and took a small Bible from a stand near the head of the sofa, opened the pages of the Holy Book, and soon was absorbed in reading them. A quarter of an hour passed, and on glancing at the sofa the face of the President seemed cheerful. The dejected look was gone, and the countenance was lighted up with new resolution and hope. The change was so marked that I could not wonder at it, and wonder led to the desire to know what book of the Bible afforded so much comfort to the reader. Making the search for a missing article an excuse, I walked gently around the sofa, and looking into the open book, I discovered that Mr. Lincoln was reading that divine comforter, Job. He read with Christian eagerness, and courage and the hope he derived from the inspired pages made him a new man.[59]

Though the influence of the Bible on Lincoln's political thought has been consistently recognized, there has been too great a tendency among scholars to reduce the richness of his use of biblical symbolism to one purpose. Thus, Lincoln's appeal to the Bible is interpreted literally in apocalyptic terms or instrumentally as a concession to public prejudice or rhetorically as a way to remake American self-government. On the contrary, Lincoln appealed to the language of the Bible in at least five different senses: theologically, to ponder God and his providence; civil theologically, as a rule and measure to judge politics; didactically and allegorically, to elucidate a political teaching; evocatively, to arouse the emotions and imagination of his audience; and existentially, to convey the core experiences of his biblical faith. The wholesale reduction of Lincoln's biblical symbolism to one level of communication inevitably leads to distorted interpretations of his civil theology.[60]

In addition to his more ancillary uses of the Bible, Lincoln turned to Scripture as a source of genuine spiritual insight bringing him in closer communion with God. There was a remarkable congruence between his private and public religious utterances contained in his own speeches and the testimony of reliable eyewitnesses who heard him invoke God in a similar manner. Though the inner recesses of Lincoln's heart were known only to himself and to God, a core of biblical faith has been delineated and the sincerity of this faith has been established. Indeed, evidence shows that Lincoln's appeal to the Bible involved a meditative unfolding of religious experience, an anguished search to know God's will, and a corresponding inchoate recognition of the promptings of divine grace calling him to be "an instrument of God" in the mysterious, but ultimately beneficent, hand of providence. The biblical teachings on faith, providence, conscience, sin, guilt, and divine judgment guided Lincoln as he shaped his own life and led a nation at war.

Chapter Three

LINCOLN AND
PROSLAVERY THEOLOGY

Lincoln's biblical republicanism developed as an urgent response to the political challenges of his own time, not as an abstract doctrine composed from some Archimedean vantage point outside the political realm. Characterizing the debate with his rivals in civil theological terms as a struggle over the moral foundations of American republicanism, Lincoln repudiated proslavery theology as both a perversion of the Bible and an abandonment of the founders' republicanism in exchange for the retrograde doctrine of divine-right absolutism. According to Lincoln, the apologists of slavery sought to transform the very ethos of the regime by replacing one version of the American dream with another: "What that substitute is to be is not difficult to perceive. It is to deny the equality of men, and to assert the natural, moral, and religious right of one class to enslave another." Indeed, Lincoln's dire prediction was confirmed by Alexander Stephens, vice president of the Confederate States of America, who forthrightly proclaimed that the Confederacy would be based on a new moral foundation, one diametrically opposed to the principles of the Declaration of Independence that had animated the old Union:

> Our new government is founded upon exactly the opposite idea; its foundations are laid, its corner stone rests upon the great truth that the negro is not equal to the white man. That slavery—subordination to the superior race, is his natural and normal condition. This, our new Government, is the first, in the history of the world, based upon this great physical and moral truth.

The struggle over slavery was at the same time a struggle over competing interpretations of Christianity and the Bible. The split in the northern and southern churches over the issues of slavery and secession gave the Civil War the character of a religious struggle. Sidney Ahlstrom explains: "Churchmen played leading roles in the moral revolutions that swept the North and the South in opposite directions between 1830 and 1860. Between 1846 and 1860, churchmen gradually converted the antislavery movement into a massive juggernaut, and dedicated the South to preserving a biblically supported social order."[1]

Specifically, George Fitzhugh, the Reverend Frederick Ross, and Stephen

A. Douglas may be considered Lincoln's proslavery rivals, since his biblical republicanism developed in response to their competing visions of American public life. Fitzhugh was a Virginia author whose works *Cannibals All!* and *Sociology of the South* propounded a radical critique of free society in the North and a corresponding vindication of slave society in the South. Ross was a Presbyterian minister who wrote a series of pamphlets entitled *Slavery Ordained of God*. Douglas was the champion of popular sovereignty, which purported to be morally indifferent to slavery by granting territorial settlers the right of self-determination in choosing to have slaves.

Given the proslavery attack upon the very foundations of free society, Lincoln viewed the Civil War as a "war upon the first principles of popular government." The liberty of the slaveholder to exploit human chattel was quite different from the liberty of the radical abolitionist to redeem the nation from the sin of slavery. In a like manner, different interpretations of the republican principle of equality competed for public authoritativeness. Stephen Douglas interpreted equality narrowly as a principle that applied exclusively to the white race. John C. Calhoun and Jefferson Davis interpreted it collectively as applying to states and political communities rather than individuals. George Fitzhugh, Senator John Pettit, and others rejected the principle altogether as fallacious. Fitzhugh candidly repudiated the principle of equal consent in the Declaration as illusory, claiming, instead, that force was the only legitimate principle of governance:

> We do not agree with the authors of the Declaration of Independence, that governments "derive their just powers from the consent of the governed." . . . All governments must originate in force, and be continued by force. . . . The ancient republics were governed by a small class of adult male citizens who assumed and exercised the government without the consent of the governed. The South is governed just as those ancient republics were.

And Pettit "shamefully" denigrated "the central idea" of the American regime as a "self-evident lie." The notorious and influential proslavery philosopher Senator J. H. Hammond of South Carolina was also in the forefront of the attack on equality, declaring in *Slavery in the Light of Political Science*, "I indorse without reserve the much abused sentiment . . . that 'slavery is the corner-stone of our republican edifice'; while I repudiate, as ridiculously absurd, that much lauded but nowhere accredited dogma of Mr. Jefferson, that 'all men are created equal.'" Indeed, these radical critiques of equality more than vindicate Lincoln's civil theological effort to "save the principles of Jefferson from total overthrow in this nation."[2]

The following passage from an article entitled "The War of The South Vindicated" published in the *Southern Presbyterian Review*, an influential sectarian journal, is paradigmatic of the South's proslavery theology:

But what if God made slavery a part of man's and woman's original curse; what if God ordained, as a part of that penalty, that the earth should be brought into universal cultivation by a universally diffused race, through slavery in some form of involuntary servitude; what if God, by a positive, divine enactment, ordained that through the history of the world, slavery should exist as a form of organized labor among certain races of men, and that lordship over such slaves should be a part of the perpetual blessings of the races of Shem and Japheth; what if God has actually embodied slavery in His moral law, and by there guarding, and protecting, and regulating it, has made it appertain to the present condition of humanity; what if He ordained and regulated it under the patriarchal, Mosaical, prophetical, and Christian dispensations; what if in the New Testament a curse is pronounced against fanatical opposition to slavery as anti-Christian, and a sentence of withdrawal from such as heretical, both in Church and State; what if, in these and other ways, God claims slavery, like other forms of government adapted to sinful human nature, as His own ordinance for good; what, then, must be thought of this war of the North against slavery, and this war of the South in its defence, as inwoven by providence into the very texture of its body politic?

With this remarkable statement, the southern clergy not only defended slavery as a moral and religious right, but they also candidly attributed it as the root cause of the Civil War. Indeed, a transformation in the southern public mind over slavery had occurred since the time of Jefferson and the Revolution. Given the profitability of slavery as well as its dwindling prestige in the world, the South took the offensive by justifying its "peculiar institution" as a moral, religious, and national right affirmed by the laws of God and the Constitution. Abandoning the founders' characterization of slavery as a necessary evil to be placed on a path of ultimate extinction, a new generation of southern fire-eaters embraced slavery as a social and political blessing. Nurtured on the proslavery teachings of John C. Calhoun, this new southern cultural elite no longer viewed slavery as an archaic convention to be ashamed of, but as a progressive institution that was intrinsically good.[3]

George Fitzhugh defiantly applauded the South for taking an unabashed, aggressive stance in promoting slavery:

Very many able co-laborers have arisen, and many books and essays are daily appearing, taking higher ground in defence of Slavery, justifying it as a normal and natural institution, instead of excusing or apologizing for it as an exceptional one. It is now treated as a positive good, not a necessary evil. The success, not the ability of our essay, may have some influence in eliciting a new mode of defence. We have for many years, been gradually and cautiously testing public opinion at the South, and have ascertained that it is ready to approve, and much prefers, the highest ground of defence.

Here, Fitzhugh proudly took credit ºfor disposing southern public opinion toward the embrace of slavery as a "positive good." Although Fitzhugh and Lincoln reached different conclusions about the status of slavery as either a national blessing or curse, both agreed that the two ways of life were philosophically incompatible; the approval of one logically implied the disapproval of the other. According to William Herndon, "George Fitzhugh's *Sociology for the South,* which attacked the mobility of market societies as an 'abyss of misery and penury,' succeeded in arousing 'the ire of Lincoln more than most proslavery books.'" To be sure, Lincoln's biblical republicanism may be viewed as a dialectical response to Fitzhugh, who brazenly announced the irreconcilability between slave and free society two years before the same theme was sounded in the House Divided speech. In 1856, Fitzhugh proclaimed: "The issue is made throughout the world on the general subject of slavery in the abstract. The argument has commenced. One set of ideas will govern and control after awhile the civilized world. Slavery will every where be abolished, or every where be re-instituted." The very phrasing of Lincoln's House Divided speech indicates that it was, to some extent, a response to Fitzhugh's argument: "Either the *opponents* of slavery, will arrest the further spread of it, and place it where the public mind shall rest in the belief that it is in the course of ultimate extinction; or its *advocates* will push it forward, till it shall become alike lawful in *all* the States, *old* as well as *new—North* as well as *South.*" Lincoln, then, was aware of the shifting sentiment in the South, and he responded to the specious arguments of men like Fitzhugh.[4]

Members of the southern elite preached the new faith of proslavery theology relentlessly and thoroughly. In *Slavery Ordained of God,* the Reverend Frederick Ross, a Presbyterian minister from Huntsville, Alabama, praised the South's new moral orientation toward slavery:

Twenty-five years ago the religious mind of the South was leavened by wrong Northern training, on the great point of the right and wrong of slavery. Meanwhile, powerful intellects in the South, following the mere light of a healthy good sense, guided by the common grace of God, reached the very truth of this great matter—namely, that the relation of master and slave is not sin; and that, notwithstanding its admitted evils, it is a connection between the highest and lowest races of man, revealing influences which may be, and will be, most benevolent for the ultimate good of the master and the slave,—conservative on the Union, by preserving the South from all forms of Northern fanaticism, and thereby being a great balance wheel in the working of the tremendous machinery of our experiment in self-government. This seen result of slavery was found to be in absolute harmony with the word of God. These men, then, of the highest grade of thought, who had turned in scorn from Northern notions, now see, in the Bible, that these notions are false and silly. They now read the Bible, never examined before, with growing respect. God is honored, and his glory will be more and more in their salvation.

Like the foregoing declamation from the *Southern Presbyterian Review,* Ross's vindication of slavery—indeed, the very title of his pamphlets, *Slavery Ordained of God*—was derived from Romans 13:1: "Let every soul be subject unto higher powers. For there is no power but of God: the powers that be are ordained of God."[5]

Responding to Ross in a private memo, Lincoln distilled the essence of proslavery theology in these terms:

> The sum of pro-slavery theology seems to be this: "Slavery is not universally *right,* nor yet universally *wrong;* it is better for *some* people to be slaves; and, in such cases it is the Will of God that they be such."
>
> Certainly there is no contending against the Will of God; but still there is some difficulty in ascertaining, and applying it to particular cases. For instance we will suppose the Rev. Dr. Ross has a slave named Sambo, and the question is "Is it the Will of God that Sambo shall remain a slave, or be set free?" The Almighty gives no audable answer to the question, and his revelation—the Bible—gives none—or, at most, none but such as admits of a squabble, as to its meaning. No one thinks of asking Sambo's opinion on it. So, at last, it comes to this, that *Dr. Ross* is to decide the question. And while he consider[s] it, he sits in the shade, with gloves on his hands, and subsists on the bread Sambo is earning in the burning sun. If he decides that God Wills Sambo to continue a slave, he thereby retains his own comfortable position; but if he decides that God wills Sambo to be free, he thereby has to walk out of the shade, throw off his gloves, and delve for his own bread. . . . But, slavery is good for some people!!! As a *good* thing, slavery is strikingly perculiar, in this, that it is the only good thing which no man ever seeks the good of, *for himself.*
>
> Nonsense! Wolves devouring lambs, not because it is good for their own greedy maws, but because it [is] good for the lambs!!!

Lincoln's reference to wolves and lambs recalls Isaiah 11:6: "Then the wolf shall be guest of the lamb." The prophet Isaiah used this picture to express the universal peace and harmony that would come about in messianic times. Lincoln humorously turned the prophetic teaching against the proslavery theologians. Instead of bringing about harmony between God's creatures, symbolized by the friendship of the wolf and lamb, proslavery theology encouraged the wolf to satisfy his ravenous appetite and provided him with an excuse to devour the lambs with impunity. And worse, it claimed that all of this was good for the lambs![6]

The influence of the southern clergy upon public opinion during the Civil War era was pervasive. In *Ordeal of the Union,* a magisterial study of the antebellum period, Allan Nevins reveals the profound influence of the *Southern Presbyterian Review* and other sectarian journals on the southern public mind. To one scholar of southern conservatism, Eugene D. Genovese, the "power of the Presbyterian divines would be hard to exaggerate." Genovese correctly notes that the South's "defense of slavery was not simply a defense of property rights or racial dictatorship" but part of a wider social and theological outlook. "The slaveholders invoked the Bible," he writes, "and their cause might not have prevailed in the deeply religious South if they had not been able to make a strong case that the Bible sanctioned slavery."[7]

Thus, slavery was not merely an economic system but part of an overarching worldview that suffused southern culture. The justifications for the extension of slavery and slave society carried with them a corresponding critique of free labor and free society. Fitzhugh and other leaders of southern public opinion like Senator John Hammond advanced what came to be known as the "mud-sill" critique of free labor, which claimed that every society was predicated on some servile class of labor, some "bottom rung" on the "social ladder." They argued further that the condition of the southern black slave was better off than the northern "wage slave": the former was paternalistically cared for by a benevolent master while the latter was callously abandoned to the vagaries of the free market. Whether the "mud-sill" was occupied by southern black slaves or the northern wage slaves, their condition was permanently fixed without the possibility of improvement. Governor James Hammond of South Carolina, a relative of the senator from the same state, propounded the theory to vindicate the superiority of southern black slavery over the wage slavery of the northern proletariat:

> The difference between us is, that our slaves are hired for life and well compensated; there is no starvation, no begging, no want of employment among our people, and not too much employment either. Yours are hired by the day, not cared for, and scantily compensated, which may be proved in the most painful manner, at any hour in any street in any of your large towns. Why, you meet more beggars in one day, in any single street of the city of New York, than you would meet in a lifetime in the whole South.

In *The Political Economy of Slavery*, the notorious fire-eater Edmund Ruffin proposed to ameliorate the plight of the northern proletariat through "the enslaving of these reckless, wretched drones and cumberers of the earth . . . thereby compelling them to habits of labor, and in return satisfying their wants for necessaries, and raising them and their progeny in the scale of humanity, not only physically, but morally and intellectually." As a radical and provocative critique of the status quo, Ruffin's argument bears comparison to Swift's "Modest Proposal," except that, unlike Swift, Ruffin was serious.[8]

The "mud-sill" critique denied the possibility of social mobility and advancement of the laboring class. In this respect, it was influenced by the pessimistic political economies of the Manchester school—for example, David Ricardo's "Iron Law of Wages" and Thomas Malthus's "Essay on Population." In *The Southern Tradition*, Eugene Genovese describes the influence of the Manchester school on the South's critique of free society. Their argument "proved especially powerful because it blended with the theological argument to condemn capitalism as a brutal and immoral system and to exalt slavery as a Christian alternative. . . . [The slaveholders] concluded that the free-labor system generated wage-slavery and the immization of the laboring classes." From a reactionary rather than a socialist perspective, the southern cultural elite portrayed capitalism as heartless and inhuman compared to the warm paternalism of their peculiar institution that provided for the slave's basic needs and rudimentary happiness.[9]

Lincoln's defense of republicanism implied a corresponding justification of free labor that held out the genuine possibility of social and economic advancement. Through his vindication of free labor against the recriminations of proslavery theology, Lincoln has provided one of the most enduring visions of the American dream, one that has resonated with countless generations of Americans:

> We know, Southern men declare that their slaves are better off than hired laborers amongst us. How little they *know*, whereof they *speak!* There is no permanent class of hired laborers amongst us [in the North]. Twentyfive years ago, I was a hired laborer. The hired laborer of yesterday, labors on his own account to-day; and will hire others to labor for him to-morrow. Advancement— improvement in condition—is the order of things in a society of equals. As Labor is the common *burthen* of our race, so the effort of *some* to shift their share of the burthen on to the shoulders of *others,* is the great, durable, curse of the race. Originally a curse for transgression upon the whole race, when, as by slavery, it is concentrated on a part only, it becomes the double-refined curse of God upon his creatures.

Because it combines a biblical justification of free labor with a republican defense of equality of opportunity, the above speech clearly manifests the symbolic form of biblical republicanism. Lincoln incorporated Jefferson's republican view of equality of opportunity as the condition sine qua non of self-government. His defense of "advancement" and "improvement" "in a society of equals" and his correlative denial of a "permanent class of hired laborers" were republican principles derived from the moral promise of the Declaration. At the same time, Lincoln's defense of free labor relied upon the biblical symbolism of labor as a "common burthen of the race" from Genesis 3:19's account of the Fall. As a punishment for man's "transgression," God announced to Adam and his ancestors that from hereafter, "In the sweat of thy face shalt thou eat bread." This curse became "double refined" when it was illegitimately concentrated upon the black race through a perversion of the Bible. Finally, Lincoln's defense of free labor was validated even further by his own experience as a self-made man. Thus, reason (based on Lincoln's own experience), revelation, and republicanism reinforced one another to vindicate free labor.[10]

Contrary to Fitzhugh, who alleged that "Christian morality is the natural morality in slave society, and slave society is the only natural society," Lincoln vehemently denied that Christianity provided a moral justification for slavery. In response to such sophistry, he summoned the "great commandment" from Matthew 22:39–40 to love one's neighbor as oneself and the Golden Rule from Matthew 7:12: "Although volume upon volume is written to prove slavery a very good thing, we never hear of the man who wishes to take the good of it, by being a slave himself." Lincoln's reference to the many "volumes" that are "written to prove slavery a good thing" was aimed at the myriad writings in support of proslavery theology.[11]

Indeed, Lincoln reserved his most vehement criticism for those who exploited the Bible to sanction the grave evil of slavery. In response to a northern Baptist group that had repudiated the South's use of Scripture to justify slavery, Lincoln stated in a letter dated May 30, 1864:

> . . . I can only thank you for thus adding to the effective and almost unanamous support which the Christian communities are so zealously giving to the country, and to liberty. Indeed it is difficult to conceive how it could be otherwise with any one professing christianity, or even having ordinary perceptions of right and wrong. To read in the Bible, as the word of God himself, that "In the sweat of *thy* face shalt thou eat bread" [Genesis 3:19] and to preach therefrom that, "In the sweat of *other mans* faces shalt thou eat bread," to my mind can scarcely be reconciled with honest sincerity. When brought to my final reckoning, may I have to answer for robbing no man of his goods; yet more tolerable even this, than for robbing one of himself, and all that was his. When, a year or two ago, those professedly holy men of the South, met in the semblance of prayer and devotion, and, in the name of Him who said "As ye would all men should do unto you, do ye even so unto them" [Matthew 7:12] appealed to the christian world to aid them in doing to a whole race of men, as they would have no man do unto themselves, to my thinking, they contemned and insulted God and His church, far more than did Satan when he tempted the Saviour with the Kingdoms of the earth. The devils attempt was no more false, and far less hypocritical. But let me forebear, remembering it is also written "Judge not, lest ye be judged" [Luke 6:37].

Lincoln's appeal to Scripture provides an important teaching on both the "use and abuse" of the Bible in politics. Remarkably, almost every sentence in this speech contains an allusion to the Bible against proslavery theology. His sarcastic jab at those "professedly holy men of the South" who "met in semblance and devotion" was most likely a reference to the Southern Presbyterian Church's official endorsement of the moral and religious right to slavery in 1864: "we hesitate not to affirm that it is the peculiar mission of the Southern Church to conserve the institution of slavery, and to make it a blessing to master and slave." In reply to this sophistry, Lincoln cited the biblical precepts of Genesis 3:19 and the Golden Rule in Matthew 7:12, and expressed amazement that anyone "professing christianity" could endorse the moral and religious right to slavery.[12]

In anticipation of what he would say in his Second Inaugural Address, Lincoln noted that both sides cited the same Bible to reach diametrically opposed conclusions. Instead of rejecting the authority of Scripture, as

some abolitionists did because it was enlisted in the cause of slavery, however, Lincoln demonstrated a much deeper understanding of revelation by
noting that the Bible itself warns against those who would twist the word of
God in service of evil ends. He thus likened the South's manipulation of
Scripture to Satan's temptation of Christ, related in Matthew 4:1–11. This
story must have been familiar to a Bible-reading nation of the nineteenth
century who would have recognized that Satan exploited the Bible in a sophistic attempt to deceive the Savior. In preparation for his ministry, Jesus
was tested in the desert three times by Satan. In the second temptation, Satan quoted Psalm 91:10–12 as a way of manipulating Jesus to test God the
Father: "The devil took him to the holy city and set him on the parapet of
the Temple. 'If you are the son of God,' he said, 'throw yourself down; for
scripture says: "He has given his angels orders about you, and they will carry
you in their arms in case you trip over a stone."'" Quoting Deuteronomy
6:16, Jesus responded, "Scripture also says, 'Do not put the Lord your God to
the test.'" Indeed, after each temptation, Jesus provided an alternative interpretation of Scripture to refute Satan. By alluding to this biblical story, Lincoln appealed to the example of Christ himself, the ultimate source of biblical authority, who warns that the letter of Scripture may be perverted against
its spirit. Thus, the Bible teaches that the wise should be on guard against
those who would use the word of God to deceive and manipulate. Christ's
example is instructive: he did not repudiate the authority of God's word because it was perverted by Satan; rather, he exposed the deception by providing the true and proper interpretation of the Bible. Following the example of
Christ, Lincoln responded to proslavery theology by quoting alternative
teachings that were in harmony with the spirit, not merely the letter, of
Scripture, namely, Genesis 3:19 and Matthew 7:12.

The proslavery interpretation of the Bible was not merely one of many
equally valid perspectives; it was perniciously false and contradicted by the
complementary teachings of reason, revelation, and republicanism. Lincoln
noted that the South's exploitation of the Bible violated "ordinary perceptions of right and wrong" and could not be "reconciled with honest sincerity." That is to say, moral conclusions drawn from Scripture that violate
one's commonsense notions of good and evil should be viewed as highly
suspect, if not altogether fallacious. Cutting through all the sophistry, Lincoln characterized slavery in commonsense terms as "robbery." It did not
take metaphysical demonstrations for ordinary people to recognize that it
was wrong to rob another of his or her very person, not to mention the
fruits of one's labor. The Decalogue's prohibition against stealing in Exodus
20:15 is written upon the human heart as well. In his Peoria Address of
1854, Lincoln likewise appealed to southerners' "ordinary perceptions of
right and wrong" and "honest sincerity" by prompting them to examine
their consciences in regard to slavery's inherent evil.

Lincoln's belief in a God who was free from contradictions, his reverence
for the sacredness of Scripture, and the human mind's ability to comprehend

the natural law elicited in him rare glimpses of the pathos of righteous indignation that departed from his usual forbearance. He considered biblical
justifications of slavery to be an insult to God's benevolence, justice, and
wisdom. Consequently, in his jeremiad, Lincoln invoked the threat of divine
judgment to awaken the southern clergy from its sophistry. In characteristically biblical terms, he placed the debate over proslavery theology on a
wider "cosmic stage" in which all of the actors must answer to God, the Di-
rector and Judge of the grand human drama. His righteous indignation was
the appropriate response to those who exploited Scripture to justify the
"monstrous injustice" of slavery. By concluding his speech with Luke 6:37
("Judge not, lest ye be judged"), however, Lincoln tempered his condemnation of slavery, consciously guarding himself against the sin of pride
whereby righteous indignation lapses into self-righteousness. Throughout
his public life, he reminded the North of its complicity in the slave trade
and showed sympathy for southerners of goodwill who were trapped by an
institution that was deeply interwoven into the fabric of their society.[13]

Another example of Lincoln's scorn for proslavery theology concerned a
story written for his friend Noah Brooks. Departing from his usual restraint,
Lincoln replied to a Confederate wife who pleaded for clemency for her husband on account of his piety: "You say your husband is a religious man; tell
him when you meet him, that I say I am not much of a judge of religion,
but that, in my opinion, the religion that sets men to rebel and fight against
their government, because, as they think, that government does not sufficiently help *some* men to eat their bread on the sweat of *other* men's faces
[Genesis 3:19], is not the sort of religion upon which people can get to
heaven!" The pathos of the statement conveys Lincoln's moral intolerance
of proslavery theology. Clearly intending for his response to be published,
Lincoln called Brooks into his study, recited the conversation to him, and
then remarked, "here is one speech of mine that has never been printed, and
I think it worth printing." Brooks copied the speech verbatim and subsequently had it printed in the *Washington Daily Chronicle* a day later. Lincoln
signed his name, adding the revealing caption, "The President's Last, Short-
est, and Best Speech." The title for the speech and the intention to have it
published demonstrate Lincoln's attentiveness to the influence of proslavery
theology on the public mind. The sociopolitical implications of proslavery
theology were enormous. In Lincoln's words, it fostered the pernicious
opinion that "the Almighty has made Slavery necessarily eternal." Although he showed clemency in pardoning the prisoner, he also chastised
the couple for their self-righteous adherence to a false doctrine, as a
teacher would reprimand a student, in the hope that it would provoke
needed reflection. Lincoln attempted to elicit guilt and shame in the Confederate wife for her thoughtlessness in accepting a doctrine that so
nakedly perverted the teachings of Scripture.[14]

A reading of the South's political theology in the works of Fitzhugh, Ross,
Samuel Seabury's *American Slavery Distinguished from the Slavery of English*

Theorists and Justified by the Law of Nature, and E. N. Elliot's *Cotton Is King,* a revealing compilation of influential proslavery authors edited in 1860, shows that southern justifications for slavery were derived primarily from about ten passages in the Bible: Genesis 9:18–27; Exodus 21:2–5, 7–11, 20–21; Leviticus 25:44–46; Colossians 3:22—"Servants, obey in all things your masters"; Colossians 4:1—"Masters, Give unto your servants that which is just and equal; knowing that ye also have a Master in heaven"; 1 Timothy 6:1–6—"Let as many servants as are under the yoke count their own masters worthy of all honour"; Titus 2:9—"Exhort servants to be obedient unto their own masters"; Ephesians 6:5–9—"Servants, be obedient to them that are your masters according to the flesh, with fear and trembling, in singleness of your heart, as unto Christ; 1 Peter 2:18—"Servants, be subject to your masters with all fear; not only to the good and gentle, but also to the froward"; and Romans 13:1—"Let every soul be subject unto the higher powers. For there is no power but of God: the powers that be are ordained of God." In his introduction to *Cotton Is King,* Elliot triumphantly announced that the proslavery exegesis of the Bible was so unassailable that it drove northern abolitionists to infidelity:

> It is due to a citizen of this State, the Rev. J. Smylie, to say that he was the first to promulgate the truth, as deduced from the Bible, on the subject of slavery. He was followed by a host of others, who discussed it not only in light of revelation and morals, but as consistent with the Federal Constitution and the Declaration of Independence; until many of those who had commenced their career of abolition agitation from reasoning from the Bible and the Constitution, were compelled to acknowledge that they both were hopelessly proslavery, and to cry: "give us an anti-slavery constitution, an antislavery Bible, and an anti-slavery God." To such straits are men reduced by fanaticism. It is here worthy of remark, that most of the early abolition propagandists, many who commenced as Christian ministers, have ended in downright infidelity.

Ironically, Elliot and Lincoln appealed to the same sources of political order—the Bible, the Declaration of Independence, the Constitution—to justify diametrically opposed versions of American republicanism. Whereas Lincoln's civil theology is best characterized as biblical republicanism, Elliot's proslavery vision is best characterized as biblical despotism.[15]

One of the most common proslavery arguments from Scripture was the "Curse of Ham," based on an interpretation of Genesis 9:18–27.[16] Proslavery theologians and philosophers interpreted this biblical passage as providing a moral imperative to enslave the African race. In his pamphlet, *The Bible Argument; or, Slavery in the Light of Divine Revelation,* Thornton Stringfellow, a doctor of divinity of Richmond, Virginia, provided a biblical exegesis from Genesis 9 that attempted to sanction the enslavement of the African race as God's will:

> The first recorded language which was ever uttered in relation to slavery, is the inspired language of Noah. In God's stead he says, "Cursed be Canaan;" "a servant of servants shall he be to his brethren." "Blessed be the Lord God of Shem; and Cannan shall be his servant." "God shall enlarge Japheth, and he shall dwell in the tents of Shem; and Canaan shall be his servant"—Genesis 9:25, 26, 27. Here, language is used, showing the *favor* which God would exercise to the posterity of Shem and Japtheth, while they were holding the posterity of Ham in a state of *abject bondage*. May it not be said in truth, that God decreed this institution before it existed; and has he not connected its *existence* with prophetic tokens of special favor, to those who should be slave owners or masters? He is the same God now, that he was when he gave these views of his moral character to the world; and unless the posterity of Shem and Japheth, from whom have sprung the Jews, and all the nations of Europe and America, and a great part of Asia, (the African race that is in them excepted,)—I say, unless they are all dead, as well as the Canaanites or Africans, who descended from Ham, then it is quite possible that his favor may now be found with one class of men who are holding another class in bondage. Be this as it may, God *decreed slavery*—and shows in that decree, tokens of good will to the master.

The particular section of Genesis alluded to by Stringfellow chronicles the fate of Noah's three sons, the original ancestors after the Flood whose descendants "overspread" and peopled the entire earth: Shem, Japheth, and Ham. The Bible relates that Noah was the first to plant vineyards and to make wine. One night, while passing by Noah's tent, Ham discovered his father intoxicated and unclothed. He then impudently summoned his two brothers to behold the spectacle. After they had arrived, Ham's brothers, in a gesture of humility, walked backwards into their father's tent to evade the embarrassing sight. When they finally reached their father, they draped a cloak over him and then left discretely. After Noah awoke from his slumber, he punished Ham for his impudence. Henceforth, God, speaking through Noah, proclaimed that Ham and his descendants (Canaan) shall be slaves to his brothers and their descendants: "Cursed be Canaan: a servant of servants shall he be unto his brethren. And he said Blessed be the Lord God of Shem; and Canaan shall be his servant. God shall enlarge Japheth, and he shall dwell in the tents of Shem; and Canaan shall be his servant." The punishment was extended to Canaan, the descendants of Ham who were identified by southern clergymen as the entire African race.[17]

Since the story from Genesis does not identify the descendants of Ham with a specific racial or ethnic group, the proslavery theologians' conclusion was without biblical foundation. It constituted nothing less than an ideological construction of the Bible to justify the doctrine of racial superiority, a doctrine that was without scriptural support, since the actual practice of slavery in biblical times was not racially based and since the Bible does not provide a moral imperative to enslave others. The belief that God had favored the white race over the black race was incompatible with divine justice and the biblical teaching that all human beings possessed a unique dignity created in the image of God (Genesis 1:27).

In 1859, just before secession, Jefferson Davis, future president of the Confederacy, avowed his commitment to proslavery theology by reiterating the Curse of Ham argument:

> It is enough for us that the Creator, speaking through the inspired lips of Noah, declared that destiny of all three races of men. Around and about us is the remarkable fulfillment of the prophecy, the execution of the decree, and the justification of the literal construction of the text.
>
> The judgements of God are not as those of man. To the former all things are accommodated, and the fate of the subject is thereby his nature, but the victim of man's decree rebels and struggles against his condition.
>
> When the Spaniards discovered this continent and reduced the sons of Shem to bondage, unsuited to that condition they pined and rapidly wasted away in unproductive labor. The good Bishop Las Casas, with philosophical humanity inaugurated the importation of the race of Ham; they came to relieve from an unnatural state the dwellers in tents, and to fulfill their own destiny, that of being "servants of servants." In their normal condition they thrived, and by their labor the land was subdued and made fruitful.

The "racist construction" of the Bible by Davis and proslavery theologians dramatically illustrates the potential limitations and dangers of interpreting Scripture out of context. Not only was their identification of the black race as the descendants of Ham without literal support from the Bible, but they also completely disregarded other crucial teachings of the Bible that contradicted their interpretation. In fact, the moral and political implication derived by Davis and proslavery theologians from Genesis 9—that a race of people are forever consigned to slavery by God—contradicted the teaching of Genesis 3:19, which declares labor to be God's punishment to the entire human race. How then should the Bible be interpreted in regard to slavery?[18]

Lincoln believed that slavery was incompatible with a just God and with a proper interpretation of the Bible. In sum, his biblical case against proslavery theology relied on the following precepts overlooked by the southern clergy: (1) the teaching that man is created in God's image (Genesis 1:27)—"So God created man in his own image, in the image of God created he him; male and female created he them"; (2) the Golden Rule (Matthew 7:12)—"Therefore all things whatsoever ye would that men should do to you, do ye even so to them: for this is the law and the prophets"; (3) Jesus' summary of the Jewish law in terms of the two great commandments (Matthew 22:37–40)—"Thou shalt love the Lord thy God with all thy heart, and with all thy soul, and with all thy mind. This is the first and great commandment. And the second is like unto it, Thou shalt love thy neighbour as thyself"; and (4) labor as the divinely ordained and inescapable condition of existence for the entire human race (Genesis 3:19)—"In the sweat of thy face shalt thou eat bread."

Although the Bible recognized the existence of slavery as an institution in ancient times, it did not sanction it; the mere historical description of a circumstance does not prove its moral right in the abstract. Proslavery philosophers noted the existence of slavery in biblical times and then drew the mistaken conclusion that God had decreed it as a categorical imperative. In *Liberty and Slavery; or, Slavery in Light of Moral and Political Philosophy,* Albert Taylor Bledsoe, a professor of mathematics at the University of Virginia, provided a syllogism to demonstrate this point: "Whatever God sanctioned among the Hebrews he sanctions for all men and all times. God sanctioned slavery among the Hebrews; therefore God sanctions slavery for all men and at all times." In Lincoln's thinking, Bledsoe commited a non sequitur in his reasoning: it does not follow that, because the institution of slavery existed in biblical times, God has sanctioned it universally as a general rule of conduct. The references to slavery in Scripture are not comparable to the commandments and moral imperatives of the Decalogue. Indeed, the proslavery philosophers failed to distinguish between practices that were sanctioned by mere convention and those that were sanctioned as a moral imperative from God himself. As Lincoln noted, proslavery theologians were selective in their use of Scripture. If applied consistently, their selective, literal interpretation of the Bible would have led to absurd moral consequences. For instance, consider the rule in Exodus 21:7—"When a man sells his daughter as a slave, she shall not go free as male slaves do." If interpreted as a moral imperative and applied consistently, this precept would have sanctioned the enslavement of white daughters in both the North and the South. And should a lapse of Sabbath observance result in the punishment of death as Exodus 31:14 seems to demand? Did the prohibition of the eating of pork and shellfish in Leviticus 11:7 apply to the great tradition of southern barbecue? We know that Jesus himself was criticized by the Pharisees for not following the letter of the law.[19]

Though the distinction between "nature" *(physis)* and "convention" *(nomos)* was of Greek origin, a parallel understanding existed in Israel. Indeed, the distinction between customs and practices that were merely conventional and therefore did not necessarily conform with the true spirit of God's Law and those practices that did was recognized by all the great teachers of Israel including the prophets, Jesus, and Paul. For example, speaking through the prophet Amos, God proclaimed: "I hate, I scorn your festivals, I take no pleasure in your solemn assemblies. When you bring me burnt offerings . . . your oblations, I do not accept them and I do not look at your communion sacrifices of fat cattle. Spare me the din of your chanting, let me hear none of your chanting, let me hear none of your strumming on lyres, but let justice flow like water and uprightness like a never-failing stream!" (Amos 5:21–27). What Amos says about the practice of religious formalism may be applied a fortiori to the custom of racial slavery in nineteenth-century

America. The teaching of Amos is clear: what really matters to God is the experiential substance of religious practice, not hollow customs that are devoid of the spirit. The fruits of true religion will "let justice flow like water and uprightness like a never-failing stream." Quoting Isaiah 29:13, Jesus would likewise admonish the Pharisees for following the letter of the law but completely disregarding its spirit: "This people honours me only with lip-service, while their hearts are far from me. Their reverence of me is worthless; the lessons they teach are nothing but human commandments" (Matthew 15:1–9). Significantly, Isaiah and Jesus both teach the people of Israel to distinguish between "human commandments" that are self-serving and divine commandments that serve God. In similarly responding to proslavery theologians, Frederick Douglass provided perhaps the most concise hermeneutic for interpreting the Bible: "That which is inhuman can't be divine!" If read in its proper context, the Bible quite simply does not impose a moral and religious obligation to enslave others.[20]

As with the Torah, the New Testament acknowledged the institution of slavery as a matter of positive law, but it never sanctioned it as an ethical norm. Slavery was merely an accepted fact of Roman life. The references to slavery in the New Testament were intended to remind both master and servant alike of their moral obligations to one another as members of a common mystical body that anticipated the imminent return of Jesus Christ. The references to slavery were therefore not a political prescription to govern society as a whole but practical advice to members of a newly formed Christian community who were focused completely upon a transcendent goal, to such an extent that it may have eclipsed their preoccupation with the more mundane concerns of secular politics. In fact, Christianity promised a spiritual equality whose radical political implications would steadily unfold throughout the history of Western civilization. In Galatians 3:28, Paul explained: "For all of you who were baptized into Christ have clothed yourselves with Christ. There is neither slave nor free person, there is not male and female; for you are all one in Christ Jesus." Furthermore, it must be emphasized that the servitude of biblical times was incomparable to African slavery in the United States. Ancient slavery was not racially based and was more akin to indentured servitude than to the racially based African slavery institutionalized throughout the South. Finally, Lincoln correctly reminded proslavery theologians that the very substance of Jesus' teaching was charity: "Thou shalt love thy neighbour as thyself" is the greatest commandment on which "hang all the law and the prophets" (Matthew 22:39–40). According to Lincoln charity (the true spirit of Christianity) and *amor sui* (or love of self, the sinful motivation behind slavery) were incompatible. While the Bible did not provide a moral imperative to enslave other human beings, as proslavery theologians contended, the very essence of Christianity included the moral imperative to charity. Proslavery theologians could not claim to be practicing true Christianity by either sanctioning or practicing ungodly and uncharitable conduct. Lincoln summed this up when he stated, "'*Give* to him that is needy' is the Christian rule of charity; but 'Take from him that is needy' is the rule of slavery."[21]

Lincoln discerned that, at its philosophical core, the political theology of the South was predicated on the doctrine of divine right, the very antithesis of American republicanism in its denial of equality and in its affirmation of the superhuman status of certain individuals: "But this argument strikes me as not a little remarkable in another particular—in its strong resemblance to the old argument for the Divine right of Kings." At bottom, proslavery theology was based upon the same despotic principle as royal absolutism. Both justifications were predicated on a master-slave relationship that denied equal consent; both regarded slavery as mutually beneficial to master, slave, and society; and both invoked divine authority to sanction despotism. Although there was no monarchy on the American continent, the principle of despotism applied just the same whether it took the form of a southern master or an English king. Demonstrating the correspondence between divine right and proslavery theology, Lincoln stated:

> It is the eternal struggle between these two principles—right and wrong—throughout the world. They are the two principles that have stood face to face from the beginning of time; and will ever continue to struggle. The one is the common right of humanity and the other the divine right of kings. It is the same principle in whatever shape it develops itself. It is the same spirit that says, "You work and toil and earn bread, and I'll eat it." No matter in what shape it comes, whether from the mouth of a king who seeks to bestride the people of his own nation and live by the fruit of their labor, or from one race of men as an apology for enslaving another race, it is the same tyrannical principle.

Lincoln repeated the argument throughout his struggle against the spread of slavery:

> Those arguments that are made, that the inferior race are to be treated with as much allowance as they are capable of enjoying; that as much is to be done for them as their condition will allow. What are these arguments? They are the arguments that kings have made for enslaving the people in all ages of the world. You will find that all the arguments in favor of king-craft were of this class; they always bestrode the necks of the people, not that they wanted to do it, but because the people were better off for being ridden. That is their argument. . . . Turn in whatever way you will—whether it come from the mouth of a King, an excuse for enslaving the people of his country, or from the mouth of men of one race as a reason for enslaving the men of another race, it is all the same old serpent. . . .

Whether it took the form of a divinely favored individual, family, class, or race, claims of the superiority of one group of people over another denied the belief in a common humanity distributed equally among all human beings. Lincoln likened the embrace of the principle of a divine right to mastery over others, in allegorical terms, as a beguiling serpent tempting the regime from its true moral path.[22]

Slavery was to be shunned not only because it was morally evil but, as Jefferson pointed out two generations earlier, because it promoted dispositions and habits that undermined the character of republican government. In true republican form, Lincoln attributed the spread of slavery to a degeneration of civic virtue. In the name of moral complacency, simple greed, and self-interest, the nation was willing to abandon its birthright:

> On the question of liberty, as a principle, we are not what we have been. When we were the political slaves of King George, and wanted to be free, we called the maxim that "all men are created equal" a self-evident truth; but now when we have grown fat, and have lost all dread of being slaves ourselves, we have become so greedy to be *masters* that we call the same maxim "a self-evident lie". . . .[23]

Stephen Douglas took a different tack in his defense of slavery. His notion of popular sovereignty would leave the debate over slavery to each individual territory. Notwithstanding Douglas's claim to moral neutrality on the issue of slavery, however, Lincoln showed that popular sovereignty did, in fact, presume an underlying moral justification. At Peoria in 1854, Lincoln exposed Douglas's "declared indifference" as a "covert real zeal for the spread of slavery." Regardless of Douglas's intention, the consequences of his popular sovereignty were proslavery in Lincoln's view. Indeed, Douglas professed a moral indifference to slavery because he denied the common humanity of the African American and affirmed the superiority of the white race. This was dramatically revealed in remarks he made during his debates with Lincoln in 1858: "I believe this government was made on the white basis. I believe it was made by white men, for the benefit of white men and their posterity for ever, and I am in favor of confining citizenship to white men, men of European birth and descent, instead of conferring it upon negroes, Indians and other inferior races." In *Lincoln's Virtues: An Ethical Biography*, an indispensable work for understanding Lincoln's moral development, William Lee Miller juxtaposes Douglas's arguments for racial supremacy to Lincoln's defense of our common humanity. Miller explains that Douglas's strategy during the debates was to discredit Lincoln as an abolitionist and to exploit public opinion against him in the virulently racist free state of Illinois, which had enacted a black exclusion law to prevent African Americans from entering. Douglas's opening speech at Ottawa on August 21, 1858, provides a vivid contrast between his and Lincoln's civil theological outlooks:

> Mr. Lincoln, following the example and lead of all the Abolition orators, who go around and lecture in the basements of schools and churches, reads from the Declaration of Independence, that all men were created equal, and then asks how can you deprive a negro of that equality which God and the Declaration of Inde-

pendence awards to him. He and they maintain that negro equality is guarantied by the laws of God, and that it is asserted in the Declaration of Independence. . . . I do not question Mr. Lincoln's conscientious belief that the negro was made his equal, and hence his brother, but for my own part, I do not regard the negro as my equal, and positively deny that he is my brother or any kin to me whatever. . . . He [Lincoln] holds that the negro was born his equal and yours, and that he was endowed with equality by the Almighty, and that no human law can deprive him of these rights which were guarantied to him by the Supreme ruler of the Universe. Now, I do not believe that the Almighty ever intended the negro to be equal to the white man.[24]

Though he misrepresented Lincoln as a radical abolitionist who sought to free the slaves at any cost, including the abrogation of the Constitution and dissolution of the Union, Douglas nonetheless grasped the civil theological grounding of Lincoln's opposition to slavery. In stark contrast to Lincoln, who included African Americans in the "all men are created equal" clause of the Declaration, Douglas rejected a common human essence between the races. He denied any fellowship between blacks and whites as members of the same human family created in the image of God. The underlying view of human nature that informed Douglas's civil theological outlook was based on a racial supremacy that debased African Americans to a subhuman status and thereby divested them of their unalienable rights as human beings. Cognizant that Douglas would exploit the issue of race against him in the forthcoming debates, Lincoln appealed to the "better angels" of his audience at Chicago on July 10, 1858:

My friends . . . I have only to say, let us discard all this quibbling about this man and the other man—this race and that race and the other race being inferior, and therefore they must be placed in an inferior position. . . . Let us discard all these things and unite as one people throughout this land, until we shall once more stand up declaring that all men are created equal.

In sum, the distinction between the two rival civil theologies can be more readily seen by contrasting Douglas's racially conscious definition of republican government at Ottawa—"by white men" and "for the benefit of the white men"—to Lincoln's view of republican government at Gettysburg, which makes no reference to race in its use of the phrase "of the people, by the people, for the people." According to Lincoln, such a government included all people by virtue of their common humanity.[25]

Lurking beneath Douglas's indifference to slavery was his contempt for the African American's humanity that permitted the continued exploitation of the entire black race as mere beasts of burden. For that reason, Lincoln characterized popular sovereignty in civil theological terms as a "false philosophy," and he repudiated Douglas's leadership as a "false statesmanship." Though it purported to be morally neutral, popular sovereignty presumed an ultimate moral commitment that was completely indifferent to the unalienable rights of African Americans. It replaced the principle of consent of the governed with the naked self-interest of the majority.[26]

Consistent with Richard John Neuhaus's view that the public square abhors a moral vacuum, Douglas, who renounced absolute moral claims in public life, could not help but invoke the Bible to justify the ethical neutrality—and the white supremacy—of popular sovereignty. When debating Lincoln, Douglas stated:

> I repeat that the principle is the right of each State, each territory, to decide this slavery question for itself, to have slavery or not, as it chooses, and it does not become Mr. Lincoln, or anybody else, to tell the people of Kentucky that they have no consciences, that they are living in a state of iniquity, and that they are cherishing an institution to their bosoms in violation of the law of God. Better for him to adopt the doctrine of "judge not lest ye be judged."

Ironically, Douglas invoked the Bible in order to banish divine authority from public life. He appealed not to the Supreme Judge and Lawgiver of the Universe, the God of Israel, but to a permissive god of ethical relativism. Lincoln exposed Douglas's appeal to the Bible as a form of sophistry that attempted to exploit Scripture to justify morally bankrupt public policies.[27]

Although the God of Israel is benevolent and merciful, he is also just, and slavery is a transgression of his justice. As revealed in the Bible, divine justice is incompatible with an ethical relativism in which "everything is permitted." The principle of moral relativism calls into question the very notion of an ultimate moral judgment. How can any decent person, let alone a just God, be morally indifferent to the monstrous injustice of slavery? At Peoria in 1854, Lincoln discerned the civil theological implications of Douglas's often repeated argument that divine authority actually sanctioned the moral relativism of popular sovereignty:

> In the course of my main argument, Judge Douglas interrupted me to say, that the principle [of] the Nebraska bill was very old; that it originated when God made man and placed good and evil before him, allowing him to choose for himself, being responsible for the choice he should make. At the time I thought this was merely playful; and I answered it accordingly. But in his reply to me he renewed it, as a serious argument. In seriousness then, the facts of this proposition are not true as stated. God did not place good and evil before man, telling him to make his choice. On the contrary, he did tell him there was one tree, of the fruit of which, he should not eat, upon pain of certain death. I should scarcely wish so strong a prohibition against slavery in Nebraska.

Whereas Lincoln interpreted God's injunction not to eat the fruit as a moral imperative, Douglas interpreted it as a mere suggestion that granted human beings moral autonomy to decide for themselves what was good and evil. Indeed, if taken to its logical conclusion, Douglas's exploitation of the Bible would obliterate all moral distinctions. In short, Douglas interpreted the Bible as conferring a moral right to do wrong.[28]

In a speech in Cincinnati, Ohio, on September 17, 1859, Lincoln twice responded to Douglas's civil theology. Lincoln first criticized Douglas's racial supremacy and his use of the Bible to justify it. Lincoln reminded his audience that the slavery found in the Bible applied to whites as well as blacks— "without reference to color." Douglas cleverly argued that slavery applied only to the black man, "the man who has a skin of a different color." Lincoln then turned the logic of his proslavery rivals against them:

> In Kentucky, perhaps, in many of the Slave States certainly, you are trying to establish the rightfulness of Slavery by reference to the Bible. You are trying to show that slavery existed in the Bible times by Divine ordinance. Now Douglas is wiser than you, for your own benefit, upon that subject. Douglas knows that whenever you establish that slavery was right by the Bible, it will occur that that Slavery was the Slavery of the *white* man—of men without reference to color—and he knows very well that you may entertain that idea in Kentucky as much as you please, but you will never win any Northern support upon it. He makes a wiser argument for you; he makes the argument that the slavery of the *black* man, the slavery of the man who has a skin of a different color from your own, is right.[29]

Lincoln's disposition to view public policy in wider theological terms is revealed further by his second response to Douglas's civil theology, in which he attacked Douglas's appeal to "the Almighty's dividing line," the belief that God had ordained America to be half slave and half free. In a speech delivered at Memphis on November 30, 1858, Douglas had stated, "The Almighty had drawn a line on this Continent, on one side on which the soil must be cultivated by slave labor; on the other by white labor." Although Douglas's reference to "the Almighty's dividing line" occupied only one sentence in his entire speech, Lincoln seized upon its profound civil theological implications: Douglas had offered an implicit theological defense for popular sovereignty by arguing that the Almighty sanctioned the permanent national division between southern slave labor and northern wage labor. As an indication of how seriously Lincoln considered ultimate justifications of public life, he responded to the dividing line argument on at least eight different occasions. In other words, his critique focused on the one sentence of Douglas's speech holding civil theological implications. To cite only one of these instances:

> Whenever you can get these Northern audiences to adopt the opinion that slavery is right on the other side of the Ohio; whenever you can get them, in pursuance

of Douglas' views, to adopt that sentiment, they will very readily make the other
argument, which is perfectly logical, that that which is right on that side of the
Ohio, cannot be wrong on this, and that if you have that property on that side of
the Ohio, under the seal and stamp of the Almighty, when by any means it es-
capes over here, it is wrong to have constitutions and laws, "to devil" you about it.

The view of law implicit in the argument above presumes that human positive law must be brought into conformity with divine law, from which human laws and enactments derive their legitimacy. Lincoln's argument identifies God as the ultimate source of legal authority. In the abstract, God's
eternal law is the measure of all constitutions, all laws. In effect, Douglas's
appeal to the dividing line argument provided a tacit moral justification of
slavery: If God, the preeminent source of legal and moral authority, had
sanctioned slavery on one side of the Ohio River, then it followed that slavery must be intrinsically right. Douglas's argument placed slavery under the
"seal and stamp of the Almighty." As Lincoln pointed out, however, it did
not follow logically that just because slavery existed on one side of the Ohio
River and was absent on the other side that God sanctioned its moral right.
It was quite possible that slavery was morally wrong even though it was
legally sanctioned. Douglas and the advocates of proslavery theology confounded positive law with natural law. In appealing to Romans 13:1, Lincoln's proslavery rivals merely pointed to the existing institution as proof
that God sanctioned it. They did not allow for the possibility of a conflict
between positive law and a divine or natural law. Their argument, based on
the principle of legal positivism, suggested that all human enactments and
policies were necessarily legitimate simply because they were commanded by
those in power or because they were part of the status quo. The southern
view of law, however, conveniently neglected another important passage
from Romans 2:14, one consistent with a more Lincolnian approach to natural law: "For the Gentiles, which have not the law, do by nature the things
contained in the law, these, having not the law, are a law unto themselves:
Which show the work of the law written in their hearts, their conscience
also bearing witness, and their thoughts the means while accusing or else excusing one another."[30]

That slavery was an institution sanctioned by the Bible and the founders
was an idea not confined merely to southerners. The very fact that the Bible
was quoted extensively by southerners to justify slavery led some of the abolitionists to renounce Scripture altogether. Indeed, an eyewitness at a Gar-
risonian convention in 1858 reported that the radical abolitionist Wendell
Phillips "denounced both George Washington and Jesus Christ as traitors to
humanity, the one for giving us the Constitution, the other, the New Testament." At least in this instance, Phillips's repudiation of America's father and
of the Bible was as much an antithesis of Lincoln's biblical republicanism as
the biblical despotism of the South. Contrary to the extreme disunionism of

northern abolitionists and southern fire-eaters alike who claimed that the Constitution affirmed a moral and national right to slavery, Lincoln contended that the proslavery interpretation of his rivals constituted both a radical departure from the founders and a perversion of the Bible. Indeed, Lincoln's characterization of proslavery theology as a rival "political faith" vying for public authoritativeness demonstrates his profound ability to probe the theological and philosophical basis of political order.[31]

Chapter Four

THE DEVELOPMENT OF
LINCOLN'S POLITICAL FAITH

Lincoln's Address to the Young Men's Lyceum of Springfield of 1838 is among the most dissected and scrutinized of his writings. Despite widely divergent conclusions, certain scholars insist that the Lyceum Address furnishes a blueprint for interpreting Lincoln's subsequent political thought. In contrast, I will argue that, although it prefigures later themes in his political thought, the Lyceum Address constitutes neither a formal guide to understanding Lincoln's subsequent thought nor the definitive statement of his civil theology. Rather, the historical context, political intention, and rhetorical style of the speech suggest that it was primarily the utterance of a young Whig who invoked the utility of religion in perpetuating the nation's political institutions against the threat of populist, or plebiscitarian, democracy. Comparing the Lyceum Address to later speeches reveals it to be an early expression of Lincoln's biblical republicanism that combined evocative biblical rhetoric with a republican devotion to ordered liberty and the rule of law.[1]

The philosophical character and coherence of Lincoln's biblical republicanism in the Lyceum Address may be defined more precisely in contradistinction to the Straussian, psychohistorian, and southern conservative interpretations of his "political religion." Despite radical disagreements over the nature of Lincoln's religion and politics, all of these scholars invest the Lyceum Address with far greater significance than it actually merits. Contrary to those who consider the Lyceum Address to be a doctrinal blueprint for understanding Lincoln's teaching on religion and politics, it is my contention that the Peoria Address of 1854 constitutes a far more profound and mature expression of his civil theology. While the Peoria Address has been acknowledged as one of Lincoln's greatest speeches, a comprehensive exploration of Lincoln's civil theological outlook in the speech has been eclipsed by the attention given to works like the Lincoln-Douglas debates and the Second Inaugural, Gettysburg, and Lyceum Addresses. This important gap in the voluminous field of Lincoln scholarship may be remedied through an exegesis of the Peoria Address as a model of biblical republicanism.[2]

Scholars differ primarily over two controversial themes in the Lyceum

Address. The first theme centers on Lincoln's appeal to a political religion. After diagnosing the threats of mob rule and vigilante justice to the perpetuation of the Union, Lincoln called for a political religion that would elicit reverence for the laws:

> Let every American, every lover of liberty, every well wisher to his posterity, swear by the blood of the Revolution, never to violate in the least particular, the laws of the country; and never to tolerate their violation by others. . . . Let reverence for the laws, be breathed by every American mother, to the lisping babe, that prattles on her lap—let it be taught in schools, in seminaries, and in colleges;—let it be written in Primmers, spelling books, and in Almanacs;—let it be preached from the pulpit, proclaimed in legislative halls, and enforced in courts of justice. And, in short, let it become the *political religion* of the nation; and let the old and the young, the rich and the poor, the grave and the gay, of all sexes and tongues, and colors and conditions, sacrifice unceasingly upon its altar.[3]

The second controversial theme in the speech concerns Lincoln's warning against the design of a cunning tyrant, "a towering genius," who will emerge as the law breaks down and who will exploit sectional animosities to satisfy his own unquenchable ambition, "whether at the expence of emancipating the slaves, or enslaving freemen":

> This field of glory is harvested, and the crop is already appropriated. But new reapers will arise, and *they,* too, will seek, a field. It is to deny, what the history of the world tells us is true, to suppose that men of ambition and talents will not continue to spring up amongst us. And, when they do, they will as naturally seek the gratification of their ruling passion, as others have *so* done before them. The question, then, is: can that gratification be found in supporting and maintaining an edifice that has been erected by others? Most certainly it cannot. Many great and good men, sufficiently qualified for any task they should undertake, may ever be found, whose ambition would aspire to nothing beyond a seat in Congress, a gubernatorial or a presidential chair; *but such belong not to the family of the lion, or the tribe of the eagle.* What! think you these places would satisfy an Alexander, a Caesar, or a Napoleon? Never! Towering genius disdains a beaten path. It seeks regions hitherto unexplored. It sees *no distinction* in adding story to story, upon the monuments of fame, erected to the memory of others. It *denies* that it is glory enough to serve under any chief. It *scorns* to tread in the footsteps of *any* predecessor, however illustrious. It thirsts and burns for distinction; and, if possible, it will have it, whether at the expense of emancipating the slaves, or enslaving freemen. Is it unreasonable then to expect, that some man possessed of the loftiest genius, coupled with ambition sufficient to push it to its utmost stretch, will at some time, spring up among us?

The psychohistorians contend that Lincoln's warnings of a Caesarean de-stroyer of liberty in the Lyceum Address were self-referential. Consequently, they argue that the speech holds the psychological key that unlocks his sub-conscious motivations as a leader. Edmund Wilson, who is credited with launching the psychological speculations about the Lyceum Address, states, "Lincoln has projected himself into the role against which he is warning." Similarly, George Forgie observes, "Lincoln had himself in mind when he composed the entire speech." And Dwight G. Anderson explains that "Lin-coln seemed to project himself into the very role which he warned his audi-ence: a towering genius who would destroy inherited institutions rather than suffer the death of political obscurity." Anderson further argues that the Lyceum Address ominously portends the secular messianism of Lin-coln's House Divided speech: "in Lincoln's mind there was a close associa-tion between the attempt to establish his divine authority and his capacity for wickedness and folly. Apparently two elements of the Lyceum speech were now being combined into one; the evil genius would realize his ambi-tion by establishing a political religion." The psychohistorians magnify Lin-coln's self-described ambition as confirmation that he had projected himself in the role of the towering genius.[4]

Their analysis unveils Lincoln's deep-seated envy and ambivalence to-ward the founders, especially George Washington, whom he regarded as his imaginary father figure. Forgie explains: "The significance of the speech is that in it Lincoln related his own conflicting desires—the humble ones in one corner and the grandiose in the other—to the structure of his broad un-derstanding of politics and the processes of history. Ambition and under-standing shaped and focused each other, and proved exceedingly durable." Charles B. Strozier's intriguing psychological profile of the president conveys Lincoln's ambivalence toward the founders in Freudian terms:

> The Oedipal implications of the speech should not be ignored. The danger the towering genius poses is the destruction of the idealized fathers' glorious work, their "temple of liberty," which they have left for us to protect and maintain. By his identification with the towering genius, Lincoln makes himself the one to carry out such a destruction, to become the jealous son displacing the am-bivalently loved father and wage a mythic battle against the collective, histori-cal fathers. His language tends to support this view. The towering genius is vi-brant, powerful, unfettered, above and beyond history itself, but the founders are now dead and their work is rotting, subject to the abuse of nature: "They [the founders] were a forest of giant oaks; but all-resistless hurricane has swept over them, and left only, here and there, a lonely trunk, despoiled of its ver-dure, shorn of its foliage; unshading and unshaded; to murmur in a few more gentle breezes, and to combat with its mutilated limbs, a few more ruder storms, then to sink, and be no more." The imagery here suggests emasculation and castration at the hands of the aspiring son.

According to the psychohistorians, Lincoln's envy involved both admiration and hatred: he admired the founders' monumental deeds but hated their unsurpassable glory that tormented him as a reminder of his own political obscurity and impotence. Like the founders, Lincoln sought to gratify his own "ruling passion" of ambition through everlasting political fame. Yet he arrived upon the political stage too late. The field of glory had already been harvested, the political edifice already established. The glorious act of founding had already been consummated. With this monumental task completed, no opportunities for greatness were left for the man of "towering genius." Unable to build up, Lincoln was compelled to tear down, the acts of creation and destruction being morally indistinguishable for the towering genius. As an envious and ambitious son driven by a paternal rivalry, Lincoln strove to transcend the founders by becoming the nation's political savior. But the nation could only be saved if it was threatened with imminent destruction in the first place. So, as the psychohistorians speculate, at the age of twenty-nine, Lincoln subconsciously revealed in the Lyceum Address his diabolical intention to provoke a fratricidal civil war to achieve monumental fame for himself as the nation's political savior. While it is conceivable that the youthful Lincoln probed the inner recesses of his own heart to understand the consequences of unbridled ambition and the psychopathology of tyranny, it does not follow that he surrendered to such dark impulses by acting upon them.[5]

Straussian scholars such as Harry V. Jaffa, Glen Thurow, Michael P. Zuckert, Laurence Berns, George Anastaplo, and Leo Paul de Alvarez interpret the Lyceum Address as a doctrinal guide for understanding Lincoln's view of religion and politics. They claim that the Lyceum Address contains an esoteric teaching that, if read carefully and in conjunction with his Temperance Address five years later, provides the key to interpreting Lincoln's subsequent political thought. Though they reach radically different conclusions than the psychohistorians, the Straussians likewise emphasize the centrality of the Lyceum Address to grasping Lincoln's political intention and motivation. In *Crisis of the House Divided,* Jaffa states that "a careful reading of the [Lyceum Address] will show that the ideas crystallized in [the Gettysburg Address in] 1863 . . . had been pondered and matured full twenty five years before." Berns explains that "no speech reveals more clearly than this what [Lincoln] regarded as the mission of his life." And Zuckert likewise reaffirms the Straussian view of the Lyceum Address as a doctrinal exposition of Lincoln's political religion:

> The theme of civil religion came early to Lincoln. In 1838, when he was only twenty-nine, he delivered an "Address on the Perpetuation of our Political Institutions," [the Lyceum Address] in which he called for a "political religion." This speech, and a companion statement made five years later [the Temperance Address of 1842] reveals more about Lincoln's thinking on civil religion than the

later speeches in which he actually preached it, because in the earlier speeches he focused far more explicitly on the reasons for, and the nature of, civil religion.[6]

In sum, the Straussians deny the sincerity of Lincoln's religious belief, interpret all of his religious utterances in purely instrumental terms, allege that he developed a theoretical doctrine of political religion comparable to the *religio catholica* of the secular political rationalist thinker Benedict Spinoza, and maintain that a combined reading of the Lyceum and Temperance Addresses provides an esoteric rationalist critique of revealed religion.[7] Jaffa once observed that "Lincoln's temperance speech contains a theological critique which parallels his critique of the dogmas of the Revolution [in the Lyceum Address]."[8] Because the Straussian interpretation of political religion implies a deep, ontological antagonism between faith and reason, they distinguish between Lincoln's exoteric (overt) and esoteric (covert) teaching.[9] Lincoln's exoteric teaching uses religion for salutary political ends and is addressed to the public; his esoteric teaching provides a covert critique of revealed religion that is conveyed "between the lines" to the enlightened reader. Consequently, Jaffa once explained, "we are entitled to think that Lincoln also had a covert argument which transcends these difficulties and that it is this argument which is the true aim of interpretation." The Straussian dualistic interpretation of political religion seems to constitute a contemporary version of the Latin Averroist "double truth" doctrine that was subsequently developed by Spinoza in the seventeenth century.[10] This doctrine holds that, while a belief may be "true" on an imaginary level, it is actually untrue from a metaphysical or philosophical standpoint. Accordingly, the Straussians claim that Lincoln's political religion operates on two levels: the public (exoteric) level in which faith is invoked for its utility and the private (esoteric) level in which it is repudiated as metaphysically false. Their depiction of "political religion" in dualistic terms thus refers to Lincoln's dual (esoteric and exoteric) teaching: "the dualistic structure of the Perpetuation Address reflects the dualistic character of the problem of civil religion as Lincoln saw it," writes Zuckert. And their cryptic references to "the problem of political religion" refer to the ostensible paradox between Lincoln's public appeal to religion and his private skepticism. This paradox is resolved by recognizing that Lincoln's speeches and writings were addressed to two different audiences. Jaffa candidly reveals Lincoln's dual intention in these terms: "to adopt the opinions of others, for public purposes, does not mean to believe in them." According to Thurow, Lincoln devised "a political religion with a dual viewpoint; one that of the nation, the other transcending it." The Straussians accomplish their interpretation of Lincoln's political religion with a dual perspective only by reducing all of his religious invocations to political rhetoric. Thus, Thurow states, "Lincoln's religion, as we know it, is part of his political rhetoric and cannot be divorced from it. In this sense at least, Lincoln's religion is political religion." While the Straussians interpret Lincoln's myriad religious utterances as purely rhetorical, however, they interpret quite literally his references in the Lyceum Address to a "sober," "cold, calculating, unimpassioned" reason as decisive evidence of his secular political rationalism. Lincoln appealed to reason against the furious passions of the mob in the following manner:

> They [the founders] *were* pillars of the temple of liberty; and now, that they have crumbled away, that temple must fall, unless we, their descendants, supply their places with other pillars, hewn from the solid quarry of sober reason. Passion has helped us; but can do so no more. It will in future be our enemy. Reason, cold, calculating, unimpassioned reason, must furnish all the materials for our future support and defence. Let those [materials] be moulded into *general intelligence, [sound] morality* and, in particular, *a reverence for the constitution and laws. . . .*[11]

The Straussians also contend that, like Spinoza, Lincoln devised a "popular religion" to accommodate the cultural prejudices of a Bible-reading nation. Like Spinoza's *religio catholica,* this popular religion harnessed and moderated the sectarian zeal implicit to religious belief and redirected it toward salutary political ends.[12] Furthermore, in accordance with Spinoza's metaphysical critique of faith as a product of the imagination and his secular rationalist view of the antipathy between reason and revelation, the Straussians depict religion in terms of emotion and sentiment rather than reason. Jaffa states, "Lincoln, however, achieved, on the level of the moral imagination, a synthesis of the elements which in Jefferson remained antagonistic." Consistent with the dual perspective of Spinoza's *religio catholica,* Lincoln's appeal to religion in the Lyceum Address and his ostensible synthesis of faith and reason occurred only at an imaginary level; these elements, however, remained antagonistic on a metaphysical level for both Lincoln and Jefferson. Thus, de Alvarez describes Lincoln's political religion in terms of a "fusion of sentiment and reason," noting that a combined reading of the Lyceum and Temperance Addresses will explain "How this fusion of sentiment and reason acts upon the passions." Although the Straussians correctly recognize the fundamental role of religion in maintaining social cohesion, they are skeptical of revelation's claim to truth and deny any philosophical compatibility between faith and reason.[13]

While the Straussians praise Lincoln's use of religious rhetoric as a "prudent" model to be emulated by future leaders, southern conservative scholars like Willmoore Kendall, George Carey, and M. E. Bradford repudiate it as a millenarian heresy that destructively confounded the sacred and secular realms. These scholars maintain that Lincoln saw the Civil War in apocalyptic terms as a crusade between the godly "children of light" and the satanic "children of darkness." They portray the sixteenth president as a secular messiah who, much like the Jacobins of the French Revolution, sought to transfigure society in accordance with the abstract rights of liberty, equality, and fraternity. His "authoritarian biblical rhetoric" sanctified the state as a sacred object of veneration. Southern conservatives agree with the psychohistorians that Lincoln was motivated by "the will to power." Like the psychohistorians, they interpret Lincoln's warnings about a towering genius as self-referential. And they argue that the Lyceum Address anticipated Lincoln's self-appointed role as the nation's savior who would mercilessly use the coercive instruments of the state in a titanic struggle to impose his utopian vision on a recalcitrant and blameless South. Like other messianic figures throughout history (Cromwell, Napoleon, Stalin, Mao, Hitler), Lincoln tempted his countrymen with the spurious charm of secular salvation. Southern conservatives allege further that Lincoln prefigured the imperial presidents of the twentieth century who were likewise driven by overweening ambition and abused their executive power in the service of utopian goals like creating a "Great Society" devoid of poverty and crime. Pointing to the Lyceum Address as an early indication of Lincoln's political messianism, Bradford states:

> Lincoln's political gnosticism does not come to a head in the House Divided speech, and does not begin there. For even in the Springfield Lyceum Address (made when he was twenty-nine), he concludes on a Puritan note: Let us re-found the Union, and the "gates of hell shall not prevail against it." The new founder, having propped up the temple of Liberty/Equality on the solid pillars of "calculating reason," will therefore be, in relation to the powers of evil (i.e., those who do not care for the arrangement) as was the faith of Peter to the Christian church after its foundation. And God is thus, by implication, the security for the quasi-religion of Equality. In a similar fashion Lincoln finds God as a verification of his rectitude in his address to Northern moderates, men who love the old "divided" house, which we find in his Second Inaugural. Here [in the Lyceum Address] is the heresy of a "political religion" at the beginning of Lincoln's political career, and also at its end.[14]

Bradford sees Lincoln's appeal to Matthew 16:18 at the end of the Lyceum Address as particularly heretical in identifying the Union with the City of God. Lincoln concluded his speech by proclaiming, "[Upon these foundations] let the proud fabric of freedom r[est, as the] rock of its basis; and as truly as has been said of the only greater institution, '*the gates of hell shall not prevail against it.*'" If placed in its proper context, however, Lincoln's reference to Matthew 16:18 was not a self-revelation of his calling to preside over a deified state. Rather, it was an example of evocative biblical rhetoric used to reinforce the central Whig teaching of the speech: the maintenance of the rule of law to ensure the Union's perpetuity. In further response to Bradford, a careful reading of the text shows that Lincoln clearly subordinated the secular realm to the spiritual realm when describing the church as a "greater institution" than the state. Lincoln's recognition of a higher spiritual authority shows that he acknowledged a sacred sphere beyond the reach of the federal government. Indeed, not only his speech but also his actions during the Civil War confirm his respect for the integrity of the spiritual realm. During the war, he pursued a policy of non-intervention with rebel churches suspected of disloyalty and counter-manded his generals for such interference if the actions of the church presented no manifest danger to the public good. After suspending an order to remove a Missouri minister suspected of Confederate sympathies, Lincoln wrote to the Union general in charge:

> But I must add that the U.S. government must not . . . undertake to run the churches. When an individual, in a church or out of it, becomes dangerous to the public interest, he must be checked; but let the churches, as such take care of themselves. It will not do for the U.S. to appoint Trustees, Supervisors, or other agents for the churches.

Lincoln's policy of noninterference with rebel churches may be contrasted to the actions of actual secular messiahs like Joseph Stalin and Mao Tse Tung who sought to crush any institution, sacred or secular, whose authority challenged their claim to omnipotence. To argue that there is a moral equivalence between the totalitarian tyrants of the twentieth century and Lincoln is to confound the wicked with the just. The failure to distinguish clearly between tyrannical and prudent leadership impairs our capacity to recognize either.[15]

Though the provocative claims of the foregoing scholars may contribute to some insight about Lincoln's religion and politics, all of them have over-stated his "call for a 'political religion,' investing it with a far broader meaning than the rather commonplace one warranted by the context, namely, adherence to legal process rather than mob action." To be sure, the Lyceum Address anticipates important republican themes found in the mature Lincoln's political thought: the commitment to ordered liberty, devotion to the Union, affirmation of America's mission to serve as an exemplar of democracy to the world, and the role of religion in perpetuating the nation's political institutions. In particular, Lincoln's interpretation of American mission in the Lyceum Address is highly consistent with his subsequent articulations during the Civil War. He described the founders' historic effort to establish successfully the democratic experiment before an "admiring world":

> Their ambition aspired to display before an admiring world, a practical demonstration of the truth of a proposition, which had hitherto been considered, at best no better, than problematical; namely, *the capability of a people to govern themselves*. If they succeeded, they were to immortalized; their names were to be transferred to countries and cities, and rivers and mountains; and to be revered and sung, and toasted through all time. If they failed, they were to be called knaves and fools, and fanatics for a fleeting hour; then to sink and be forgotten.[16]

The initial success of the American experiment was a rebuke to critics of democracy who had long argued that the people were incapable of governing themselves, that republican government was doomed inevitably to vibrate perpetually between the poles of tyranny and anarchy. Though self-government had been established successfully in America, its perpetuation was far from assured: an internal corruption threatened its viability. Lincoln predicted that the greatest threat to American democracy would come not from abroad but from within, from plebiscitarian tendencies implicit to democratic government itself. Echoing Washington's admonition in the Farewell Address, he warned of the dangers of the "mobocratic spirit" visiting the land. The furious passions of the mob threatened to overwhelm the established legal process. Confidence in the nation's political institutions would be undermined: "By such examples . . . the lawless in spirit, are encouraged to become lawless in practice; and having been used to no restraint, but dread of punishment they thus become, absolutely unrestrained." The habitual breakdown of the rule of law disposed citizens to accept lawlessness, providing a climate for aspiring tyrants to exploit sectional divisions for personal gain. The towering ambition of an American Caesar would seek political glory "whether at the expense of emancipating the slaves, or enslaving freemen." Lincoln feared that, if the populist tendencies of democracy went unchecked, America would surely demonstrate to the world not the viability but rather the "absurdity" of self-government. He thus invoked a political religion to confirm fidelity to the regime's political institutions in response to the internal corruption of republican government.[17]

The historical context, political intention, and literary form of the Lyceum Address suggest that it was primarily the rhetorical utterance of a young Whig who upheld the rule of law against the growing tendency of mobocracy unleashed during the Age of Jackson. The Whig Party, of which the young Lincoln was a self-proclaimed stalwart, was formed in opposition to the plebiscitarian excesses of Jacksonian romantic democracy of the nineteenth century. The Whigs accused the Jacksonian Democrats of circumventing established legal procedure and bypassing the checks and balances of representative government in favor of a more direct democracy, one wedded to a populist president who would be unfettered by the rule of law. Like Caesar and Napoleon, this champion of the people would wield his egalitarian scythe to level society, sweeping away all threats to his power. He would flatter the people to satisfy his own ambition at the expense of the nation's constitution and liberties. Lincoln used the term "political religion" in this context in an effort to maintain public adherence to the rule of law and established legal procedure as the indispensable means to perpetuating the nation's liberty and its political institutions. In fact, the much analyzed term "political religion" occurs only once in the Lyceum Address after a long rhetorical flourish. Lincoln's language was obviously rhetorical in its use of repetition and religious imagery. Would it not be patently absurd for him to expect the "lisping babe" to swear "reverence for the laws"? Moreover, his appeal to "the blood of the Revolution" was a rhetorical flourish designed to arouse the audience's appreciation of the founders' sacrifice. When he spoke of "blood," Lincoln intended to remind his listeners that public sacrifice is the price of liberty.[18]

To be sure, Lincoln's denunciation of mobocracy was a consistent theme throughout his early days as a Whig. A year before the Lyceum Address he delivered another speech that repudiated the "lawless mobocratic spirit." Robert V. Bruce describes the Lyceum Address in this context "as the high flown rhetoric of an aspiring young politician." Garry Wills also notes the rhetorical context of the Lyceum Address as a Whig response to the excesses of Jacksonian democracy: "The importance of the Lyceum speech in Lincoln's life has more to do with his literary development than with his psyche. As calmer scholars have pointed out, the political point of the speech was conventional—a Whig denunciation of Jacksonian usurpations, of 'King Andrew' and his high-handed ways."[19]

The institutional role of the lyceums as a forum for aspiring young statesmen to practice their oratorical abilities further confirms the rhetorical context of the speech. Thomas F. Schwartz explains the role of the Illinois lyceums during the antebellum period: "Lyceums offered an early form of popular education through lectures and debates. . . . Advancement of individual skills also played an important role. The associations provided young professional men with an opportunity for demonstrating their oratorical ability before an audience." Schwartz then demonstrates the thematic continuity between the institutional purpose of the lyceum and Lincoln's address of 1838: "Clearly, the focus of the Young Men's Lyceum was to nurture civic responsibility," and, fittingly, Lincoln's "emphasis was on civic responsibility and the preservation of the republic." More specifically, the theme and language of Lincoln's Lyceum Address corresponded to a former speech delivered by another lyceum speaker two years earlier. Indeed, Lincoln composed his speech during the "Golden Age of Oratory" in American history, when the spoken word was valued above the written word, and when aspiring young leaders practiced a cult of filial piety toward the founders, especially George Washington, who was revered as *pater patriae*. In a regime without a hereditary aristocracy, the natural aristocracy of the Republic's founders served as an inspiration to would-be leaders.[20]

The Lyceum Address should be viewed as an important document in tracing the contours of the American republican tradition from the founding generation to the mid-nineteenth century. Its call for a return to the founding principles of the regime as a source of political renewal was characteristically republican. Lincoln explained that the mobocratic spirit could only be exorcised through a rededication to the sacred principles of the Revolution. Although a cause-and-effect relationship cannot be demonstrated between Washington's Farewell Address and Lincoln's Lyceum Address, the remarkable similarities between the two texts reveal an important continuity between the republican outlook of the nation's political founder and its savior.

The parallel themes of the two addresses are unmistakable: both speeches begin by surveying the benefits and blessings of the Union; both uphold the
rule of law against the mobocratic spirit; both invoke the role of religion in
maintaining the nation's republican institutions; both are dominated by the
theme of the Union's perpetuity; both speak of America's mission to serve as
a model of democracy to the world; and both warn against the influence of
designing tyrants who will exploit sectional differences for personal ambition. Consequently, the two texts may be understood as parallel covenants
of American republicanism.[21]

The parallels between the two are not merely coincidental, given the influence of Washington on Lincoln. If Jefferson's Declaration furnished Lincoln with a political creed, Washington's magnanimity provided him with an
inspirational model of statesmanship. Psychohistorians are correct in noting
that Washington represented a political father figure to Lincoln, although
they conclude mistakenly that the latter was driven to patricide by a vaulting
and unbounded ambition to surpass Washington's fame. The nineteenth-
century cult of filial piety revered Washington as a role model for American
youth. Indeed, as a young man, Lincoln had read David Ramsay's *Life of
George Washington* (1807) and Parson Mason Weems's renowned *Life of Washington* (1800). The inclusion of Washington's Farewell Address in these famous biographies provides an important textual link between the Farewell
and Lyceum Addresses. Years later, in his Address to the New Jersey Senate at
Trenton, Lincoln described the influence of Weems's biography upon the formation of his character: "May I be pardoned if, upon this occasion, I mention that away back in my childhood, the earliest days of my being able to
read, I got hold of a small book, such as one as few of the younger members
have ever seen, 'Weem's Life of Washington.' I remember all the accounts
there given of the battlefields and the struggles for the liberties of the country, and none fixed themselves upon my imagination so deeply as the struggle here at Trenton, New Jersey." Perhaps it was no coincidence that Lincoln
invoked Washington's name at the end of the Lyceum Address, hoping "that
during his long sleep we permitted no hostile foot to pass over or desecrate
his resting place." In fact, Lincoln had a penchant for concluding his ora-
tions with a reference to George Washington. For example, he ended his
Temperance Address in 1842, delivered on Washington's birthday, with an
"unrestrained apostrophe" to the first president:

> This is the one hundred and tenth anniversary of the birth-day of Washington.
> We are met to celebrate this day. Washington is the mightiest name of earth—
> *long since* the mightiest in the cause of civil liberty; *still* mightiest in moral re-
> formation. On that name, an eulogy is expected. It cannot be. To add bright-
> ness to the sun, or glory to the name of Washington, is alike impossible. Let
> none attempt it. In solemn awe pronounce the name, and in its naked death-
> less splendor, leave it shining on.

And at Peoria in 1854, Lincoln appealed to Washington's example in opposing the extension of slavery: "If we do not know these things, we do not know that we ever had a revolutionary war, or such a chief as Washington." Similarly, at the end of his celebrated Cooper Institute Address of 1860, he rebuked "Disunionists" for attempting to "unsay what Washington said, and undo what Washington did." Bidding a final farewell to his hometown of Springfield to face the crisis of secession as the next president of the United States, Lincoln once again compared himself to Washington: "I now leave, not knowing when, or whether ever, I may return, with a task before me greater than that which rested upon Washington." From Lincoln's perspective as president-elect, the task of confronting a divided nation in which seven states had already seceded from the Union before he took office was greater than the task of leading the Continental army to end a foreign occupation. Lincoln's consistent gestures of filial piety demonstrate the republican continuity between his leadership and Washington's.[22]

The Straussian, psychohistorian, and southern conservative interpretations of Lincoln's political religion evince the same fatal flaw: they all place far too much emphasis upon a particular passage or certain implication of the Lyceum Address. By interpreting the Lyceum Address as either the definitive or the most profound expression of Lincoln's political theology, they abstract from the work's historical, political, and literary context and disregard primary textual evidence that contradicts their interpretation. Given the wise hermeneutic of "understanding an author as he would understand himself," it should be asked whether Lincoln's own speeches and deeds confirm the interpretations of these scholars. On the contrary, nowhere does Lincoln suggest that his early works provide a blueprint for understanding his subsequent political thought. Lincoln used biblical language in different senses. Those who insist on interpreting his evocative biblical rhetoric literally will inevitably view his utterances in millenarian terms. While focusing upon his rhetorical flourishes, they ignore Lincoln's consistent affirmation of the mysterious character of the divine will. Similarly, those who insist on doubting the sincerity of Lincoln's biblical faith will inevitably view him as a rationalist who exploited religion for political purposes. In so doing, however, they ignore the manifest intention of his public and private religious utterances and the coherence between his private and public faith. Ultimately, the most adequate response to allegations by psychohistorians and southern conservatives that Lincoln projected himself in the Lyceum Address as an American Caesar driven by a lust for power must involve a demonstration of his prudent leadership.[23]

In *Lincoln's Sacred Effort,* Lucas E. Morel provides a balanced interpretation of the Lyceum Address that acknowledges its relevance to Lincoln's civil theology without exaggerating its significance. Morel places the Lyceum Address in its proper context as a Whig protest against Jacksonian romantic democracy. In particular, he suggests that the speech was written in response to President Martin Van Buren's Inaugural Address, delivered before Lincoln's speech and dedicated to the same broad theme of the perpetuation of the nation's political institutions, but from the differing standpoint of a Jacksonian Democrat. As the handpicked successor of Andrew Jackson, Van Buren believed that the democratic excesses of mid-nineteenth-century America would be corrected spontaneously. Though he was cognizant of the danger of mob rule that was sweeping the nation, Van Buren suggested that the problems of self-government could be remedied through an appeal to more democracy. In opposition to this romantic faith in the ability of republican government to heal itself, Lincoln emphasized the need for strenuous moral habituation and civic virtue to restrain the impulses of unbridled democracy. According to Lincoln, the perpetuation of the nation's political institution required a "political religion" that should "be taught in schools, in seminaries, and in colleges" and "preached from the pulpit." While Morel correctly observes the young Lincoln's emphasis on the instrumental role of religion in maintaining political order, he sees no necessary incompatibility between the truth and utility of religion. He also points out an important implication of the speech: the preaching of political religion presumes a preacher, a member of the nation's natural aristocracy (the cultural elite) who can articulate a compelling moral vision of public life. Lincoln would become that preacher, not as a result of an esoteric teaching in the Lyceum Address that provided a rationalist critique of revealed religion, as Straussian scholars have contended, but because of his more mature reflections on religion conveyed in subsequent speeches like the Peoria Address. The Lyceum Address merely hints at the possibility of a much deeper synthesis of the biblical and republican traditions, realized in the Peoria Address, against the "New Creed" of slavery's extension.

THE PEORIA ADDRESS

The Peoria Address of 1854 represents the most mature and profound expression of Lincoln's biblical republicanism to date. It was delivered in response to the infamous Kansas-Nebraska Act of the same year. Ralph Lerner explains that, at Peoria, Lincoln reshaped "the debate raging over the extension of slavery into a debate over the moral foundations of popular government." William Lee Miller sees the Peoria Address in 1854 as a crucial stage in Lincoln's ethical development, where he had "lifted himself to a new intellectual and moral level." By repealing the Missouri Compromise's ban on slavery, the Kansas-Nebraska Act polarized sectional conflict with increasing vigor. Indeed, it marked an important turning point in Lincoln's life and the life of the nation. After 1854, Lincoln would direct his energies to resisting the concrete threat of slavery's extension and nationalization. From this time onward, he would consistently invoke the Declaration as the nation's moral covenant.[24]

The Kansas-Nebraska Act was authored principally by Stephen A. Douglas, coauthor of the Compromise of 1850, longtime political nemesis of Abraham Lincoln in Illinois, his opponent in the debates of 1858, and his rival, once again, in the presidential election of 1860. The unintended consequence of this policy was to explode the combustible issue of the extension of slavery after it had been left precariously unresolved four years earlier by the Compromise of 1850. Based on his vision of manifest destiny and, perhaps, in hopes of securing a transcontinental railroad route through the Midwest, Douglas, who was then chairman of the Senate Committee on Territories, sponsored a bill that would expedite the settlement and statehood of the northern portion of the Louisiana Purchase known as the Nebraska Territory. The Missouri Compromise of 1820 had barred slavery from all territory in the Louisiana Purchase north of the famous 36° 30' line of demarcation, including the Nebraska Territory. Recognizing that the southern-dominated Senate would consent neither to the admission of another free state in the Union nor to a transcontinental railroad route through northern territory, Douglas agreed to an explicit repeal of the Missouri Compromise, thereby opening up the virgin Nebraska Territory for new slave states. During the negotiations, the Nebraska Territory was divided into a southern portion (Kansas) and a northern portion (Nebraska). In an effort to diffuse sectional strife that further polarized it, Douglas proposed that the question of involuntary servitude in the territories be resolved through the principle of popular sovereignty: the right of territorial settlers to choose for themselves whether to adopt slavery. In defense of his scheme, Douglas trumpeted popular sovereignty as a "Sacred Right" of self-government based on the democratic principle of self-determination. He contended further that popular sovereignty was consistent with both the letter and spirit of the Compromise of 1850 whereby the new territories gained in the Mexican War (Utah and New Mexico) were organized without explicit mention of slavery. As an author of this earlier compromise measure, Douglas interpreted the Compromise of 1850's silence over slavery to imply the doctrine of popular sovereignty. Such was the ominous birth of the Kansas-Nebraska Act, which exacerbated sectional conflict, caused an incipient civil war in Kansas, precipitated a political realignment culminating with the formation of the Republican Party, and led to the emergence of Lincoln in national politics. The history of this act provides an object lesson on the dangers of pursuing a short-term policy of political expediency at the expense of the long-term public good. Douglas attempted to ignore the long-term question of slavery, hoping that the issue would somehow resolve itself. He mistakenly believed that conflict would abate if divisive moral questions were kept out of politics. What Douglas did not appreciate, and what Lincoln did, was that determinations about the public good necessarily involve questions of morality and that the long-term interest of the nation is necessarily guided by an underlying vision of justice. Without a legitimate ethical vision to serve as a moral compass, the ship of state will sail blithely toward the rocks of political chaos.

The Kansas-Nebraska Act stirred Lincoln to reenter politics after he had retired from public life to focus on his law career. He believed that popular sovereignty constituted an abandonment of the founding ideals of the republic for the short-term interest of a few. By extending slavery into the virgin territories and by promoting the belief in the public mind that the institution was either a matter of moral right or moral indifference, the Kansas-Nebraska Act placed the nation on a path never envisioned by the founders. Six years after the Peoria Address, in a campaign autobiography for the presidency, Lincoln explained his motivations for reentering public life: "I was losing interest in politics, when the repeal of the Missouri Compromise aroused me again."[25]

The often quoted testimony of William Herndon that his law partner's ambition was "a little engine that knew no rest" seems to support the sinister interpretation that Lincoln's motivation to reenter politics was driven by an insatiable will to power. The identification of Lincoln with the towering genius of the Lyceum Address, however, fails to distinguish between a noble ambition that serves the public good and a base ambition that transgresses moral boundaries. True, Lincoln was ambitious, but his ambition had limits. In an early campaign circular, the youthful Lincoln candidly admitted: "Every man is said to have his peculiar ambition. Whether it be true or not, I can say for one that I have no other so great as that of being truly esteemed of my fellow men, by rendering myself worthy of their esteem." In a speech at Lewiston, Illinois, on August 17, 1858, Lincoln revealed his twin motives as an aspiring leader in these terms, "While pretending no indifference to earthly honors, I *do claim* to be actuated in this contest by something higher than an anxiety for office." In the same speech, Lincoln ironically professed his willingness to die in behalf of the core principles of the regime: "Think nothing of me . . . but come back to the truths that are in the Declaration of Independence. You may do anything with me you choose, if you will but heed these sacred principles. You many not only defeat me for the Senate, but you may take me and put me to death."[26]

William Lee Miller explains that Lincoln's propensity to attribute to himself the twin motives of both principle and recognition recurs throughout his public service: "while he does not claim to be indifferent to political success, he does claim that he stands for something higher." The foregoing statements by Lincoln provide needed balance to distorted interpretations that have focused upon his self-described ambition as if it were a character defect and a premonition of his role as the Caesarean usurper described in the Lyceum Address. Lincoln aspired to be "worthy" of public esteem, an important qualification that acknowledges a moral boundary to ambition. The desire for recognition may be ordered, as in the case of Washington, to serve the common good. In fact, there is no necessary disjunction per se between recognition and principle. Without ambition to spur greatness, Lincoln may never have exerted the Herculean effort needed to resist the tide of slavery's spread.[27]

Indeed, Lincoln's principled decision to reenter politics in response to the new threat unleashed by the Kansas-Nebraska Act manifests a biblical magnanimity (greatness of soul) that combines a pagan nobility with a Christian humility to serve others for the glory of God. The scriptural basis for this biblical magnanimity is derived from the precepts of Matthew 5:16 ("So let your light shine before men, that they may see your good works and glorify [not you but] your Father who is Heaven") and Luke 11:33 ("No man, when he hath lighted a candle, putteth it in a secret place, neither under a bushel, but on a candlestick, that they which come in may see the light"). Thus the Bible teaches that the gifts of the spirit should not be despised in wretched pusillanimity but manifested for the glory of God.

Thomas Aquinas provides an account of Christian magnanimity that balances the quest for worldly greatness with a spiritual humility to serve God and others:

> There is in man something great that he possesses through the gift of God; and something defective that accrues to him through the weakness of nature. Accordingly magnanimity makes a man deem himself worthy of great things in consideration of the gifts he holds from God; Thus if his soul is endowed with great virtue, magnanimity makes him tend to perfect works of virtue; and the same it so be said of the use of any other good, such as science or external fortune. On the other hand, humility makes a man think of his own deficiency, and magnanimity makes him despise others in so far as they fall away from God's gifts. Yet humility makes us honor others and esteem them better than ourselves, in so far as we see some of God's gifts in them.

Based on Aquinas's teaching, Kenneth L. Deutsch describes the virtue of biblical magnanimity in terms of a dynamic tension between "human grandeur and human limitations":

> Through the realization of the "image of God" in the world, human persons are not totally wretched. Man is responsible for his good actions as well as his evil deeds. As a humble creature, man knows that his powers are gifts from God. Aquinas does not present a drama of God's grandeur as contrasted with puny man. The drama is shifted to man; it is concerned with the tension between human grandeur and human limitations. Magnanimity, for Aquinas, is a virtue of human social and political hope, to be realized through one's own human strength and good deeds; honor must be viewed as the natural consequence of good deeds and not merely as an end in itself. . . . From the very outset of his discussion of magnanimity Aquinas is careful to reconcile it with humility. There is no necessary conflict between humility and magnanimity. . . .[28]

Lincoln truly embodied such a characterization of biblical magnanimity. In terms that bear comparison to Aquinas's description of magnanimity, Lincoln remarked in a speech at Springfield, Illinois, on October 30, 1858:

Ambition has been ascribed to me. God knows how sincerely I prayed from the first that this field of ambition might not be opened. I claim no insensibility to political honors; but today could the Missouri restriction be restored and the whole slavery question replaced on the old ground of "toleration" by *necessity* where it exists, with unyielding hostility to the spread of it, on principle, I would, in consideration, gladly agree, that Judge Douglas should never be *out*, and I never *in*, an office, so long as we both or either, live.

Though conscious of his own talents in relation to other human beings, Lincoln humbly sought to attune himself to the divine measure and consistently affirmed the sovereignty and mystery of God's will against human pretensions of power and knowledge. His earnest desire to be "worthy" of recognition coincides remarkably with the foregoing account of biblical magnanimity in which "honor must be viewed as the natural consequence of good deeds and not merely as an end in itself." In speech and deed, Lincoln manifested a biblical magnanimity through his scrupulous adherence to high ethical standards in both his private and public life, his prudential balancing of moral principle and political practice, his lack of self-righteousness toward his enemies, his humility, his clemency toward the South, his compassion, and his personal sacrifice in the service of others. Finally, an insight into Lincoln's humility can be found in his admiration of William Knox's poem "Mortality," a poignant reflection on the ephemeral character of human striving, which begins with the line "Oh, why should the spirit of mortal be proud." In his eulogy to Zachary Taylor, Lincoln first praised the deceased president for "verifying the great truth, that 'he who humbleth himself, shall be exalted' (Matthew 23:12)." He then quoted Knox's "Mortality" in contemplation of the limits of human ambition.[29]

Through its multifaceted and profound integration of the biblical and republican precepts of American order against the palpable resurgence of slavery, the Peoria Address is a more paradigmatic expression of Lincoln's biblical republicanism than his earlier declamations. By illustrating so richly the various elements of biblical republicanism described in the earlier chapters of this work, the speech provides a case study of the symbolic form of Lincoln's civil theology. Lincoln delivered the Peoria Address as a reply to Douglas, who toured Illinois in September 1854 in defense of his Kansas-Nebraska Act. The early exchange between the two men may be seen as a prelude to their great debates four years later in 1858. In fact, Lincoln would repeat many of the arguments in the Peoria Address during his debates with Douglas.

Lincoln announced the subject of his speech, "The repeal of the Missouri Compromise, and the propriety of its restoration," in the first sentence. This seemingly narrow topic would involve a much deeper reflection about slavery's relationship to American republicanism. Lincoln's civil theological intention to articulate and clarify the nation's political creed is evident throughout the speech. He uses the expressions "ancient faith" and "old faith" synonymously on five different occasions, in contradistinction to the

"New Faith" of slavery's extension preached by the Kansas-Nebraska Act. Repudiating Douglas's affirmation of popular sovereignty as a sacred right of self-government, he declared "**my ancient faith** teaches me that 'all men are created equal'; and that there can be no moral right in connection with one man's making a slave of another." After reciting the celebrated prologue of the Declaration, he explained: "I have quoted so much at this time merely to show that according to **our ancient faith**, the just powers of governments are derived from the consent of the governed." Seeking a restoration of the founders' policy, he observed: "We thereby restore **the national faith**, the national confidence, the national feeling of brotherhood." Predicting a substitution of political standards, he warned, "Little by little, but steadily as man's march to the grave, we have been **giving up the OLD for the NEW faith**." Noting the Kansas-Nebraska Act's radical departure from the founders' original intent, he asked, "Is there no danger to liberty itself, in discarding the earliest practice, and first precept of our **ancient faith**?" (emphasis added). Remarkably, Lincoln's sole, passing reference to "political religion" in the Lyceum Address, which was itself delivered in the context of a long rhetorical flourish, has received greater scholarly attention than his various references to the "national," "old," and "ancient" political faith in the Peoria Address. These references are far more civil theological than rhetorical in character, since they denote more than an instrumental use of religion to buttress the rule of law. All of them affirm a political creed based on the universal moral principles of the Declaration. All of them juxtapose two rival views of political life competing for public authoritativeness.[30]

After concisely stating his subject, Lincoln prefaced his speech by publicly avowing that as a statesman he was bound by just means and ends. He would rely upon rational persuasion as the legitimate mode of political discourse. The mental habits of practicing law would equip Lincoln with the logical tools necessary to combat popular sovereignty. Speaking as one who had mastered the lawyer's art, he pledged to "strictly confine [himself] to the naked merits of the question." He then disavowed sectionalism and affirmed his nationalist aim to uphold the Union: "I also wish to be no less than National in all the positions I may take; and whenever I take ground which others have thought, or may think, narrow, sectional and dangerous to the Union, I hope to give a reason, which will appear sufficient, at least to some, why I think differently." Indeed, the centrality of the Union to biblical republicanism is evident in Lincoln's use of the term more than thirty times throughout the speech.[31]

The argument and design of the Peoria Address are as follows: Lincoln first traced the history of slavery in the territories from the Northwest Ordinance in 1787 to the repeal of the Missouri Compromise by the Kansas-Nebraska Act in 1854. Throughout this survey, he cited important legal and historical precedents to show that the Kansas-Nebraska Act violated the spirit and letter of the founders' intention to contain the spread of slavery in the virgin territories. The Peoria Address then contains an important interlude in which Lincoln made a concession to the insoluble problem of racial adjustment in his time. Here he prudently moderated his condemnation of slavery by acknowledging the necessary limits of politics. Some have appealed to this section of the speech as evidence that Lincoln was a racist, though a careful reading of the text does not bear out the interpretation. The next section considered arguments in favor of abolishing the Missouri Compromise. True to his reputation as a formidable lawyer armed with iron-clad logic, Lincoln examined each of the arguments for the repeal on its own terms and then refuted them. In the most significant section of the speech, he considered whether the "avowed principle" of the Kansas-Nebraska Act was "intrinsically right." Here Lincoln attempted to prick the nation's conscience by reminding his fellow countrymen of the inherent turpitude of slavery and its antipathy to the founding principles of American republicanism expressed in both the Declaration and the Constitution. Lincoln emphasized that slavery was the only evil that seriously threatened the Union. His moral case against slavery in this section is complemented by the legal and historical case against it earlier in the speech. The case against the extension of slavery in the Peoria Address involved a prudent balancing of both moral obligation to the natural law and legal obligation to the Constitution. Lincoln concluded his speech in a spirit of filial piety by establishing the republican continuity between himself and his symbolic republican family including George Washington as father and Henry Clay and Daniel Webster as elder siblings. The Peoria Address thus manifests the republican lineage of Lincoln who invokes Jefferson and Washington as preeminent influences of the founding generation and Clay and Webster as heirs of the second generation who carried the banner of liberty and Union. Indeed, Lincoln situated himself within this continuous tradition of republicanism. Each section of the Peoria Address integrates biblical and republican tradition in justification of the "national faith" against the social and political heresies of slavery and of disunion.[32]

In his analysis of Lincoln's rhetoric in the Second Inaugural Address, Ronald C. White, Jr., points out that Lincoln had a "penchant for beginning speeches with historical perspective." In tracing antecedents to the Second Inaugural, White notes that Lincoln also began the Lyceum Address of 1838 by grounding himself in history to convey the wider significance of his speech. Consistent with this rhetorical form, the Peoria Address begins with a short history of the federal policy of restricting slavery in the territories from the Northwest Ordinance (1787) to the repeal of the Missouri Compromise by the Kansas-Nebraska Act (1854). From the outset of the speech, Lincoln distinguished carefully between the "EXISTING institution, and the EXTENSION of it." His intention was made clear by capitalizing the letters of each word for emphasis. The crucial legal distinction between the existence and extension of slavery corresponded to federal authority over the institution. The jurisdiction of the national government did not apply to slavery where it already existed in the southern states; in Lincoln's view, however, it did apply to the territories. Consequently, the federal government was legally prohibited from interfering where slavery existed but was legally authorized to regulate it in those territories under federal jurisdiction, thereby preventing its extension. Taken together, Lincoln's disavowal of a "narrow, sectional" politics as "dangerous to the Union" and his legal fidelity to the distinction between "the EXISTING institution of slavery, and the EXTENSION of it" established his credentials as a moderate antislavery leader. He thereby distinguished himself from the disunionist extremism of radical abolitionists like Garrison and Phillips who repudiated the Constitution for its concessions to slavery.[33]

The Peoria speech marked the beginning of one of the most important political realignments in American history. At the time, Lincoln was without a firm national party. The Whig Party to which he belonged was in dissolution as a result of the Compromise of 1850, which split it along sectional lines: northern "conscience Whigs" opposed the compromise's concessions to slavery while southern "cotton Whigs" supported its terms. The Kansas-Nebraska Act precipitated a shift in coalitions leading to the creation of the Republican Party, a new coalition made up of former northern Democrats and Whigs who opposed slavery's extension. Through his moral stewardship at Peoria, Lincoln would begin to establish himself as the leader of the incipient Republican Party in the West. The party was united through its shared moral consensus on the evil of slavery and the legal right to restrict it in the territories.

The Peoria Address thus provides an indispensable historical, legal, political, and moral case against slavery from the founding era to the sectional conflict of the mid-nineteenth century. Lincoln's historical case study cited important precedents for the restriction of slavery in the territories. In particular, he appealed to the Northwest Ordinance of 1787, a federal act that barred slavery from all nationally owned territory west of the Appalachian Mountains to the Mississippi River and north of the Ohio River to the Great Lakes. This vast territory was originally owned by the state of Virginia and then ceded to the United States government around the time of the Articles of Confederation. As a federal act initially passed under the Articles of Confederation and subsequently reconfirmed by the Constitution of 1787, the Northwest Ordinance organized the settlement of the only nationally owned territory held at that time. The explicit prohibition of slavery by Article 6 of the ordinance resulted in the formation of the free states of Ohio, Indiana, Illinois, Michigan, and Wisconsin. George Anastaplo points out that the policy fortuitously helped to ensure a Union victory during the war, since the free states carved from the Old Northwest were indispensable to the federal cause. Jefferson drafted an earlier version, the ordinance of 1784, which sought to prohibit slavery in the territories but was defeated by one vote. The subsequent ordinance of 1787, which did succeed in prohibiting slavery, was enacted under the Articles of Confederation and then reaffirmed by the Constitution's First Congress of 1789. The Northwest Ordinance provided a compelling legal precedent that justified the federal use of authority to restrict slavery in all newly acquired territories.[34]

Claiming his republican legacy, Lincoln pointed to the example of Thomas Jefferson:

> The question of ceding these territories to the general government was set on foot. Mr. Jefferson, the author of the Declaration of Independence, and otherwise a chief actor in the revolution; then a delegate in Congress; afterwards twice President; who was, is, and perhaps will continue to be, the most distinguished politician of our history; a Virginian by birth and continued residence, and withal a slave-holder; conceived the idea of taking that occasion, to prevent slavery ever going into the north-western territory. He prevailed on the Virginia Legislature to adopt his views, and to cede the territory, making the prohibition of slavery therein a condition of the deed.

The precedent established by Jefferson in the Northwest territories was even more compelling, given the republican tradition of filial piety. By citing the authority of Jefferson, the founding father of the Democratic Party, Lincoln portrayed Douglas and the Nebraska Democrats as unfaithful sons unworthy of their father's republican legacy:

> But *now* new light breaks upon us. Now congress declares this ought never to have been; and the like of it, must never be again. The sacred right of self-government is grossly violated by it! We even find some men, who drew their first breath, and every other breath of their lives, under this very restriction, now live in dread of absolute suffocation, if they should be restricted in the "sacred right" of taking slaves to Nebraska. That *perfect* liberty they sigh for—the liberty of making slaves of other people—Jefferson never thought of; their own father never thought of; they never thought of themselves, a year ago.[35]

Lincoln attributed the political disorder to a breakdown in moral consensus over the meaning of first principles such as liberty. The public teaching of the Kansas-Nebraska Act transformed the meaning of liberty from Jefferson's original understanding of the term as a God-given promise of freedom for all human beings to the "sacred right" of holding slaves. Lincoln referred to this transformation in civil theological terms as the substitution of one "sacred right" for another. The "sacred right" held by Douglas was, in fact, a sham; it was no right at all, but the naked assertion of power by the white majority over the black minority. Thus, later in the speech, Lincoln would blame the doctrine of popular sovereignty for forcing "so many really good men amongst ourselves into an open war with the very fundamental principles of civil liberty—criticizing the Declaration of Independence, and insisting that there is no right principle of action but *self-interest*."[36]

At Peoria, Lincoln anticipated the *Dred Scott* decision of 1857 that affirmed a national right to slavery based on the Fifth Amendment's liberty clause. He warned of the South's aggressiveness in demanding federal extension of slavery, claiming "the constitutional right to take and to hold slaves in the free states." Indeed, the Taney Court subsequently interpreted "liberty" as the freedom of the slaveholder to take his chattel (moveable property) wherever he pleased without interference by the national government. Given the logic of the Taney Court, the South was perfectly consistent in demanding a federal slave code to protect and encourage its national right. Contrary to Taney's sophistry, however, Lincoln distinguished between liberty and license. Authentic freedom must be exercised within legitimate moral boundaries; the entitlement of rights implies reciprocal duties and obligations. According to Lincoln, genuine liberty did not entail "the right to do wrong."[37]

Like the Northwest Ordinance, the Missouri Compromise of 1820 provided another important legal precedent authorizing federal restriction of slavery. While the Missouri Compromise prohibited slavery in the Louisiana Territory, north of the 36° 30′ line of demarcation, it made no mention of the institution south of that line. Though this silence led to the toleration of the institution south of the demarcation line, it by no means affirmed a national right to slavery. Lincoln then referred to the authority of Henry Clay, the author of the Missouri Compromise, against the Kansas-Nebraska Act. As a Whig, westerner, and moderate antislavery statesman for the Union, Clay represented Lincoln's political role model among the second generation of American leaders. Describing the Kentuckian as his "beau-ideal of a statesman," Lincoln campaigned for Clay, modeled his Whig politics after him, and delivered a stirring eulogy for him in Springfield. Clay's compromise was lauded as a Union-saving measure by all, including Douglas, who now repudiated it as a violation of the "sacred right" to hold slaves. Lincoln then quoted from a public address in which Douglas had earlier described the Missouri Compromise as "canonized in the hearts of the American people, as a sacred thing which no ruthless hand would ever be reckless enough to disturb." This exposed Douglas's disingenuous attempt to impress upon the "public mind" the belief that popular sovereignty constituted a "sacred right" of self-government and that the principle of popular sovereignty demanded the repeal of the Missouri Compromise.[38]

After citing legal and historical precedents for the restriction of slavery in the Northwest and Louisiana Territory, Lincoln turned to the territories acquired by the United States as a result of the Mexican War from 1846 to 1848. As a Whig member serving a single term in the U.S. House of Representatives at the time, Lincoln opposed the Mexican War. During the conflict, the Whigs in the House of Representatives proposed a series of resolutions to exclude slavery from all new territory acquired from Mexico. These various proposals were collectively known as the Wilmot Proviso. Harry Jaffa quite properly notes that the principle behind the Wilmot Proviso represented the acorn that would evolve into the mature oak tree of the Republican Party. Although the proviso passed in the House, it was defeated in the

Senate, where policies were contingent on the approval of the southern states. Lincoln mentioned this history to reveal his consistent opposition to slavery's extension: "'The Wilmot Proviso' or the principle of it, was constantly coming up in some shape or other, and I think I may venture to say I voted for it at least forty times; during the short term I was there." This important deed matches Lincoln's antislavery speech, thereby testifying to his principled opposition to the institution. To be sure, Lincoln consistently opposed slavery from his first public condemnation of the institution in the Illinois legislature in 1837 to his repeated support for the Wilmot Proviso in the U.S. House of Representatives roughly ten years later.[39]

By the time of the peace treaty with Mexico in 1848, the United States had obtained the territories of California, Utah, and New Mexico. Douglas, who was then serving in the Senate, proposed an extension of the Missouri Compromise to the new territories ceded by Mexico. With the Wilmot Proviso dead, Douglas's proposal offered a plausible means for restricting slavery in the northern portion of the new territory. Lincoln, however, opposed the extension of the compromise line, which "gave up the Southern part to slavery, while we were bent on having it all free." His effort to prohibit slavery throughout the entire territory gained in the Mexican War further demonstrates Lincoln's moral resolve not to compromise with the institution when legally authorized to resist its spread. Fortuitously, the influx of free white labor to California precipitated by the discovery of gold in 1848 ensured that its settlers would exclude slavery and apply for admission to the Union as a free state. With California seeking admission to the Union as a free state, the year 1850 marked a watershed in sectional tension: "The Union, now, as in 1820 was thought to be in danger; and devotion to the Union rightfully inclined men to yield somewhat, in points nothing else could have so inclined them." Lincoln then offered a concise summary of the complex and multifaceted Compromise of 1850:

> The south got their new fugitive-slave law; and the north got California (the far best part of our acquisition from Mexico) as a free State. The south got a provision that New Mexico and Utah, *when admitted as States,* may come in *with* or *without* slavery as they may then choose; and the north got the slave-trade abolished in the District of Columbia. The north got the western boundary of Texas, thence further back eastward than the south desired; but, in turn, they gave Texas ten millions of dollars, with which to pay her old debts.

According to Lincoln, the Compromise of 1850 did not constitute an abandonment of the antislavery cause but an accommodation to the limits of politics. It prudently achieved what was politically possible under the circumstances. It was a necessary Union-saving measure involving a quid pro quo. "The North consented to this provision, not because they considered it right in itself; but because they were compensated" with concessions from the South.[40]

Douglas, who drafted the Compromise of 1850, defended the Kansas-Nebraska Act of 1854 by claiming that it was consistent with both the spirit and letter of the former. In reply, Lincoln accused Douglas of committing a non sequitur: the provision of the Compromise of 1850 that allowed New Mexico and Utah to come into the Union did not mandate a repeal of the earlier Missouri Compromise of 1820. Once again, Lincoln exposed Douglas's duplicity. When he initially sponsored the bill, Douglas recommended that the Kansas-Nebraska Act should neither expressly affirm nor deny the Missouri Compromise. Lincoln noted that an earlier version of the Nebraska Bill was assailed by proslavery forces for not containing an express repeal of the Missouri Compromise. In order to gain support for his measure, Douglas thus acquiesced by agreeing to an explicit repeal. Lincoln argued that the legal status of the Missouri Compromise was still binding notwithstanding the provisions of the Compromise of 1850 that applied to a different territory and a different set of circumstances. Furthermore, he argued that the United States had a compelling moral obligation to enforce its legal right to restrict slavery in the territories and to combat the pernicious teaching of popular sovereignty:

> This *declared* indifference, but as I must think, covert *real* zeal for the spread of slavery, I can not but hate. I hate it because of the monstrous injustice of slavery itself. I hate it because it deprives our republican example of its just influence in the world—enables the enemies of free institutions, with plausibility, to taunt us as hypocrites—causes the real friends of freedom to doubt our sincerity, and especially because it forces so many really good men amongst ourselves into an open war with the very fundamental principles of civil liberty—criticising the Declaration of Independence, and insisting that there is no right principle of action but *self-interest.*"[41]

Lincoln believed that the purported claim of popular sovereignty to be ethically neutral toward slavery was disingenuous, since an aggressive proslavery coalition bent on extending the institution succeeded in gaining an explicit repeal of the Missouri Compromise. More important, the public teaching of popular sovereignty espoused a creed of moral relativism that was antithetical to the moral foundations of American republicanism. With unusual candor, Lincoln used the strong language of hatred to characterize his personal feelings toward slavery. The institution was odious "because of the monstrous injustice of slavery itself." At Peoria, Lincoln publicly declared his unqualified condemnation of slavery in principle. Slavery was further detestable because of its consequences; it threatened the very integrity of American republicanism. The institution undermined America's moral credibility in the eyes of the world. By abandoning the moral high ground of the Declaration to the moral relativism of popular sovereignty, America would be, in effect, forfeiting its symbolic role as a standard-bearer of democratic government to the friends of freedom throughout the world. Lincoln reminded his countrymen of the gross incompatibility between the founding creed of the Declaration based on universal principles of natural right and the creed of popular sovereignty based on the principle of the will of the stronger. The acceptance of popular sovereignty as a new national faith would confirm the cynical view of Old World despots that the only true principle of governance is "the will of the stronger over the weaker." American republicanism would become a sham. It would merely replace "the will of the stronger" with "the will of the [white] majority over the black minority." Thus, Lincoln explained that popular sovereignty "forces so many really good men into an open war with very fundamental principles" of the regime. His description of a war between "fundamental principles" battling for "the public mind" corresponds with his civil theological view of different political faiths competing for public authoritativeness. Once sanctioned by the state, popular sovereignty would have steadily debauched the public mind by teaching citizens not to care about "the monstrous injustice" of slavery.

At this point in the speech, Lincoln tempered his prior condemnation of slavery by acknowledging the practical difficulty of its abolition. It was necessary for Lincoln as a credible antislavery leader seeking elective office to distinguish himself from the radical abolitionists. Humbly sympathizing with those southern people who acknowledged the evil of slavery but whose circumstances prevented a simple solution to it, Lincoln stated:

> Before proceeding, let me say I think I have no prejudice against the Southern people. . . . They are just what we would be in their situation. If slavery did not now exist amongst them, they would not introduce it. If it did now exist amongst us, we should not instantly give it up. This I believe of the masses north and south. . . . When southern people tell us they are no more responsible for the origin of slavery, than we; I acknowledge the fact. When it is said that the institution exists; and that it is very difficult to get rid of it, in any satisfactory way, I can understand and appreciate the saying. I surely will not blame them for not doing what I should not know how to do myself.

Lincoln then humbly acknowledged his own limitations in providing a practical solution to ending slavery:

> If all earthly power were given me, I should not know what to do, as to the existing institution. My first impulse would be to free all the slaves, and send them to Liberia,—to their own native land. But a moment's reflection would convince me, that whatever of high hope, (as I think there is) there may be in this, in the long run, its sudden execution is impossible. If they were all landed there in a day, they would all perish in the next ten days; and there are not surplus shipping and surplus money enough in the world to carry them there in many times ten days.[42]

Lincoln has been criticized for condemning slavery without providing any viable solution for incorporating blacks into American society once they were freed. This criticism overlooks the necessary political priority at the time. All of Lincoln's gifts and energy were needed to respond to the threatened expansion of slavery and its corrupting effect upon the moral foundations of American republicanism. The tangible threat of slavery's spread, not the utopian dream of perfect racial equality, was the immediate and compelling issue facing the nation in 1854. To be sure, the issue of abolition and racial adjustment would have been moot had slavery been allowed to spread into the territories. Lincoln consistently emphasized the priority of first disposing public opinion toward legitimate moral ends before proceeding on to derivative questions of policymaking: "he who moulds public opinion goes deeper than he who enacts public policy—he makes public policy possible." In the context of the mid-nineteenth century, given the universal prejudice against blacks, the success of any scheme of emancipation or racial integration first depended upon preparing public opinion to support it. Before a policy of emancipation and integration could take place, it was first necessary for the American public to recognize the African American's humanity and to acknowledge the inherent evil of slavery. No progress toward these loftier goals could ever be made if the American people saw African Americans as subhuman, devoid of natural rights.[43]

Although he hated slavery in principle and would not himself enslave another human being, Lincoln disclaimed advocating the full political and social equality of blacks at this moment in his public life:

> What then? Free them all, and keep them among us as underlings? Is it quite certain that this betters their condition? I think I would not hold one in slavery, at any rate; yet the point is not clear enough for me to denounce people upon. What next? Free them, and make them politically and socially, our equals? My own feelings will not admit of this; and if mine would, we well know that those of the great mass of white people will not. Whether this feeling accords with justice and sound judgment, is not the sole question, if indeed, it is any part of it. A universal feeling, whether well or ill-founded, can not be safely disregarded. We can not, then, make them equals. It does seem to me that systems of gradual emancipation might be adopted; but for their tardiness in this, I will not undertake to judge our brethren of the south.

The foregoing, some argue, provides evidence that Lincoln was a racist. A careful reading proves otherwise. In moderating his earlier condemnation of slavery, Lincoln made a necessary concession to the racial prejudices of his audience. It would have been political suicide for a leader running for elected office in the mid-nineteenth century to endorse the full social and political equality of blacks. Furthermore, Lincoln's use of conditional language provided an important qualification to his remarks. His statement "My own feelings will not admit of this" cannot be taken categorically in view of the following qualification: "*and if mine would,* we know that the great mass of white people will not" (emphasis added). Lincoln candidly acknowledged that public opinion would not support full social and political equality at this time, regardless of the policy's inherent right or wrong. The conditional phrase, "Whether this feeling accords with justice and sound judgment, is not the sole question," further conveys the moral dubiousness of denying full social and political equality to blacks. In presenting the various dimensions of biblical republicanism, the introduction of this work emphasized the role of Lincoln as an agent of civil theology, a member of the natural aristocracy, who disposed the climate of public opinion toward a just moral end. Because the role of leader in guiding public opinion is necessarily constrained under the circumstances, however, statesmen must strike a prudent balance between guiding public opinion and bowing to its recalcitrance. The attempt to reap a premature harvest before public opinion has sufficiently ripened will yield bitter fruit; a sweeter crop may be produced through a more patient cultivation.[44]

The inability to confer full civil and political rights upon blacks did not contradict Lincoln's claim that they were nevertheless entitled to the natural rights of life, liberty, and the pursuit of happiness promised by the Declaration. One may distinguish between natural rights that are antecedent to government and social and political rights that are conferred by government. Lincoln believed that, at the very least, all human beings, regardless of their social status in society, were entitled to the God-given right to enjoy the fruits of their own labor. To deprive another human being of the fruits of his or her labor was to steal from another.[45]

The moral recognition of the African American's humanity was a recurrent theme throughout the Peoria Address. If the African American was a human being, it followed that he was entitled to the natural rights in the Declaration. Lincoln envisioned the supreme task of political leadership to be moral. Statesmen must take their initial bearings, not from formalistic metaphysical doctrines, but from man's inherent moral awareness. Neither relative nor "evanescent," this awareness is "eternal," for it attends the promptings of transcendence that clamor steadfastly to the human spirit. Statesmen must cultivate the nation's moral impulses and subsequently direct them toward the common good. At the end of the speech, Lincoln criticized Douglas for denying the African American's humanity and the corresponding claim to natural rights:

> In the course of his reply, Senator Douglas remarked, in substance, that he had always considered this government was made for the white people and not for the negroes. Why, in point of mere fact, I think so too. But in this remark of the Judge, there is a significance, which I think is the key to the great mistake . . . which he has made in this Nebraska Bill. It shows that the Judge has no very vivid impression that the negro is a human; and consequently has no idea that there can be any moral question in legislating about him. In his view, the question of whether a new country shall be slave or free, is a matter of as utter indifference, as it is whether his neighbor shall plant his farm with tobacco, or stock it with horned cattle. Now whether this view is right or wrong, it is very certain

that the great mass of mankind take a totally different view. They consider slavery a great moral wrong; and their feelings against it, is not evanescent, but eternal. It lies at the very foundation of their sense of justice; and it cannot be trifled with. It is a great and durable element of popular action, and, I think, no statesman can safely disregard it.[46]

Douglas conceived of a Union that was exclusive to white men. He would repeat this vision of white supremacy in his subsequent debates with Lincoln in 1858. In response, Lincoln conceded that the founders were white and that the Constitution was established for a predominantly white public. Nonetheless, this "point of mere fact" did not deny the universal implications of the founders' view of equality as an aspiration for all human beings. Douglas committed another logical fallacy: it did not follow that because equality applied to whites at the time of the founding that it ought not to apply universally to all human beings in the future. In fact, as Lincoln reminded Douglas, the Little Giant's narrow application of equality to white males of the founding generation could be used to exclude groups of white people as well, since full social political equality was denied to propertyless white males until the Age of Jackson.

At Peoria, Lincoln affirmed that the initial moral claim concerning slavery's inherent good or evil must be preeminent in the determination of public policy. The resolution of this moral claim was a necessary condition for further public dialogue on slavery. The teaching of popular sovereignty was particularly pernicious because it dulled the nation's moral conscience through its moral indifference to "the monstrous injustice of slavery." Douglas trivialized the gravity of human servitude by comparing the decision of settlers to hold slaves with their decision to plant tobacco or stock cattle. These choices were morally incomparable, since slaves were human beings created in the image of God, not plants or animals. Thus, the institution of slavery was different in kind from other domestic institutions like industry and agriculture. By confounding slavery with these other institutions, Douglas inappropriately trivialized "the very foundation of [mankind's] sense of justice." Significantly, Lincoln identified the moral claim against slavery and for freedom as "a great and durable source of popular action." In his view, public policy had to be grounded upon the rectitude of substantive moral claims.

During a prior interlude in the Peoria Address, Lincoln bowed to a "universal feeling, whether well or ill-founded," that could not be "safely disregarded." The constraints of public opinion prevented him from demanding full social and political equality for blacks. At the end of the Peoria Address, however, he appealed to the universal moral condemnation of slavery in the court of worldwide public opinion. The mass of humanity consider slavery a "great moral wrong; and their feelings against it, is not evanescent, but eternal. It lies at the very foundation of their sense of justice; and it cannot be trifled with." Here Lincoln referred to a biblical understanding of morality and the eternal origin of humanity's intuitive grasp of right and wrong. This moral awareness should guide leaders in the determination of public policy: "no statesman can safely disregard it." In sum, the defining parameters of public opinion at this time permitted the containment of slavery where the government was constitutionally authorized to do so but prohibited immediate emancipation and the granting of full social and political equality for blacks.

Lincoln's moral argument against slavery in the Peoria Address presumed the biblical teaching that all human beings were endowed by God with a prearticulate moral awareness, a natural inclination that "seeks to do good and avoids evil." Consonant with the teaching of Jeremiah 31:33 ("I will put my law in their inward parts, and write it in their hearts"), he affirmed the biblical view of a universal moral law that God has impressed upon the human heart and mind. Although this law is of divine origin, it is known naturally, through unassisted human reason. Its promptings are recognized through the activity of conscience.[47] In Deuteronomy 30:11–14, Moses described the voice of conscience to the people of Israel as a moral law that has been stamped upon their hearts so it may be known by all. According to Moses, the inner voice of conscience was neither an ethereal abstraction to be discovered only by the enlightened few nor a remote vestige of another time or place to be discovered only in some far-off land by daring adventurers:

> For the commandments which I command thee this day, it is not hidden from thee, neither is it far off. It is not in heaven, that thou shouldest say, "Who shall go up for us to heaven, and bring it unto us, that we may hear it, and do it?" Neither is it beyond the sea, that thou shouldest say, "Who shall go over the sea for us, and bring it unto us, that we may hear it, and do it?" But the word is very nigh unto thee, in thy mouth, and in thy heart, that thou mayest do it.

Indeed, Lincoln's appeal to southerners' intuitive recognition of the African American's humanity was informed by a biblical understanding of conscience as described throughout Scripture by Moses, the prophets, and the apostle Paul:

> Equal justice to the south, it is said, requires us to consent to the extending of slavery to new countries. That is to say, inasmuch as you do not object to my taking my hog to Nebraska, therefore I must not object to you taking your slave. Now, I admit this is perfectly logical, if there is no difference between hogs and Negroes. But while you thus require me to deny the humanity of the negro, I wish to ask whether you of the south yourselves, have ever been willing to do as much? It is kindly provided that of all those who come into the world, only a small percentage are natural tyrants. That percentage is no larger in the slave States than in the free. The great majority, south as well as north, have human sympathies, of which they can no more divest themselves than they can of their sensibility to physical pain. These sympathies in the bosom of southern people, manifest in many ways, their sense of the wrong of slavery,

and their consciousness that, after all, there is humanity in the negro. If they deny this, let me address them a few plain questions. In 1820 you joined the north, almost unanimously, in declaring the African slave trade piracy, and in annexing to it the punishment of death. Why did you do this? If you did not feel that it was wrong, why did you join in providing that men should be hung for it? The practice was no more than bringing wild negroes from Africa, to sell to such as would buy them. But you never thought of hanging men for catching and selling wild horses, wild buffaloes or wild bears.

Again, you have amongst you, a sneaking individual, of the class of native tyrants known as the "SLAVE-DEALER." He watches your necessities, and crawls up to buy your slave at a speculating price. If you cannot help it, you sell to him; but if you can help it, you drive him from your door. You despise him utterly. You do not recognize him as a friend, or even as an honest man. Your children must not play with his; they may rollick freely with the little negroes, but not with the "slave-dealers" children. If you are obliged to deal with him, you try to get through the job without so much as touching him. It is common with you to join hands with the men you meet; but with the slave dealer you avoid the ceremony—instinctively shrinking from the snaky contact. If he grows rich and retires from business, you still remember him, and still keep up the ban of non-intercourse upon him and his family. Now why is this? You do not so treat the man who deals in corn, cattle or tobacco.

And yet again; there are in the United States and territories, including the District of Columbia, 433,643 free blacks. At $500.00 per head they are worth over two hundred millions of dollars. How comes this vast amount of property to be running about without owners? We do not see free horses or free cattle running at large. How is this? All these free blacks are the descendants of slaves, or have been slaves themselves, and they would be slaves now, but for SOMETHING which has operated on their white owners, inducing them, at vast pecuniary sacrifices, to liberate them. What is that SOMETHING? Is there any mistaking it? In all these cases it is your sense of justice, and human sympathy, continually telling you, that the poor negro has some natural right to himself—that those who deny it, and make merchandise of him, deserve kickings, contempt and death.[48]

Lincoln presumed that the evil of slavery could be recognized intuitively by his audience. By prompting his audience to acknowledge the common humanity of the African American, Lincoln pointed to the self-evident truth of human equality affirmed by the Declaration and known intuitively by all. If African Americans were truly human, as even their southern masters seemed to admit, then they were entitled to the same God-given, inalienable rights as whites. Rather than offering a rational demonstration of the evil of slavery, Lincoln compelled his listeners to discern their internal moral tensions. Whether or not they admitted it, southerners knew in their hearts that slavery was wrong. If slavery was indeed a social and political blessing, as George Fitzhugh and others argued, why did decent southern people shun the slave trader? Why did they seek to free their slaves at vast pecuniary sacrifice? Why did they prohibit the foreign slave trade? Why did they make participation in the foreign slave trade a capital offense? Lincoln's capitalization of the word "SOMETHING" emphasized to his audience the moral phenomenon given concretely to human experience. He presumed a noetic apprehension (an intuitive grasp) of slavery's evil.[49] The inner voice of conscience cried out against the evil of slavery despite sophistic arguments to the contrary. Avoiding self-righteous invective, Lincoln subtly allowed the southerners to draw their own moral conclusions. Since the moral phenomenon was intuitively recognized by the audience, it did not require a formal rational demonstration to prove slavery's inherent nobility or baseness.

Lincoln's ethics were far more Aristotelian and Thomistic than Kantian. He presumed that the process of moral judgment began with an apprehension "that" something could be intuitively recognized by human experience as good or evil before proceeding on to a discursive reasoning of "why" it is wrong or to a systematic account of "what" makes it wrong. For Kant, the order of moral inquiry is reversed: the formal account and rational demonstration of why something is good or evil seems to precede the commonsense acknowledgment that something can be grasped initially as evil without relying upon discursive reasoning. In the Peoria Address, Lincoln magnified this "SOMETHING" to his audience as an element that "has operated on white owners inducing them, at vast pecuniary sacrifices, to liberate their slaves." Indeed, this "SOMETHING" was tantamount to a biblical understanding of conscience that could not be laid aside and that persisted despite specious arguments to the contrary. In pricking the nation's conscience at Peoria, Lincoln awakened his audience to the common humanity of the African American.

A biblical view of conscience and moral inclination is clearly revealed in another important passage from the Peoria Address in which Lincoln diagnosed slavery as part of the inherent selfishness of human nature:

> Slavery is founded in the selfishness of man's nature—opposition to it, is [in] his love of justice. These principles are an eternal antagonism; and when brought into collision so fiercely, as slavery extension brings them, shocks, and throes, and convulsions must ceaselessly follow. Repeal the Missouri compromise—repeal all compromises—repeal the declaration of independence—repeal all past history, you still can not repeal human nature. It still will be the abundance of man's heart, that slavery extension is wrong; and out of the abundance of his heart, his mouth will continue to speak.

The final sentence of the passage refers to Luke 6:45: "A good man out of the good treasure of his heart bringeth forth that which is good, and an evil man out of the evil treasure of his heart bringeth forth that which is evil: for out of the abundance of the heart his mouth speaketh." A parallel statement of this biblical view of moral inclination is found in Matthew 15:18–19: "But those things which proceed out of the mouth come forth from the heart; and they defile the man. For out of the heart proceed evil thoughts, murders, adulteries, fornications, thefts, false witness, blasphemies." In civil theological terms, the biblical teaching reminded the audience of a divine law antecedent to human convention. Human enactments cannot erase the law God has inscribed upon the human mind and heart. Consonant with Augustine's teaching on fallen human nature, Lincoln viewed slavery as a manifestation of the *libido dominandi,* the lust for power. Slavery was not merely a social problem that could be adjusted through bureaucratic manipulation; it was a "monstrous injustice" deeply rooted in the very "selfishness of human nature." Lincoln's critique of slavery thus relied upon a biblical view of human nature, one that recognized the human heart's capacity for both good and evil, thereby rejecting the Enlightenment teaching of man's natural goodness or the opposite view of humanity's utter depravity.[50]

It is important to note that Lincoln's appeal to a prearticulate moral awareness was only the "starting-point for all virtuous considerations, feelings and interior actions." Although the intuitive grasp of slavery's evil established a common ground for further inquiry on the issue, it did not provide or seek to provide concrete determinations of public policy. While Lincoln believed that, on the most important questions, abstract moral claims must be resolved before proceeding to legal determinations and derivative questions of practical judgment, he did not believe that subsequent deliberations concerning how best to apply the principle under the circumstances were irrelevant to public life. On the contrary, he maintained that the discursive processes of argumentation, debate, and deliberation were essential to the prudent determination of public policy. For this reason, he was highly critical of the radical abolitionists whose condemnation of slavery was based upon either sentiment or the abstract moral evil of slavery without regard for the circumstances surrounding it. Although moral inclination provided a common reference point for dialogue, it was by no means decisive in shaping public policy. Prudent leaders must harmonize principle with legal, social, and political circumstances as well. Presuming slavery's evil, Lincoln himself once remarked: "I am naturally anti-slavery. If slavery is not wrong, nothing is wrong. . . ." In the same utterance, however, he made it clear that his fidelity to the Constitution prevented him from acting upon his abstract moral judgments; he could only strike against slavery where he was legally authorized to do so: "I understood, too, that in ordinary civil administration this oath even forbade me to practically indulge my primary abstract judgment on the moral question of slavery."[51]

Once Lincoln established the humanity of African Americans, he insisted that the principle of consent ought to be applied to them as members of the human race. Douglas's conception of liberty was a sham because it deprived an entire class of human beings of the natural right to equal consent. Responding to the rival interpretation of self-government propounded by Douglas, Lincoln explained:

My faith in the proposition that each man should do precisely as he pleases with all which is exclusively his own, lies at the foundation of the sense of justice there is in me. I extend the principles to communities of men, as well as to individuals. I so extend it, because it is politically wise, as well as naturally just: political wise, in saving us from broils about matters which do not concern us. Here, or at Washington, I would not trouble myself with the oyster laws of Virginia, or the cranberry laws of Indiana.

By acknowledging that under the American form of government there are discrete levels of authority at the community and state level that prohibited the national government from intervening beyond its legitimate scope of power, Lincoln further demonstrated his fidelity to the Constitution and the doctrine of federalism. Though national power was augmented as a necessary consequence of the Civil War, Lincoln did not endorse the bureaucratic welfare state.[52]

Although human beings have the God-given freedom to do what they will with their own property, they do not have a right to treat other human beings as property. As free and rational agents, human beings must consent to be governed rather than being ruled despotically as one would govern an animal. Lincoln stated:

The doctrine of self-government is right—absolutely and eternally right—but it has no just application, as here attempted. Or perhaps I should rather say that whether it has such just application depends upon whether a negro is *not* or *is* a man. If he is *not* a man, why in that case, he who *is* a man may, as a matter of self-government, do just as he pleases with him. But if the negro is a man, is it not to that extent, a total destruction of self-government, to say that he too shall not govern *himself?* When the white man governs himself that is self-government; but when he governs himself, and also governs *another* man, that is *more* than self-government—that is despotism. If the negro is a man, why then my ancient faith teaches me that "all men are created equal;" and that there can be no moral right in connection with one man's making a slave of another.

Lincoln emphasized the centrality of equal consent as the "sheet anchor of American republicanism." The "ancient faith" of American republicanism forbade the embrace of a moral right to slavery. America's political creed was fundamentally opposed to ethical relativism and the misinterpretation of liberty as "the right to do wrong."[53]

After vindicating the republican principle of equal consent against Douglas's reinterpretation of the term, Lincoln then considered the threat that slavery posed to the Union's perpetuity. Using evocative biblical rhetoric from the Book of Job, he characterized slavery as "the great Behemoth of danger" to the Union. He emphatically denied that the Kansas-Nebraska Act was a "Union saving measure" like the Missouri Compromise of 1820 and the Compromise of 1850. In fact, it was just the opposite; it was a pernicious measure designed, as if by some evil genius, to destroy the Union. He even predicted the incipient civil war of "Bleeding Kansas" that would erupt two years later: "Some yankees, in the east, are sending emigrants to Nebraska, to exclude slavery from it. . . . But the Missourians are awake too. They are within a stone's throw of the contested ground. . . . Through all this, bowie knives and six shooters are seen plainly enough; but never a glimpse of the ballot box." Lincoln teaches political prudence through his willingness to tolerate slavery rather than risk disunion at this time: "Much as I hate slavery, I would consent to the extension of it rather than see the Union dissolved, just as I would consent to any GREAT evil, to avoid a GREATER one. But when I go to Union saving, I must believe at least, that the means I employ has some adaptation to the end." Again, Lincoln's use of capitalization throughout the Peoria address conveys an important intention: it should leave no doubt in the mind of his audience that the author considered slavery a GREAT evil and that this GREAT evil could only be tolerated to avoid a GREATER evil. As the art of the possible rather than the ideal, politics necessarily involved choosing the lesser of two evils. The dissolution of the Union constituted the GREATER evil because it extinguished the American experiment, "the last best hope of earth" and its promise of freedom to all human beings.[54]

Lincoln's affirmation of his priorities in the Peoria Address of 1854 is remarkably consistent with his controversial reply to Horace Greeley, eight years later, when as president he explained that his "paramount object" during the war was to preserve the Union, not to free the slaves. But Lincoln saw no necessary disjunction between preserving the Union and black freedom. Later in the Peoria Address, he would make clear that the preservation of the Union meant preserving the principles for which it stood, including the promise of freedom to all human beings. The preservation of the Union was the sine qua non of black freedom. At Peoria and throughout his public life, Lincoln consistently opposed the extremism of southern fire-eaters and northern abolitionists alike:

> Stand with anybody that stands RIGHT. Stand with him while he is right and PART with him when he goes wrong. Stand WITH the abolitionist in restoring the Missouri Compromise; and stand AGAINST him when he attempts to repeal the fugitive slave law. In the latter case you stand with the southern disunionist. What of that? You are still right, In both cases you are right. In both cases you oppose the dangerous extremes. In both you stand on middle ground and hold the ship level and steady. In both you are national and nothing less than national. This is good old whig ground.

Lincoln's political prudence manifests an openness to discuss the merits of an argument on its own terms; it is devoid of ideological blinders by which zealots cling to partisan dogma. While some scholars have focused upon Lincoln's evocative rhetoric as evidence that he was a moral idealist, others read the above passage as confirmation that he was a political opportunist, completely unprincipled in his commitment to preserve the Union. Both interpretations are flawed, since each fails to recognize prudence as the preeminent virtue of statesmanship in harmonizing moral principle under the circumstances.[55]

After presenting the legal and ethical case against the repeal of the Missouri Compromise, Lincoln combined both arguments to vindicate the founders from the belief that they envisioned either a moral or national right to slavery:

> I particularly object to the NEW position which the avowed principle of this Nebraska law gives to slavery in the body politic. I object to it because it assumes there can be MORAL RIGHT in the enslaving of one man by another. . . . I object to it because the fathers of the republic eschewed, and rejected it. The argument of "Necessity" was the only argument they ever admitted in favor of slavery. . . . They found the institution existing among us, which they could not help; and they cast blame upon the British King for having permitted its introduction. BEFORE the constitution, they prohibited its introduction in the north-western Territory—the only country we owned, then free from it. At the framing and adoption of the constitution, they forbore to so much as mention the word "slave" or "slavery" in the whole instrument. In the provision for the recovery of fugitives, the slave is spoken of as a "Person Held To Service OR Labor." In that prohibiting the abolition of the Africa slave trade for twenty years, the trade is spoken of as "The migration or importation of such persons as any of the States now EXISTING, shall think proper to admit," &c. these are the only provisions alluding to slavery. Thus, the thing is hid away, in the constitution, just as an afflicted man hides away a wen or a cancer, which he dares not cut out at once, lest he bleed to death; with the promise, nevertheless, that the cutting begin at the end of a given time.[56]

Lincoln's capitalization of "MORAL RIGHT" magnified the centrality of anchoring politics upon a solid ethical foundation. The prior determination of MORAL RIGHT must serve as an ultimate rule and measure to guide public policy. By assuming that "there can be a MORAL RIGHT in the enslaving of one man by another," the principle of Kansas-Nebraska paved the way for the indefinite perpetuation of slavery as a national institution. In this crucial paragraph, Lincoln provided unsurpassed clarity and profundity in articulating the complex and paradoxical relationship of slavery to American republicanism. The contemporary recovery of his teaching may help to elucidate a problem that continues to torment the American mind: How could a nation pledge itself to a creed of equality yet enslave other human beings? The contemporary answer to this question mistakenly concludes that the founders sanctioned slavery as a national right and that a new founding had to be undertaken by subsequent generations in which the errors of the Revolutionary generation were corrected through a more egalitarian vision of democracy. A more radical contemporary interpretation repudiates the Constitution altogether as an irredeemable political fraud conceived in slavery and dedicated to the proposition of white supremacy.[57]

According to Lincoln, the founders never sanctioned slavery as a national right; rather, they viewed it primarily as a state institution tolerated by the national government. The concessions made to slavery at the convention were done out of necessity to secure ratification of the Constitution. The founders' very choice of language conveyed the moral dubiousness of the institution. Their unwillingness to use the word "slave" or "slavery" was a deliberate attempt to avoid a moral approbation of the institution. In *Abraham Lincoln: A Constitutional Biography* and other important works on the subject of slavery and the Constitution, George Anastaplo demonstrates the founders' principled opposition to the institution. During the proceedings of the Constitutional Convention, James Madison "thought it wrong to admit in the Constitution the idea that there could be property in men." Likewise, Roger Sherman, the author of the Great Compromise that saved the Constitution, "was against . . . acknowledging men to be property, by taking them as such under the character of slaves." The remarks of Sherman and Madison at the Constitutional Convention clearly contradict Taney's assertion in *Dred Scott* that the right to property in a slave was expressly and distinctly affirmed in the Constitution. George Mason, a southerner and author of the Virginia Declaration of Rights, described slavery as an offense to God and warned of divine retribution: "Every master of slaves is born a petty tyrant. They bring the judgement of heaven on a Country. As nations can not be rewarded in the next world they must be in this. By an inevitable chain of causes & effects providence punishes national sins, by national calamaties." In retrospect, Mason's words seem almost prophetic. Perhaps the most biting condemnation of slavery at the Constitutional Convention came from Governor Morris, who referred to it as "a nefarious institution . . . the curse of heaven on the States where it prevailed." And Luther Martin, a delegate from Maryland, condemned slavery as being "inconsistent with the principles of the revolution and dishonorable to the American character to have such a feature in the Constitution."[58]

In sum, Lincoln characterized slavery as an anomaly in the Constitution tolerated in practice as a necessary evil but never sanctioned in principle. It is worth repeating that under the federal division of power the national government was prohibited from restricting slavery where it already existed. Slavery was tolerated only as an existing institution, not affirmed as a national right enshrined by the Constitution. Like Plato, who used a medical analogy to convey the relative health or sickness of a regime, Lincoln diagnosed slavery as a cancer that threatened to ravage the body politic. The founders hoped that the disease of slavery would be arrested and placed on a path of ultimate extinction. Ashamed of the affliction, they hid the institution away and never explicitly sanctioned or upheld it as either a moral or national right. They could not excise the cancer of slavery at the time of the Constitution for fear that it would cause the political death of the Union.

Contrary to the founders' hopes and expectations, however, the disease persisted, and it spread. Lincoln's vivid and coarse references to a diseased body in need of surgery to remedy a terminal affliction communicated the complex issue of slavery's relationship to the Constitution in terms understandable to a frontier audience.

In civil theological terms, Lincoln warned of the transformation in the ethos of the regime. He repudiated "the spin" of popular sovereignty and its claim to be an authoritative account of American public life. The founders' "political faith," based on the principle of equality, and the policy of restricting slavery was being superseded by a rival political faith that affirmed the moral right to slavery and the national right to its extension:

> But now it is to be transformed into a "sacred right." Nebraska brings it forth, places it on the high road to extension and perpetuity; and with a pat on its back, says to it, "Go, and God Speed you." Henceforth it is to be the chief jewel of the nation—the very figure-head of the ship of State. Little by little, but steadily as man's march to the grave, we have been given up the OLD for the NEW faith. Near eighty years ago we began by declaring that all men are created equal; but now from that beginning we have run to the other declaration that for SOME men to enslave others is a "sacred right of self-government." These principles can not stand together. They are as opposite as God and mammon. . . . Let no one be deceived. The spirit of seventy-six and the spirit of Nebraska, are utter antagonisms; and the former is being rapidly displaced by the latter.

The metaphor of popular sovereignty superseding equality as "the chief jewel of the nation—the very figure-head of the ship of State" reveals the extent to which Lincoln saw the American regime as being defined by an overarching end (telos). He would use the jewel metaphor once again when he asked Governor Michael Hahn of Louisiana during that state's reconstruction in 1864 to extend the franchise to blacks. The granting of black suffrage would "keep the jewel of liberty within the family of freedom." Lincoln thus likened liberty and equality as precious gems and family heirlooms that should be passed on from generation to generation. By analogy, the founders' legacy of liberty should be bequeathed unto the entire family of mankind. All Americans regardless of race, creed, or color may claim their rightful inheritance to liberty as human beings created in the image of God and endowed by their Creator with unalienable rights. Lincoln's consistent use of the gem metaphor in lamenting the eclipse of equality as "the jewel of the nation" at Peoria and black suffrage as the "jewel of liberty" in his letter to Governor Hahn demonstrates the connection in his mind between the preservation of a moral Union and the eventual promise of black freedom.[59]

The Kansas-Nebraska Act attempted to replace the nation's jewel of liberty with the stone of servitude. Consistent with his subsequent understanding of the "house divided" metaphor, used four years later to describe the struggle between incompatible moral justifications for public mind, Lincoln observed that the two principles of equal consent and popular sovereignty could not stand together; they were as opposite as God and mammon. Lincoln's reference to God and mammon comes from Matthew 7:24—"No one can serve two masters. He will either hate one and love the other, or be devoted to one and despise the other. You cannot serve God and mammon." Here he used biblical language in both an evocative and a didactic sense to express the incompatibility between the founding principles of American republicanism and the principles behind the Kansas-Nebraska Act. Mammon, an Aramaic word meaning wealth or property, is appropriate in this context, since the only real justification for slavery is greed and naked self-interest: "slavery is founded in the selfishness of man's nature." Lincoln portrayed the struggle against the spread of slavery in biblical terms reminiscent of Paul's many allusions to the struggle between the spirit and the flesh. His concluding phrase of the paragraph, "Let no one be deceived. The spirit of seventy-six and Kansas Nebraska are utter antagonisms," recalls Paul in Galatians 6:7— "Be not deceived; God is not mocked: for whatsover a man soweth that shall he also reap." Quoting this passage, Lincoln used biblical language in a didactic sense to convey the incompatibility between the founders' and Douglas's interpretation of consent of the governed. Popular sovereignty was a sham form of consent, a deception that seduced the nation from its "ancient faith." Lincoln's reference to Galatians 6:7 also appealed to biblical language in an evocative sense to convey the gravity of the situation for his listeners, who would decide the moral destiny of their regime.

The biblical language of the Peoria Address culminates with an invocation of Revelation 7:9–13, 7:17, and 22:14, which chronicle an apocalyptic vision of the last days and the subsequent transfiguration of the Christian community, whose redemption is symbolized through the purification of their white baptismal robes with the blood of the lamb:

> Our republican robe is soiled, and trailed in the dust. Let us repurify it. Let us turn and wash it white, in the spirit, if not the blood, of the Revolution. Let us turn slavery from its claims of "moral right," back upon its existing legal rights, and its arguments of "necessity." Let us return it to the position our fathers gave it; and there let it rest in peace. Let us re-adopt the Declaration of Independence, and with it, the practices, and policy, which harmonize with it. Let north and south—let all Americans—let all lovers of liberty everywhere—join in the great and good work. If we do this, we shall not only have saved the Union, but we shall have so saved it, as to make, and to keep it, forever worthy of saving. We shall have so saved it, that succeeding millions of free happy people, the world over, shall rise up, and call us blessed, to the latest generations.

The epilogue of Revelation warns Christians of a coming temptation: "Blessed are they who wash their robes so as to have the right to the tree of life and enter the city through its gates. Outside are dogs, the sorcerers, the

unchaste, the murderers, the idol worshipers, and all who love and practice deceit." Allegorically, Lincoln likened the washing of the baptismal
robe with the blood of the lamb to the washing of the nation's republican
robe with the blood of the Revolution. Just as the Christian's white robe
had been tainted by sin but redeemed through the blood of Christ, so the
nation's republican robe had been stained by the sin of slavery but could
be washed clean through the blood of the Revolution, which symbolically
represented the ancient faith of the founders. Didactically, Lincoln's appeal to the Book of Revelation preached a continual recurrence to first
principles of republicanism. Only a return to this simple faith in the purity of its principles would ensure the nation's safe passage through the
coming trial.[60]

Significantly, Lincoln emphasized that the Union must be "worthy of
saving." This aspiration to make the Union worthy of saving provides a
more complete understanding of his view of the inseparability of liberty
and Union. The Union was worth preserving because of what it represented, that is, the moral ends to which it was dedicated: "the chief jewel
of the nation," "the figure-head of the ship of State." Lincoln's civil theological reasoning is parallel with the natural law teaching of Thomas
Aquinas: the moral obligations of the natural law provide a rule and measure for positive law. Public policy and positive law must always take their
bearings from fundamental moral precepts. "Practices and policies" of
American government should be harmonized with the general precepts of
the natural law, which are affirmed by the Declaration. Finally, Lincoln
ended his speech with a poignant reminder of American mission. Using
evocative biblical language from the Magnificat in Luke 1:48, he noted that
the vindication of the American experiment in republicanism through the
Union's perpetuation would cause "succeeding millions of free happy people, the world over, [to] rise up, and call us blessed, to the latest generation." Just as the Virgin Mary would bring glad tidings to the world that
would cause rejoicing, so the United States would bring hope for those
seeking freedom and opportunity. Like John Winthrop, Lincoln affirmed
the biblical belief in mission, a unique national destiny for the American
people that held worldwide significance.

Before concluding his Peoria Address, Lincoln made an extemporaneous
reply to Douglas, who had interrupted his speech by citing the Bible in defense of popular sovereignty. Lincoln's impromptu digression shows how seriously he took theological and scriptural justifications of public life:

> In the course of my main argument, Judge Douglas interrupted me to say, that
> the principle [of] the Nebraska bill was very old; that it originated when God
> made man and placed good and evil before him, allowing him to choose for
> himself, being responsible for the choice he should make. At the time I thought
> this was merely playful; and I answered it accordingly. But in his reply to me he

renewed it, as a serious argument. In seriousness then, the facts of this proposition are not true as stated. God did not place good and evil before man, telling him to make his choice. On the contrary, he did tell him there was one tree, of the fruit of which, he should not eat, upon pain of certain death. I should scarcely wish so strong a prohibition against slavery in Nebraska.

Lincoln refuted Douglas's claim by providing a proper understanding of Scripture that viewed divine law in terms of a moral imperative from God. Human freedom must be exercised responsibly in accordance with the dictates of the moral law.[61]

In accordance with his tendency to characterize alternative accounts of public life in civil theological terms, Lincoln compared the principle of Kansas-Nebraska with the divine right of kings:

> But this argument strikes me as not a little remarkable in another particular—in its strong resemblance to the old argument for the "Divine Right of Kings." By the latter, the King is to do just as he pleases with his white subjects, being responsible to God alone. By the former the white man is to do just as he pleases with his black slaves, being responsible to God alone. The two things are precisely alike; and it is but natural that they should find similar arguments to sustain them.

Absolute sovereigns claimed for themselves the principle of *potestas soluta legibus,* a power freed from law, to justify their despotism over others. The king's interpretation of God's will was unbounded and not subject to constitutional limitations by a competing secular or spiritual authority. Lincoln discerned that the monarch's claim to be exempt from a law that he imposed upon others was repugnant to the principles of republicanism and that it substituted a government of laws for that of men. Yet the Kansas-Nebraska Bill adopted the same principle of absolutism. White people imposed a rule upon others they would not prescribe for themselves. Lincoln argued that, once the axiom of equality was denied as a necessary condition of public life, the principle of slavery could be used to justify the enslavement of white people as well.[62]

Lincoln concluded the Peoria speech by tracing his republican pedigree. His credentials were based upon the legacy handed down to him by his elderly siblings, Clay and Webster, and, ultimately, from George Washington, the father of the republican family. His final paragraph reaffirmed the "national axioms and dogmas of American republicanism" as a necessary condition of shared public life. Without a shared consensus on the meaning of first principles there could be no real civic life. Thus, Lincoln explained, "To deny these things is to deny our national axioms, or dogmas, at least; and it puts an end to all argument." Indeed, Lincoln was ominously correct in this prediction, for in rejecting the "ancient faith" of equality in favor of a new faith of human inequality the South would put an end to all argument by firing upon Fort Sumter six years later.

While the Lyceum Address prefigures certain themes found in the mature Lincoln's political thought, it is neither a systematic treatise on his political theology nor a literal declamation of his millenarian intent. The emphasis placed upon the Lyceum Address should not eclipse Lincoln's mature reflections on religion and politics expressed more fully and richly in the Peoria Address, which is exemplary of his civil theology of biblical republicanism.

Chapter Five

SLAVERY, EQUALITY, AND THE UNION

Consent of the governed, the Union, and opposition to slavery are quintessential themes of Lincoln's biblical republicanism, linked by the central idea of equality. A biblical republican conception of consent and equality recurs throughout Lincoln's critique of slavery, his appeal to the Declaration of Independence, and his moral justification for the Union. To consider each theme solely in the abstract, apart from its inseparable relation to the others, distorts and narrows the depth and richness of Lincoln's civil theological intention. To interpret Lincoln's view of equality apart from the issue of slavery reinforces the misconception that he espoused a radical egalitarianism that was contrary to the nation's founding principles. To interpret his view of the Union apart from equality as a moral principle leads to the false conclusion that Lincoln faced a dilemma of choosing between a Union without black freedom or black freedom without a Union. In truth, Lincoln saw the great themes of slavery, the Declaration, and the Union as intimately related. His critique of slavery, his defense of consent, and his correlative justification of republican government were all predicated upon a biblical view of human nature and equality.

In the allegorical drama of biblical republicanism, the subjugation of the thirteen colonies under England corresponds to the servitude of the Hebrew tribes under Egypt; the American people, God's "almost chosen people," represent the Jews, God's chosen people; the divine right of kings is symbolic of Pharaoh's claim to mastery over the Israelites; the founders collectively play the role of Moses, the deliverer of his people from slavery and their lawgiver, who establishes a "more perfect Union" among the Hebrews. The Declaration represents the American Decalogue, the moral covenant handed down from God promulgating the basic precepts of the nation's political faith. The Fourth of July thus becomes the American Passover, a sacred day of political renewal. The challenge of proslavery theology is tantamount to an idolatry forsaking the "ancient faith" of the fathers for the false gods of the pagans. Lincoln plays the role of both prophet and political savior. He is the preacher of the nation's republican faith, who calls his errant people back to their ancestral ways. And the Union that Lincoln saves represents the apostle Paul's description of the *corpus mysticum* (mystical body) in Romans 12, whose animating spirit and inclusive principles unite people of diverse races, creeds, and colors.

The republican history of the United States symbolically parallels the history of the Jewish people conveyed by Moses in Deuteronomy 6:20–25:

> And when thou shalt say unto thy son, We were the Pharaoh's bondsmen in Egypt; and the Lord brought us out of Egypt with a mighty hand: And the Lord showed signs and wonders, great and sore, upon Egypt, upon Pharaoh, and upon all his household, before our eyes: And he brought us out from thence, that he might bring us in, to give us the land which he swore unto our fathers. And the Lord commanded us to do all these statutes, to fear the Lord our God, for our good always, that he might preserve us alive, as it is at this day. And it shall be our righteousness, if we observe to do all these commandments before the Lord our God, as he hath commanded us.

Throughout the Book of Deuteronomy, Moses' lawgiving is coupled with his warnings to Israel against sliding into the pagan beliefs and practices of the surrounding peoples. Fidelity to the moral covenant provided a standard by which to measure Israel's success or failure as a nation. Indeed, the symbolism and language of Deuteronomy informs Lincoln's biblical republicanism. For instance, Lincoln used the term "bondsman" from Deuteronomy in his Second Inaugural Address as a synonym for the slave, and his warnings to the American people of breaking their moral covenant in the Declaration likewise parallels the language and symbolism of Deuteronomy:

> When we were the political slaves of King George, and wanted to be free, we called the maxim that "all men are created equal" a self-evident truth; but now when we have grown fat, and have lost all dread of being slaves ourselves, we have become so greedy to be *masters* that we call the same maxim "a self-evident lie." The fourth of July has not quite dwindled away; it is still a great day—*for burning fire-crackers!!!*[1]

Just as fidelity to the covenant received on Mount Sinai by the Jews represented a standard to measure their spiritual success as a people under God, so the moral covenant of the Declaration provided a standard to measure the political success of the American people. The failure of America to live up to its ancient faith made the celebration of July Fourth a hollow ritual, devoid of meaning and moral substance.

In view of the parallel history between Israel and America, it was altogether fitting that African American slaves appropriated the biblical allegory of Exodus and applied it to their own experience. The slaves took the moral high ground by invoking America's own biblical symbolism against itself. This transfer of moral authority to the slaves was especially vivid in the case of Frederick Douglass, a former slave, who accepted the republican principles of the Declaration per se but repudiated the failure to apply them consistently to all human beings. Like Lincoln, Douglass challenged the hypocrisy of the American regime on the Fourth of July from within

the American tradition itself. The symbolic role of Egyptian master and Hebrew slave that once constituted the allegorical self-interpretation of Americans in their revolutionary struggle against the British was ironically
turned against the American defenders of slavery by Lincoln, Douglass,
and the slaves themselves.

Human nature is the bedrock of any civil theology. Lincoln, who consistently emphasized that public opinion must be "in accordance with the philosophy of the human mind," subscribed to a sound philosophical anthropology that was informed by a biblical understanding of human nature.
First, Lincoln's view of human nature was biblical because it was realistic.
That is to say, it recognized the human inclination for both good and evil.
Reinhold Niebuhr tersely captures the Bible's teaching on human nature in
relation to self-government when he notes, "Man's capacity for justice
makes democracy possible; but man's inclination to injustice makes democracy necessary." Indeed, the Bible teaches that "the same radical freedom
which makes man creative also makes him potentially destructive and dangerous, that the dignity of man and the misery of man therefore have the
same root." This realistic view of human nature may be contrasted to either
Rousseau's optimistic view of man's natural goodness or to Hobbes's pessimistic view of his utter depravity. Second, Lincoln's view of human nature
was biblical because it affirmed the Judeo-Christian teaching of man created
in the image of God (Genesis 1:27). Sympathizing with a group of African
Americans, Lincoln remarked, "It is difficult to make a man miserable while
he feels he is worthy of himself, and claims kindred to the great God who
made him." According to Lincoln, all human beings regardless of race, creed,
or color possessed a unique rational and spiritual dignity that placed them
equally in the middle station in the hierarchy of being, above beasts, yet be-
low God. Lincoln's biblical view of human nature thus involved "an appreciation of the unique worth of the individual which [made] it wrong to fit him
into any political program as a mere instrument." The sacredness of human
life was derived from man's kinship with the Creator. This divine kinship constituted the very basis of political rights and obligations. A truly just government must recognize each citizen's claim to "humanity." To exploit human
beings as raw material violated the order of God's Creation and degraded its
inherent dignity. The impulse to control others as if they were a mere means
to an end was rooted in man's inherent lust for power and his prideful inclination to become God. Third, Lincoln's view of human nature was biblical because it "assume[d] a source of authority from the standpoint of which the individual may defy the authorities of this world." For Lincoln, the will of the
people was not absolute. It was accountable to the ultimate authority of God,
whose eternal law governs the universe. Lincoln rejected proslavery justifications precisely because they did not correspond to universal precepts of
moral right found in the Declaration and the Bible. Finally, as seen in the
Peoria Address, Lincoln's view of human nature was biblical because it presumed a Judeo-Christian understanding of moral inclination and conscience;

it presumed the human mind's access to a natural law that God had, metaphorically speaking, impressed upon his creature's mind and heart.[2]

Critics of Christianity may legitimately blame the Church for its historical persecution of non-Christians, its millenarian crusades, its corruption, and its worldliness—all of which, it should be noted, are contrary to the teachings of the Church's Founder. Machiavelli and others have claimed that Christianity is either apolitical or antipolitical, that its otherworldliness encourages a pusillanimous retreat from politics. The derailments of Christianity, however, should not obscure its positive contribution to republican government. For Niebuhr, "Biblical faith is unique in offering . . . insights into the human situation which are indispensable to democracy."[3]

What specifically then is the contribution of Christianity to republican government? Paradoxically, while the Incarnation offered the possibility of a more intimate union with God through the living example of his only begotten son, it also heightened humanity's awareness of the distance between mortals and God through Christ's model of purity. The defining event of Christianity, God's sharing our humanity, intensified both the intimacy with God and the awareness of human fallibility.[4] Thus, in Philippians 2:5–10, Paul exhorted his listeners to imitate Jesus, "Who, being in the form of God, did not count equality with God something to be grasped. But he emptied himself, taking the form of a slave, becoming as human beings are; and being in every way like a human being, he was humbler yet, even to accepting death, death on a cross." Humanity became more conscious of its own imperfection and its need for divine grace in comparison to the concrete model of perfection and humility provided by Jesus Christ. Thus, on the one hand, Christianity contributed to an understanding of democracy by affirming the equal, spiritual dignity of all human beings as children of God; on the other, it taught that all human beings are equally sinful and in need of divine grace. Unlike pagan philosophers who emphasized human inequality, Christianity radically affirmed the spiritual equality of mankind. Jesus preached to the politically marginalized in pagan society: slaves, women, and the lowly. The spiritual equality of the Kingdom of Christ exalted the meek and humble: "But many that are first shall be last; and the last shall be first" (Matthew 19:30). Paul extended the universal implications of Jesus' teaching in Galatians 3:28: "There is neither Jew nor Greek, there is neither bond nor free, there is neither male nor female: for ye are all one in Christ Jesus."[5]

C. S. Lewis explains how the Bible's realistic view of human nature provides an ultimate moral justification for self-government that bears comparison to Lincoln's biblical republicanism:

> I am a democrat because I believe in the Fall of Man. I think most people are democrats for the opposite reason. A great deal of democratic enthusiasm descends from the ideas of people like Rousseau, who believed in democracy because they thought mankind so wise and good that everyone deserved a share in government. The real reason for democracy is just the reverse. Mankind is so

fallen that no man can be trusted with unchecked power over his fellows. Aristotle said that some people were only fit to be slaves. I do not contradict him. But I reject slavery because I see no men fit to be masters.[6]

Because all human beings have an inherent tendency to abuse power, no human being, no matter how virtuous, can be entrusted with absolute power. Lord Acton presumed this biblical understanding of human nature in his famous aphorism: "Power tends to corrupt and absolute power corrupts absolutely. Great men are almost always bad men, even when they exercise influence and not authority; still more when you superadd the tendency or the certainty of corruption by authority." James Madison conveyed a similar view in the *Federalist:* "If men were angels no government would be necessary. If angels were to govern men, neither internal nor external controuls on government would be necessary." Given the human propensity to sin, absolute power in any form will inevitably degenerate into despotism. Christianity's heightened awareness of human imperfection forbids anyone from wielding absolute power. Because republican government recognizes the baser motives and inclinations as an intrinsic part of human nature, it attempts to limit their potential for mischief by checking and dispersing power. Lincoln's terse definition of democracy accords with this biblical view of human nature and equality: "As I would not be a *slave* so I would not be a *master*. This expresses my idea of democracy. Whatever differs from this, to the extent of the difference, is no democracy." Lincoln's case for democracy and against slavery also relied upon the biblical precept of the Golden Rule: "Do unto others as you would have them do unto you." Because no one would wish to be treated as a slave himself, no one was entitled to enslave another: "I never knew a man who wished to be himself a slave. Consider if you know any good thing, that no man desires for himself."[7]

It may be argued, however, that perhaps slavery is actually good for people in the same way medicine is good for children who shun its unpleasant taste but nevertheless benefit from its effects. Perhaps the irrationality of human nature prevents an honest acceptance of slavery. That is to say, if a truly rational person knew what was actually good for him, he would consent to becoming a slave. On the contrary, the Golden Rule would still forbid the enslaving of another person given the biblical view of human nature it presumes: no one is obliged to become the slave of another because no imperfect human being is entitled to absolute power over his or her fellows. Indeed, the teaching of Christianity dictates that man's equal dignity as a rational and free being created in the image of God entitles him to the rights of life, liberty, and the pursuit of happiness regardless of differences in intellectual abilities. Thus, in view of this biblical understanding of human nature, Lincoln interpreted equality as a principle of justice, fairness, and reciprocity in dealing with other human beings: "This is a world of compensations; and he who would *be* no slave, must consent to *have* no slave. Those who deny freedom to others, deserve it not for themselves; and, under a just God, can not long retain it."[8]

Lincoln's realistic view of human nature also implies a distinct human essence that is fundamentally the same throughout space and time. It views man in terms of an immutable nature that God has created and distributed equally to all people: "human nature . . . is God's decree, and can never be reversed." Differences in intellectual abilities are therefore differences in degree, not in kind; they do not constitute a different human essence or species. Affirming this biblical teaching of the unity of human nature, Lincoln stated: "Human nature is the same—people at the South are the same as those at the North, barring the difference in circumstances." Lincoln's teaching presumes a transcendent God who is the Father of all people and the Creator of a universal human community. All human beings regardless of race, creed, or color are descended from two original ancestors (Genesis 1:27–28). And, like Adam and Eve, all members of the human race have a natural inclination for both good and evil.[9]

Lincoln's humility and his realistic view of human nature provided him with the needed sobriety in judging others. His abhorrence of slavery did not lapse into self-righteousness. Unlike the abolitionists of his time who portrayed southerners as morally depraved, Lincoln refused to take solace in self-righteous dichotomies that saw northerners as the children of light, pure in their moral convictions, and southerners as the children of darkness, fundamentally evil at their core and beyond redemption: "I have no prejudice against the Southern people. They are just what we [northerners] would be in their situation." Unlike the abolitionists, notes Niebuhr, Lincoln understood "that good men may inherit social attitudes and become the bearers of social evil, although their own consciences are not perverse, but merely conventional." In his Second Inaugural Address, Lincoln pointed out that both North and South alike were culpable before God: slavery was a national sin. Lincoln appreciated fully that the absence of slavery in the North made it easier for northerners to be self-righteous and to seek moral solace in grandiose schemes of social transfiguration.[10]

Lincoln reiterated a sober and realistic view of human nature throughout his public life. After he had won a bitter election in 1864, he replied to a group of serenaders: "Human-nature will not change. In any future great national trial, compared with the men of this, we shall have as weak, and as strong; as silly and as wise; as bad and as good. Let us, therefore, study the incidents of this, as philosophy to learn wisdom from, and none of them as wrongs to be revenged." A spirit of charity and forbearance animates this speech. Considering the historical circumstances of the 1864 election, it is remarkable that one does not find even a suggestion of malice. Again, describing human nature, Lincoln once observed: "Like causes produce like effects. . . . Will not the same cause that produced agitation in 1820 when the Missouri Compromise was formed—that which produced the agitation upon the annexation of Texas and at other times—work out the same results always? Do you think that the nature of man will be changed—that the same causes that produced agitation at one time will not have the same effect at another?" In both passages, Lincoln looked to the dynamics of human nature as the basis for normative political guidance. Although circumstances may differ throughout time and place, human nature itself remains constant and therefore should be consulted when determining public policy.[11]

In view of the Bible's realistic teaching on human nature, Lincoln discerned that the motivation to enslave others was rooted in pride and the lust for power and greed. He saw the proclivity for evil as an inherent, not an incidental, trait. Human nature was not a tabula rasa (a blank slate) that could be perverted or perfected entirely through social environment. In Calvinistic and Augustinian terms, Lincoln interpreted slavery as being "founded in the selfishness of man's nature," a manifestation of the lust for power and the love of self. Lincoln's diagnosis of the inherent selfishness of human nature was concretely experiential: "The Bible says somewhere that we are desperately selfish. I think we would have discovered that fact without the Bible." Concrete experience confirmed the biblical teaching on human nature. Since slavery was rooted in man's fallen nature, it could not be simply eradicated through bureaucratic manipulation or an appeal to reason alone. A change of heart was needed; the peaceful extinction of slavery required a moral conversion of the American people as a whole. It required an act of will as well as an act of intellect. Yet, increasingly, the debauched climate of public opinion reinforced the baser motives of human nature that clung to slavery despite all rational arguments to the contrary. Prosperity enticed citizens to ignore the evil of slavery; greed sustained the institution; and pride justified it. Lincoln sought to arouse the nation's conscience against these temptations. He appealed to the Golden Rule by asking his fellow citizens to remember the nation's political slavery under England reminding them that moral decadence had induced forgetfulness. The greed and pride of Americans had become so swollen that they became indifferent to the suffering of others: "we have grown fat, and have lost all dread of being slaves ourselves, we have become so greedy to be masters that we call [equality] 'a self-evident lie.'" Quite early in his life, Lincoln perceived that the servitude of another race enhanced the status of poor southern whites. In addition to its financial benefits, it provided southerners with a sense of superiority, mastery, and control over a vulnerable minority.[12]

Although Lincoln acknowledged man's inclination for evil, he also recognized his inclination for good. While pride and love of self were ineradicable parts of human nature, there were redemptive elements as well. Lincoln believed that man was inclined toward the good on account of the moral law that God had impressed upon his mind and heart. According to Lincoln, the right to enjoy the fruits of one's labor has been "[m]ade so plain by our good Father in Heaven, that all feel and and understand it, even down to brutes and creeping insects." He attributed man's moral awareness to a divine source. "God reigns over you, and has inspired your mind, and given you a sense of propriety," noted Lincoln, and thus, despite the infirmity of their nature, human beings still had access to God's providential order. For this reason, he presumed that the abhorrence of slavery could be intuitively grasped by conscience: "I am naturally anti-slavery. If slavery is not wrong, nothing is wrong. I can not remember when I did not so think, and feel." Lincoln's view of equality can be understood further in terms of mankind's equal access to the natural law—that is, the rational creature's participation in God's eternal law. Appealing to the nation's "honest impulses, and sense of right," he invoked "the *love of liberty* which God has planted in our breasts." And he reminded his fellow citizens that the "great mass of mankind" "consider slavery a great moral wrong; and their feeling against it, is not evanescent but eternal. It lies at the very foundation of their sense of justice." Slavery was primordially wrong because it "repress[ed] all tendencies in the human heart to justice and mercy." Indeed, slavery would continue to be wrong "so long as the moral constitution of men's minds shall continue to be the same." Popular sovereignty's purported moral indifference to slavery violated those inherent notions of right and wrong that God had given to human beings so that they could exercise their freedom responsibly. Thus, Lincoln argued: "When he [Douglas] invites any people willing to have slavery, to establish it, he is blowing out the moral lights around us. When he says 'he cares not whether slavery is voted down or voted up,' that it is the sacred right of self-government, he is in my judgment penetrating the human soul and eradicating the light of reason and the love of liberty in this American people."[13]

Lincoln's biblical case against slavery was complemented by natural theology. As seen, his view of the harmony between reason and revelation was influenced by James Smith's *The Christian's Defence* and Robert Chambers's *Vestiges of the Natural History of Creation*. Based on the teachings of these authors, he viewed the precepts of the Bible as confirmed by unassisted human reason: "I think that if anything can be proved by natural theology, it is that slavery is morally wrong. God gave man a mouth to receive bread, hands to feed it, and his hand has a right to carry bread to his mouth without controversy." Thus, in Lincoln's view, reason and revelation complemented each other in guiding public life. Playfully elaborating the political implications of this natural theology, he stated:

> I hold that if there is one thing that can be proved to be the will of God by external nature around us, without reference to revelation, it is the proposition that whatever any one man earns with his hands and by the sweat of his brow, he shall enjoy in peace. I say that whereas God Almighty has given every man one mouth to be fed, and one pair of hands adapted to furnish food for that mouth, if anything can be proved to be the will of Heaven, it is proved by this fact, that that mouth is to be fed by those hands, without being interfered with

by any other man who has also his mouth to feed and his hands to labor with. I hold if the Almighty had ever made a set of men that should do all the eating and none of the work, he would have made them with mouths only and no hands, and if he had ever made another class that he had intended should do all the work and none of the eating, he would have made them without mouths and with all hands. But inasmuch as he has not chosen to make man in that way, if anything is proved, it is that those hands and mouth are to be co-operative through life and not to be interfered with. That they are to go forth and improve their condition as I have been trying to illustrate, is the inherent right given to mankind directly by the Maker.

Indeed, Lincoln's case for natural theology coincides with Paul's teaching in Romans 2:14–15 of a universal moral law known by means of unassisted human reason: "For the Gentiles, which have not the law, do by nature the things contained in the law, these, having not the law, are a law unto themselves. Which show the work of the law written in their hearts, their conscience also bearing witness, and their thoughts the mean while accusing or else excusing one another."[14]

Since both northerners and southerners invoked the same Bible to justify their policies, a literal appeal to the authority of Holy Scripture did not provide an explicit answer to the issue of slavery. This is not to deny the Bible's moral guidance or to espouse a purely subjective interpretation of the Good Book. Rather, it is to say that, if leaders wish to invoke the Bible in the public life, they should follow Lincoln's example of confirming their interpretation of biblical teaching through reason, the common language of the public square. If one's interpretation of the Bible leads to a moral conclusion that is repugnant to "ordinary perceptions of right and wrong" and reason, it stands that the interpretation is flawed. This was the case of proslavery theology. As seen, Lincoln's invocation of the Bible did not stand alone as a literal appeal; the moral precepts of reason, revelation, and republicanism confirmed one another. Thinking in terms that bear comparison to the thought of Thomas Aquinas, Lincoln argued that a reflection upon the rational design of creation and the purposiveness of human physiognomy affirmed the biblical precept of Genesis 3:19 that all human beings must toil for the fruits of their labor. The very fact that human beings are endowed naturally with the power of practical reason must suppose a telos, an end, a crowning activity, a final fulfillment or a perfection of this function. Lincoln's affirmation of the rational and spiritual dignity of each human being necessarily leads to an exploration of his view of the self-evident character of human equality found in the Declaration of Independence.

THE DECLARATION

Lincoln considered the Declaration of Independence to be the moral foundation of American republicanism. Its animating principles provided the key for understanding his vision of the Union and his defense of equality. Indeed, he celebrated the Declaration as the inspirational source of American leadership: "[A]ll the political sentiments I entertain have been drawn . . . from the sentiments which originated, and were given to the world from this hall [Independence Hall] in which we stand. I have never had a feeling politically that did not spring from the sentiments embodied in the Declaration of Independence." At Gettysburg, he poetically distilled the nation's birthright, relying on the Declaration of Independence as his inspirational source. The resounding "four score and seven years ago" of the Gettysburg Address placed the Republic's birth at 1776, the year of independence. This historical detail is noteworthy, for Lincoln maintained that a tacit Union among the colonies existed before the Constitution of 1787:

> [I]n legal contemplation, the Union is perpetual, confirmed by the history of the Union itself. The Union is much older than the Constitution. It was formed in fact, by the Articles of Association in 1774. It was matured and continued by the Declaration of Independence in 1776. It was further matured and expressly declared and pledged, to be perpetual, by the Articles of Confederation in 1778. And finally, in 1787, one of the declared objects for ordaining and establishing the Constitution, was *"to form a more perfect union."*

Unlike the despotisms of Europe that were established upon the accidents of birth, the United States justified its founding upon a creed of civil and religious liberty enshrined by the Declaration of Independence, "the foundation of the American experiment." By defining the spirit of collective American identity, the Declaration consummated the nation's free birth, and it reminded succeeding generations of their moral obligation to preserve and extend the legacy of freedom.[15]

The Declaration proclaimed the moral end to which the Union was dedicated. Lincoln read the Constitution in view of the Declaration. Indeed, the founding principles of the Declaration animated the Constitution in the following ways: its commitment to liberty was reaffirmed in the Constitution's preamble; its principle of equality undergirded the Constitution's prohibitions against titles of nobility and religious tests; its principle of consent was proclaimed in the opening lines, "We the people"; and its preference for a republican form of government was made legally binding in Article 4 of the Constitution. Furthermore, the First Amendment's prohibition against an establishment of religion and its guarantee of free exercise was itself an expression of the principle of equality affirmed by the Declaration. The First Amendment granted citizens the equal rights of conscience before God and forbade the government from preferring one sect to another. Lincoln consistently emphasized the continuity between the Declaration and the Constitution as two complementary and founding documents of American republicanism. The Constitution provided the specific institutions and framework whereby the aims of the Declaration could be realized prudently.[16]

The Declaration functioned as the nation's moral compass. Lincoln believed that its guiding needle had been meticulously calibrated so that navigators could plot the ship of state's destination toward republican shores. The principles of the Declaration were necessary truths, which were universal, unchanging, and absolute, that is, *not relative* to human will, whim, or caprice. Lincoln's acknowledgment of an objective truth that is rationally accessible is fundamental to his interpretation of the Declaration as a founding document. The general precepts of the Declaration were independent of time and place. In the abstract, they applied to free governments everywhere and at all times. They provided a normative standard for human law. Thus, Lincoln stated:

> I have never manifested any impatience with the necessities that spring from the actual presence of black people amongst us, and the actual existence of slavery amongst us where it does already exist; but I have insisted that, in legislating for new countries, where it does not exist, there in no just rule other than that of moral and abstract right![17]

The principles of the Declaration were not only universal but also self-evident. Reiterating the teachings of Aristotle and Thomas Aquinas, Harry V. Jaffa explains: "A self-evident truth is not one which everyone necessarily admits to be true; it is one the evidence for which is contained in the terms of the proposition, and which is admitted to be true to everyone who already grasps the meaning of the terms." Applying Euclidean terminology, Lincoln characterized the self-evident truths of the Declaration as axiomatic: "The principles of Jefferson are the definitions and axioms of free society." In his view, public order required a consensus on such principles; their validity must be accepted as a condition of political reflection. That is to say, he believed that the axioms of the Declaration must serve as the starting point of civil discourse, just as the law of noncontradiction serves as the starting point for speculative discourse.[18]

Axioms and definitions are indemonstrable. They are grasped intuitively, not discursively. The negation of an axiom precludes any further inquiry into the subject matter and is therefore logically impossible. In order to discern Lincoln's view of self-evident truth, it is instructive to consider the impossibility of rejecting the first principles of speculative reasoning, for one who rejects the law of noncontradiction undermines the very rationality upon which this rejection is predicated. By analogy, Lincoln exposed Stephen Douglas's moral indifference to slavery as a negation of practical reason: "When he [Douglas] says he 'cares not whether slavery is voted down or voted up',—that it is a sacred right of self-government—he is in my judgment penetrating the human soul and eradicating the light of reason and the love of liberty in this American people." According to Lincoln, the "light of reason" apprehended self-evident truths that were consonant with the pursuit of liberty and human happiness.[19]

By virtue of its moral imperatives, the Declaration constituted a bulwark against despotism: "The assertion that 'all men are created equal' was of no practical use in effecting our separation from Great Britain; and it was placed in the Declaration, not for that, but for future use. Its authors meant it to be, thank God, it's now proving itself, a stumbling block to those who in after time might seek to turn a free people back into the hateful paths of despotism." This "national charter of freedom," this "magna charta of human liberty," placed both negative prohibitions and positive injunctions upon the activity of government. Lincoln defended the practical relevance of the Declaration's normative guidance. Some ideas have enormous political consequences: "I submit that the proposition that the thing which determines whether a man is free or a slave, is rather concrete than abstract. I think you would conclude that it was, if your liberty depended upon it."[20]

Although the principles of the Declaration served as an aspiration, they did not constitute a blueprint for a utopia! While they were universally applicable in the abstract, their actualization depended upon prudential determinations; the concrete application of rights to groups of individuals must be weighed against the public interest and the constraints of political order. Lincoln's commitment to both liberty and Union revealed that the aspirations of the Declaration must be applied under the circumstances and in accordance with the rule of law. Contrary to the demands of the radical abolitionists, he denied that human positive law should enforce grandiose projects of revolutionary transformation. Consistent with his Whig politics, Lincoln saw the Constitution as "the only safeguard of our liberties."[21]

While law had a normative function in guiding the country toward legitimate moral ends, it could neither forcibly reconstitute people's inner dispositions nor transfigure society overnight. Given the limitations of human nature, Lincoln believed that law should not attempt to purge away all of society's vices; it must tolerate some as necessary evils. Because the institution of slavery was inextricably woven into the material of southern society, it had to be removed gradually. Providing the South was willing to compromise, slavery had to be removed without tearing apart the entire social fabric of southern life, including those noble elements that were worth preserving.

Indeed, politics is the art of the possible, not the ideal. Consequently, statesmen must do what they can to promote the nation's moral imperatives. Indeed, for Lincoln, it was the preeminent task of American statesmanship to ensure that public sentiment was consonant with the Declaration: "Our government rests in public opinion. Whoever can change public opinion can change the government, practically just so much." The *Dred Scott* decision and the Kansas-Nebraska Act degraded public opinion by transforming the discussion of slavery from that of a necessary evil into that of a positive good. In Lincoln's view, this blatant disregard of moral imperative violated national fidelity, debauched civic virtue, and summoned the ghastly specter of despotism to haunt the land.[22]

The Declaration contained both positive injunctions and negative prohibitions against slavery that obligated succeeding generations. Negatively, it prohibited the nation from identifying slavery as morally right. Positively, it enjoined the nation to abolish slavery when circumstances permitted. Contrary to what the champions of popular sovereignty demanded, Lincoln refused to acknowledge slavery as anything other than a moral evil. The pernicious institution could be tolerated only insofar as it was a necessary evil. Yet the toleration of slavery as a necessary evil did not overturn the moral imperatives of the Declaration that mandated its eventual abolition when circumstances permitted:

> It may be argued that there are certain conditions that make necessities and impose them upon us, and to the extent that a necessity is imposed upon a man he must submit to it. I think that was the condition in which we found ourselves when we established this government. We had slavery among us, we could not get our constitution unless we permitted them to remain in slavery, we could not secure the good we did secure if we grasped for more, and having by necessity submitted to that much, it does not destroy the principle that is the charter of our liberties. Let that charter stand as our standard.[23]

By refusing to identify slavery as a moral right, the founders intended to place the institution on a path to ultimate extinction. Both the letter and the spirit of the Declaration necessitated its abolition at some point within the legal framework of the Constitution. Lincoln argued that the founders had anticipated succeeding generations to complete their work, not to forsake their design by promoting the institution as a "sacred right of self-government." Vindicating the Declaration against the pernicious claims of proslavery theology, he exclaimed:

> In those days, our Declaration of Independence was held sacred by all and thought to include all; but now, to aid in making the bondage of the negro universal and eternal, it is assailed, and sneered at, and construed, and hawked at, and torn, till, if its framers could rise from their graves they could not at all recognize it. All the powers of earth seem rapidly combining against him. Mammon is after him; ambition follows, and philosophy follows, and the Theology of the day is fast joining the cry.[24]

To be sure, Lincoln interpreted American history as the unfolding of implications within the Declaration. As the history of Israel was judged in terms of its fidelity to God's covenant, so Lincoln measured the history of America in terms of its fidelity to the Declaration of Independence, its moral covenant of public life. Because the nation was capable of infidelity to its

covenant, its progress was measured by the fulfillment of its moral obligations rather than from a dialectical necessity. The moral imperatives of the
Declaration obligated statesmen to strive constantly to apply prudently the
principles of the founding:

> And although it was always submitted patiently to whatever of inequality there
> seemed to be as matter of actual necessity, its constant working has been a
> steady progress towards the practical equality of all men. The late Presidential
> election was a struggle, by one party, to discard that central idea, and to substi-
> tute for it the opposite idea that slavery is right, in the abstract, the working of
> which, as a central idea, may be the perpetuity of human slavery, and its exten-
> sion to all countries and colors.[25]

Among the republican principles contained in the Declaration, Lincoln
assigned preeminence to the self-evident truth of human equality: "Public
opinion, on any subject, always has a *'central idea,'* from which all its minor
thoughts radiate. That 'central ideal' in our political public opinion at the
beginning was, and until recently has continued to be, 'the equality of all
men.'" According to Lincoln, equality was "the father of all moral principle." It was the common denominator in his interpretation of the Declaration, of the principle of consent of the governed, and of the Union. Indeed,
Lincoln interpreted equal consent to be the very essence of self-government.
However, does not experience seem to suggest that human beings are inher-
ently unequal? Do not they differ in intellectual, artistic, physical, moral,
and spiritual capacities? If it is manifestly true that certain individuals are either stronger, taller, or more intelligent than others, then in what sense can
it be said that all men are created equal?[26]

Lincoln understood the self-evident truth of equality in view of humanity's relationship to the subhuman and superhuman. Slavery was wrong because it degraded African Americans "[f]rom the rank of a man to that of a
brute." His interpretation of equality presupposed a biblical understanding
of a hierarchical chain of being in which man is the in-between participant.
Human life occupies the realm in between time and eternity, mortality and
immortality, ignorance and certitude. The term "equality" may be expressed
negatively in the following way: since man is neither a beast (subhuman)
nor a god (superhuman), he may not govern other human beings in the
same way he would govern a beast. Correlatively, he may not govern other
human beings from the privileged standpoint of divine omnipotence and
omniscience. Because human beings are neither more than human nor less
than human, they are equally human and therefore must be treated accordingly. All human beings possess the same essence as a rational being regardless of differences in abilities and are therefore neither beasts nor gods. This
is what is meant by the self-evident truth of human equality.[27]

In defending the common humanity of the African American, Lincoln
conceived of human equality in view of the aforementioned hierarchy of be-

ing. Man's dignity was derived from his likeness to God. Lincoln viewed the Declaration as a fitting tribute to the Creator's justice, for its assertion of equality celebrated the biblical understanding of man created in the image of God:

> This was [the authors of the Declaration's] majestic interpretation of the economy of the Universe. This was their lofty, and wise, and noble understanding of the justice of the Creator to His creatures. Yes, gentlemen, to *all* His creatures, to the whole family of man. In their enlightened belief, nothing stamped with the Divine image and likeness was sent into the world to be trodden on, and degraded, and imbruted by its fellows.

Thus, to submit another human being to the lash on account of his or her skin color was to degrade the inherent goodness of Creation. To judge another from the standpoint of divine omnipotence and omniscience was to act as if one were God.[28]

If the African American was a human being, then it followed that his inherent dignity as a rational being that was created in God's image must be acknowledged. Lincoln blamed the "popular sovereigns . . . [for] blowing out the moral lights around us; teaching that the negro is no longer a man but a brute; that the Declaration has nothing to do with him; that he ranks with the crocodile and the reptile; that man, with body and soul, is a matter of dollars and cents." Here, Lincoln poetically depicted the Declaration as a moral light that illuminated the truth of human equality. The treatment of human beings as property divested individuals of their "God-given rights to enjoy the fruits of their own labor." It degraded their spiritual dignity by relegating them to the status of beasts and things. Discerning the manifest injustice of slavery, Lincoln stated: "Equal justice to the south, it is said, requires us to consent to the extending of slavery to new countries. That is to say, inasmuch as you do not object to my taking my hog to Nebraska, therefore I must not object to you taking your slave. Now I admit this is perfectly logical, if there is no difference between hogs and negros." Lincoln, it is clear, understood equality in terms of a common human essence.[29]

Although Lincoln argued for the equality of all men, he did not believe that human beings were equal in all respects, only in their possession of a common rational and spiritual dignity. Specifically, he interpreted the Declaration's affirmation of equality to mean the equality of opportunity. To be sure, his view is eminently reconcilable with the principle of merit. In fact, equality of opportunity and merit are related. The former is the condition of the latter: genuine merit can only be ascertained on the condition that a competing individual is considered to be neither subhuman nor superhuman. In assessing the talents of an individual, one would not apply the same standard that one would to an animal or to God. That is to say, the rewards or penalties of society ought not to be distributed on the basis of a claim that certain people are either more or less than human. Lincoln distinguished between equality of opportunity, rights, and equality of condition in the following manner:

> I think the authors of [the Declaration] intended to include *all* men, but they did not intend to declare all men equal *in all respects*. They did not mean to say all are equal in color, size, intellect, moral developments, or social capacity. They defined with tolerable distinctness, in what respects they did consider all men created equal—equal in "certain inalienable rights, among which are life, liberty, and the pursuit of happiness."[30]

Politically speaking, equality of opportunity had a positive and a negative implication: positively, it enjoined government to promote, at the very least, a fit habitation for human life so that people may cultivate their talents and compete fairly for status, wealth, and honor within society; negatively, it prohibited government from imposing undue penalties or conferring rewards that discriminated on the basis of race, creed, or color. A truly just nation could not legitimately take away its citizens' hope for personal improvement: "Free labor has the inspiration of hope; pure slavery has no hope. The power of hope upon human exertion, and happiness, is wonderful." Lincoln's belief in the possibility of improvement of condition led him to reject George Fitzhugh's argument that the slave laborers of the South fared better than the industrial laborers of the North.[31]

Lincoln believed that, if government could not actively promote the full social and political equality of the African American, then, at the very least, it must work toward ending slavery prudently. Lincoln used biblical language didactically to convey this important point:

> It is said in one of the admonitions of the Lord, "As your Father in Heaven is perfect, be ye also perfect." The Savior, I suppose, did not expect that any human creature could be perfect as the Father in Heaven; but He said, "As your Father in Heaven is perfect, be ye also perfect." He set that up as a standard, and he who did most towards reaching that standard, attained the highest degree of moral perfection. So I say in relation to the principle that all men are created equal, let it be as nearly reached as we can. If we cannot give freedom to every living creature, let us do nothing that will impose slavery on any other creature.

By means of this didactic analogy from Matthew's gospel, Lincoln affirmed a republican commitment to both freedom and authority, liberty and order. The moral aspiration of equality must be counterbalanced against competing legal and constitutional claims.[32]

Most important, Lincoln viewed equality as a principle of justice and reciprocity in two related senses: equality before the law, and equality of rights, privileges, and immunities. According to Lincoln, it was a matter of simple distributive justice to guarantee all citizens equality before the law and equality of rights, privileges, and immunities. If justice is provisionally defined as rendering one his or her due, then equality as a principle of distributive justice may be defined as rendering members of society their fair due as human beings. It demands that the privileges and immunities of society be distributed equally among citizens regardless of their race, creed, or color. Likewise, equality before the law suggests that it is unjust to impose harsher legal penalties on individuals based on their race, creed, or color. In the words of Justice John Marshall Harlan, the law and the Constitution are "colorblind." By treating African Americans as beasts of burden, society failed to render them their due as human beings and therefore acted unjustly. As Lincoln noted, slavery "repress[es] all tendencies in the human heart to justice and mercy."33

The principle of consent is a logical consequence of equality. Because he envisioned self-government and equality to be correlative, Lincoln explained: "As I would not be a *slave,* so I would not be a *master.* This expresses my idea of democracy. Whatever differs from this, to the extent of the difference is no democracy." Since all human beings possessed an equal dignity as rational and spiritual beings, they must not govern others of the same species as they would an animal—that is, despotically. If everyone is equal in the possession of the same human essence, then no one is entitled to rule over another as if that person were subhuman. Likewise, because all human beings are equal, no one is entitled to lord over others as if he or she were a god elevated above the rest of humanity. Unlike an animal, a human being must consent to be governed. Thus, Lincoln stated: "No man is good enough to govern another man, without the other's consent. I say this is the leading principle—the sheet anchor of American republicanism." Significantly, Lincoln denied that any human being was "good enough" to govern another without the other's consent. This denial was predicated on a biblical view of human nature that presumed man's fallen nature. Indeed, slavery violated both the republican principle of consent and the Golden Rule: "The master not only governs the slave without his consent; but he governs him by a set of rules altogether different from himself."34

To demonstrate the correspondence between equality and self-government, Lincoln rhetorically asked: By what principle may one justly enslave another human being? His argument made use of a categorical imperative to reveal the rational dignity of African Americans:

> You do not mean *color* exactly?—You mean the whites are *intellectually* the superiors of the blacks, and, therefore have the right to enslave them? Take care again. By this rule, you are to be slave to the first man you meet, with an intellect superior to your own.
>
> But, say you, it is a question of *interest;* and, if you can make it your *interest,* you have the right to enslave another. Very well. And if he can make it his interest, he has the right to enslave you.

Significantly, Lincoln considered the abstract claim of slavery without reference to race. To be sure, any standard that was used to justify slavery could be turned around to justify one's own enslavement regardless of race. In Kant's words, the maxim that justified slavery could not be universalized. Accordingly, the only fair principle of governance was to recognize the equal dignity of all human beings and its correlative, consent of the governed. Lincoln's argument may be summarized in the following way: (1) those who deny the equality of others on the basis of a certain principle may by that same standard justify their own servitude; (2) no person would honestly consent to his own servitude; and (3) therefore it is unjust to endorse the slavery of others.[35]

The viability of republican government depends upon the recognition of each citizen's basic humanity. If human dignity is derived from man's participation in transcendence, then, ultimately, the defense of human equality relies upon a transcendent foundation. Lincoln's concrete struggle with the moral question of slavery led him to the conclusion that moral discourse could not be conducted in a political vacuum. The vindication of human dignity depended upon the ultimate nature of reality: politics and ethics relied upon a supreme moral justification and grounding. If the universe is chaotic, if intelligent life is an accident, if all human experience is subjective, if man differs from an animal by degree and not in kind, then it follows that there can be no absolute or fixed basis to oppose slavery. All standards would be relative and conventional.

Like Jefferson in the *Notes on the State of Virginia,* Lincoln maintained that the denial of equality to one group of people promoted a master-slave relationship among the citizenry that corrupted the manners of society and undermined the integrity of self-government. He predicted that, if left unchecked, the habits of despotism would eclipse republican government:

> Our reliance is in the *love of liberty* which God has planted in our bosoms. Our defense is in the preservation of the spirit which prizes liberty as the heritage of all men, in all lands, every where. Destroy this spirit, and you have planted the seeds of despotism around your own doors. Familiarize yourselves with the chains of bondage, and you are preparing your own limbs to wear them. Accustomed to trample on the rights of those around you, you have lost the genius of your own independence, and become the fit subjects of the first cunning tyrant who rises.[36]

By assigning preeminence to the principle of equality in the Declaration, Lincoln did not undertake a "new founding" of the Union, as Garry Wills has contended in his work *Lincoln at Gettysburg.* Rather, he extended and applied more consistently an axiomatic principle that was already present at the nation's founding. By so doing, Lincoln clarified the anomalous status of slavery within American republicanism in a manner consistent with both the letter and the spirit of the founders. Lincoln's view of the Declaration as a founding document was derived from important antecedent sources of the founding and the antebellum period. The "refounding thesis" ignores the continuity of equality in the republican tradition. If Lincoln is to be repudiated for his commitment to the Declaration, then so must many of the key founders, e.g., Thomas Jefferson, John Adams, James Wilson, James Madison, and George Mason in addition to Lincoln's Whig predecessors Daniel Webster and Henry Clay. This is not to say that Lincoln's interpretation was the only understanding of the founding; rather, his interpretation was concordantly and authoritatively derived from important antecedent sources during the founding and antebellum periods. In response to Garry Wills's allegation that Lincoln refounded the American regime by making equality the central proposition of the regime, Harry Jaffa has shown that the language of equality was adopted by the constitutions and bills of rights of seven of the original thirteen states.[37] The reaffirmation of the Declaration of Independence by the Republican Party's platform in 1856 and 1860 further confirms Lincoln's view of the Declaration as a founding document of American republicanism. If Lincoln is to be repudiated for his defense of equality in the Declaration, then so must the entire Republican Party. This would have left the proslavery philosophy of the South and Douglas's popular sovereignty as the only alternatives to the founders' legacy.[38]

Lincoln's interpretation of the Declaration as a charter of liberty that conveyed the general precepts of American republicanism coincided remarkably with Jefferson's view. Indeed, Jefferson once explained that, at the time of the nation's founding, the Declaration elicited a moral consensus upon the first principles of republicanism: "All American Whigs thought alike on these subjects. . . . Neither aiming at originality of principle or sentiment, nor yet copied from any particular and previous writing, it was intended to be *an expression of the American mind.* All its authority rests on the harmonizing sentiments of the day [italics added]." Jefferson's description of the Declaration as "an expression of the American mind" that "rest[ed] on the harmonizing sentiments of the day" is highly significant. It suggests that, contrary to the refounding thesis, the Declaration was indeed viewed as a founding document.[39]

Lincoln's view of the Declaration as a bulwark against despotism was likewise derived from Jefferson's interpretation of the document. Jefferson proclaimed that "the flames kindled on the 4th of July, 1776, have spread over too much of the globe to be extinguished by the feeble engines of despotism, they will consume these engines and all who work them." In addition, both Jefferson and Lincoln viewed the Declaration in civil theological terms as a moral covenant whose originating principles constituted a source of political renewal. Employing evocative biblical rhetoric to convey this point, Jefferson stated: "the sacred attachments of our fellow citizens to the event of which the paper of July 4th, 1776, was but the Declaration, the genuine effusion of the soul of our country at that time. Small things may, perhaps, like relics of saints, help to nourish our devotion to this holy bond of our

Union, and keep it longer alive and warm in our affections." Once again, Jefferson revealed the extent to which the Declaration was representative of the public ethos at the time of the founding. Significantly, he referred to the document as "the genuine effusion of the soul of our country at that time." Finally, Jefferson's and Lincoln's view of the Declaration coincide in this important respect: both affirm the universality of the Declaration's moral imperatives.[40]

Consonant with the self-understanding of American republicanism, Jefferson interpreted equality to mean the equality of opportunity: "the mass of mankind have not been born with saddles on their back." Indeed, the Virginian's theory of liberal education and his distinction between a natural and an artificial aristocracy relied upon equality of opportunity as a necessary condition of societal advancement and progress. It is fair to say that Lincoln's view of the Declaration and equality was derived, in part, from Jefferson's republicanism.

James Madison also viewed the Declaration as a founding document of American republicanism. While considering the first principles of the nation, the mature Madison noted the following in a letter to Jefferson: "And on the distinctive principles of the Government of our own State, and of that of the United States, the best guides are to be found in—1. The Declaration of Independence as the fundamental act of Union of these States." Furthermore, in *Federalist 39*, Madison stated: "It is evident that no other form [of government] would be reconcilable with the genius of the people of America, with the fundamental principles of the Revolution; or with that honorable determination which animates every of freedom, to rest all our political experiments on the capacity for self-government." Madison's allusions to the "genius of the people of America" and "the fundamental principles of the revolution" are inconceivable as anything other than tacit references to the Declaration.[41]

In *Federalist 43*, Madison's description of the ends of republican government invokes the language of the Declaration: "The transcendent law of nature and nature's God . . . declares that the safety and happiness of society are the objects at which all political institutions aim and to which all institutions must be sacrificed." He noted further that the possibilities of 1787 were constrained by the principles of 1776:

> In a confederacy founded on republican principles, and composed of republican members, the superintending government ought clearly to possess authority to defend the system against aristocratic or monarchic innovations. . . . Whenever the States may choose to substitute other republican forms, they have a right to do so and to claim the federal guaranty for the latter. The only restriction imposed on them is that they shall not change republican for antirepublican Constitutions; a restriction which, it is presumed, will hardly be considered a grievance.

Madison presumed a republican consensus at the time of the founding that rejected aristocratic and monarchic forms of governance. As testified by both Jefferson and Madison, the Declaration promulgated the first principles of republicanism. It was "an expression of the American mind" that articulated "the distinctive principles of the Government . . . of the United States." Lincoln's critics commit a non sequitur in arguing that the Constitution's explicit failure to mention equality constitutes a repudiation of the Declaration's principles. The preamble's affirmation of "We the people" implies equal consent, as does its affirmation of liberty. Furthermore, the Constitution's prohibitions against titles of nobility, religious tests, and nonrepublican forms of government can only be understood in light of the nation's commitment to the principles of equality and consent of the governed. Indeed, the spirit of 1776 guided the founders at the Constitutional Convention of 1787. Lincoln's interpretation of liberty and Union envisioned a correspondence between the Declaration and Constitution as complementary charters of American republicanism.

THE UNION

Some have interpreted Lincoln's devotion to the Union as a romantic abstraction. Alexander Stephens believed that it "had risen to the sublimity of religious mysticism." Others have viewed his appeal to it as Machiavellian, motivated exclusively by a realpolitik concern for self-preservation devoid of higher moral aspirations. Neither the romantic nor the realpolitik interpretation of Lincoln's devotion to the Union is correct. On the contrary, Lincoln's commitment was prudent in recognizing that the higher moral aspirations of liberty and equality were inextricably linked to the Union's perpetuity. The latter were the sine qua non of the former. The dissolution of the Union not only would have undermined the safety of the people by inviting domestic anarchy and foreign invasion, but it also would have extinguished the pursuit of happiness by relinquishing the Declaration's moral promise of liberty. Lincoln's Whig predecessor, Daniel Webster, conveyed this moral interpretation of the Union most elegantly: "Liberty and Union, now and forever, one and inseparable!"[42]

Lincoln's devotion to the Union combined a fidelity to both the Declaration as the moral foundation of American republicanism and the Constitution as its legal framework. As seen, the preservation of a moral Union dedicated to the principles of civil and religious liberty in the Declaration constituted the end of Lincoln's biblical republicanism. At Peoria, he made it clear that the Union must be "worthy of saving" in light of the principles for which it stood. Two years later, in 1856, he reiterated that "The Union must be preserved in the purity of its principles." Pondering the significance of the Union en route to his inauguration, he linked the preservation of the Union to the moral aspirations of the Declaration in a speech at Trenton, New Jersey, on February 21, 1861. Speaking of the founders' aspirations, he stated:

> I recollect thinking then, boy even though I was, that here must have been something more than common that those men struggled for. I am exceedingly anxious that that thing which they struggled for; that something even more than National Independence; that something that held out a great promise to all the people of the world to all time to come; I am exceedingly anxious that this Union, the Constitution, and the liberties of the people shall be perpetuated in accordance with the original idea for which that struggle was made. . . .

Of course, the original idea of the revolution was the promise of liberty to all. Lincoln's vision of the Union was both inclusive and moral. He distinguished his vision of the Union from a "free love" arrangement devoid of fidelity. He believed that the preservation of the Union had universal significance in determining the fate of democracy throughout the world. The dissolution of the United States would extinguish "the last, best hope of earth."[43]

But how did the Union provide hope to other peoples? First, America provided hope as a haven and refuge for the persecuted and oppressed. Immigrants from throughout the world flocked to the United States during the mid-nineteenth century, and continue to do so today. Given the despotic practice of slavery down South, it was no coincidence that the bulk of these immigrants (primarily German, Scandinavian, and Irish) settled in the North, awarding it a clear population advantage during the Civil War. The Union promised the rights of citizenship not on the basis of a common racial, ethnic, or class identity but on a shared commitment to the political principles of the Declaration. These principles, not the accidents of birth, constituted the authentic basis of a shared political community and would transform the many ethnic groups into one body politic. Hence the nation's motto: *E Pluribus Unum*, "out of many, one."

Borrowing from Paul's description of the mystical body of Christ in 1 Corinthians 12, Lincoln described the Union as a *corpus mysticum* whose diverse members were unified, not racially through a common blood, but philosophically, through a common political faith in the creed of the Declaration. Using allegorical, didactic, and evocative biblical language, Lincoln described the Declaration as the animating spirit of the Union:

> We have besides these men—descended by blood from our ancestors—among us perhaps half our people who are not descendants at all of these men, they are men who have come from Europe—German, Irish, French and Scandinavian—men that have come from Europe themselves, or whose ancestors have come hither and settled here, finding themselves equals in all things. If they look back through this history to trace their connection with those days by blood, they find they have none, they cannot carry themselves back into that glorious epoch and make themselves feel that they are parts of us, but when they look through that old Declaration of Independence they find that those old men say that "We hold these truths to be self-evident that all men are created equal," and then they feel that that moral sentiment taught in that day evidences their

relation to those men, that it is the father of all moral principle in them, and that they have a right to claim it as though they were blood of blood and flesh of flesh of the men who wrote that Declaration, and so they are. That is the electric cord in that Declaration that links the hearts of patriotic and liberty-loving men together, that will link those patriotic hearts as long as the love of freedom exists in the minds of men throughout the world.[44]

America also provided hope and inspiration to foreign revolutionaries struggling against tyranny. In the mid-nineteenth century the United States was virtually a remote republican island surrounded by a sea of despotism. Perhaps this is difficult for people at the dawn of the twenty-first century to appreciate fully, having recently seen the triumph of democracy over communist regimes in eastern Europe. Indeed, some scholars have even suggested that this triumph was inevitable. In the context of the mid-nineteenth century, however, the fate of democracy looked bleak. In the historic year of 1848, a series of revolts unleashed in the wake of the French Revolution convulsed the European Continent in an attempt to establish democratic government. That year, Lincoln lauded the "right of revolution as a most valuable, a most sacred right—a right which, we hope and believe is to liberate the world." Although he consistently defended the right to revolution against tyranny, he also maintained that free elections constituted the lawful and prudent response in cases where constitutional government continued to be based on the principle of consent and committed to the protection of individual rights.[45]

By the outbreak of the American Civil War in 1860, all efforts to establish democracy in Europe were ruthlessly suppressed by the traditional, hereditary dynasties. The Habsburgs in Austria, the Hohenzollerns in Prussia, the Romanovs in Russia, and the Bourbons in Spain and France reasserted their power and restored the ancien régime. Lincoln did not exaggerate when he noted that the success of the Confederacy would put "an end to free government upon the earth." Giuseppe Garibaldi of Italy and Louis Kossuth of Hungary were two notable nineteenth-century revolutionaries who sought refuge in America after their failed attempts to build democracy in Europe. Garibaldi was so grateful for America's refuge that, after he finally liberated Italy, he wrote Lincoln seeking to return the favor by volunteering to lead an army against the South. The collapse of self-government in the New World would reverberate throughout the Old World, leading to despair for those struggling against the heel of tyranny. It seemed that the United States in the mid-nineteenth century was the only beacon of democratic government to provide inspiration, and now that was threatened by the affirmation of slavery as a moral and religious right and by the anarchy of secession and Civil War.[46]

Finally, America provided hope for material and moral advancement in the race of life. It promised that people would be judged on the basis of merit rather than the accidents of birth, race, creed, color, or gender.

Lincoln's struggle to preserve the Union may be viewed as a struggle to preserve the American dream. In view of his ability to articulate the core moral aspirations of the Union, he has been celebrated as the statesman who has provided the most compelling vision of the promise of America to succeeding generations:

> This is essentially a People's contest. On the side of the Union, it is a struggle for maintaining in the world, that form, and substance of government, whose leading object is, to elevate the condition of men—to lift artificial weights from all shoulders—to clear the paths of laudable pursuits for all—to afford all, an unfettered start, and a fair chance, in the race of life. Yielding to partial and temporary departures, from necessity, this is the leading object of the government for whose existence we contend.[47]

Lincoln's vision of the Union has inspired generations of immigrants to leave their native lands to find opportunity and freedom in the New World. The survival of the United States during the Civil War would prove to the world that it was possible for the people to govern themselves and that they could grow and prosper in doing so. He thereby characterized the Civil War as a "struggle for maintaining in the world, that form, and substance of government, whose leading object is to elevate the condition of men—to lift artificial weights from all shoulders—to clear the paths of unfettered start, and a fair chance, in the race of life." Lincoln consistently reaffirmed his vision of the American dream throughout his presidency. One cannot read his speeches and writings without thinking of the countless immigrants who flocked to America after the Civil War, and who continue to do so today:

> It is not merely for to-day, but for all time to come that we should perpetuate . . . free government . . . in order that each of you may have . . . an open field and a fair chance for your industry, enterprise and intelligence; that you may have all the equal privileges in the race of life, with all its desirable human aspirations.[48]

Because Lincoln envisioned a Union that was inclusive to all human beings, he opposed mid-nineteenth century nativist movements as a threat to American republicanism. Because it denied equality to people of foreign ancestry and falsely affirmed the superiority of native-born, Anglo-Saxon Americans, nativism betrayed America's mission to serve as a haven and refuge for the persecuted and dispossessed. Speaking of the surge in popular support for the nativist, Know-Nothing party in the mid-nineteenth century, he said:

> Our progress in degeneracy appears to me to be pretty rapid. As a nation, we began declaring that *"all men are created equal."* We now practically read it "all

men are created equal *except negroes.*" When the Know-Nothings get control, it will read "all men are created equal except negroes, *and foreigners, and catholics.*" When it comes to this I should prefer emigrating to some country where they make no pretense of loving liberty—to Russia, for instance, where despotism can be taken pure, and without the base alloy of hypocracy.

Nativism as well as slavery undermined America's mission to serve as an exemplar of democracy to the world. Lincoln believed that black freedom and white freedom were inseparably linked. Once the principle of equal consent was denied as a common reference between individuals in society, justifications for the mastery of one group over another (whether based on the accidental qualities of heredity, race, ethnicity, or intelligence) could be used to deprive not only blacks of their rights but other groups of people as well:

> Understanding the spirit of our institutions to aim at the *elevation* of men, I am opposed to whatever tends to *degrade* them. I have some little notoriety for commiserating the oppressed condition of the negro; and I should be strangely inconsistent if I could favor any project for curtailing the existing rights of *white men,* even though born in different lands, and speaking different languages from myself.[49]

Like his Whig predecessor Daniel Webster, Lincoln emphasized the inseparability of liberty and Union. This inseparability suggested that the perpetuity of a Union committed to the moral aspirations of liberty and equality could only be achieved through a federal constitution that was committed to a particular legal framework. The Constitution of 1787 established not any Union, but a "more perfect Union." It did this by expanding the scope of national power to remedy the mischief of faction and domestic anarchy under the Articles of Confederation. According to both Webster and Lincoln, authentic liberty could only be preserved under the auspices of a national Union that possessed sufficient power and energy to meet the exigencies of government.[50]

In order to explain the corresponding moral and legal roles of the Declaration and Constitution as sources of liberty and Union, Lincoln invoked a biblical metaphor from Proverbs 25:11—"A word fitly spoken is like apples of gold in pictures of silver." Indeed, the didactic use of this biblical passage effectively conveyed the reconciliation between legal and moral obligation within the American political tradition:

> All this is not the result of accident. It has a philosophical cause. Without the *Constitution* and the *Union,* we could not have attained the result; but even these, are not the primary cause of our great prosperity. There is something back of these, entwining itself more closely about the human heart. That something is the principle of "Liberty to all"—the principle that clears the *path* for

all—gives *hope* to all—and, by consequence, *enterprize*, and *industry* to all.

The *expression* of that principle, in our Declaration of Independence, was most happy, and fortunate. . . . The assertion of that *principle*, at *that time*, was *the* word, *"fitly spoken"* which has proved an *"apple of gold"* to us. The *Union*, and the *Constitution*, are the *picture of silver*, subsequently framed around it. The picture was made, not to *conceal*, or *destroy* the apple; but to *adorn*, and *preserve* it. The *picture* was made for the apple—*not* the apple for the picture.

So let us act, that neither *picture*, or apple shall ever be blurred, or bruised or broken.

That we may so act, we must study, and understand the points of danger.[51]

Although the moral principles of the Declaration were ontologically prior to the Constitution, they required legal and institutional support. The Constitution and the Union represented the picture of silver: "The *picture*—was made for the apple—*not* the apple for the picture." At the time of the Revolution, the assertion of liberty was a "word, *'fitly spoken.'*" The metaphor traced the historical evolution of American liberty, which, when incorporated into the nation's political institutions, has "proved [to be] an apple of gold" that has yielded freedom and prosperity to the nation. Lincoln warned, however, that the nation must act so "that neither *picture*, or apple shall ever be blurred, or bruised or broken." The apple of gold (liberty) was enhanced and protected by the picture frame (rule of law). Without the frame, the golden apple would become bruised or smashed. By analogy, the moral aspirations of the Declaration were supported by the legal and sociopolitical framework of the Constitution and the Union. Without the institutional framework provided by the Constitution (the picture of silver that protects the golden apple), ordered liberty would tend to degenerate into the extremes of anarchy and tyranny. Conversely, without the Union's commitment to liberty as a moral aspiration (without the golden apple), liberty may be viewed in terms of either proslavery theology or popular sovereignty. Thus, authentic liberty presumed the reconciliation of both the moral obligation to the principles of the Declaration and the legal obligation to the Constitution. Liberty and Union were as inseparable as the apple of gold and the picture of silver.

Lincoln's view of the inseparability of liberty and Union stood in contrast to other contemporary approaches to law and morality. The radical abolitionists, whose motto was "no Union with slaveholders," demanded "Liberty first and Union afterwards." In Lincoln's view, the dissolution of the Union would have made any opposition to slavery a moot point. On the other side of the political spectrum during the Civil War era, Stephen A. Douglas before the war and the War Democrats during the war essentially demanded a Union without liberty, without the promise of freedom for all human beings. In order to appreciate Lincoln's view of the inseparability of liberty and Union, one need only consider what "Liberty" would have meant in a Union that was dedicated to the ethically neutral principle of popular sovereignty or to a Union presided over by the War Democrat George B. McClellan, who ran against Lincoln in the 1864 election and who sought to reverse the many strides toward black freedom that were achieved during the war. He, and the Democratic Party, inveighed against the Emancipation Proclamation as the act of a dictator and sought its retraction, a step Lincoln was unwilling to take despite great political pressure and despite the possibility that it would have improved his sagging popularity in the summer of 1864.[52]

William Lloyd Garrison, who publicly burned a copy of the Constitution on the Fourth of July to show his contempt for the document, is perhaps the best representative of the radical abolitionists' moral idealism before the war. Invoking divine justice, he agitated for a revolutionary transfiguration of society that would usher in a new order purified from the corruption of human servitude:

> Let the American Union perish; let these allied States be torn with faction, or drenched in blood; let this republic realize the fate of Rome and Carthage, of Babylon and Tyre; still, those rights would remain undiminished in strength, unsullied in purity, unaffected in value, and sacred as their Divine Author. . . . Man is superior to all political compacts, all government arrangements, all religious institutions. As means to an end, these may sometimes be useful, though never indispensable; but that end must always be the freedom and happiness of man, INDIVIDUAL MAN. . . . [The Union] was conceived in sin, and brought forth in iniquity; and its career has been marked by unparalleled hypocrisy; by high-handed tyranny, by a bold defiance of the omniscience and omnipotence of God.[53]

Another abolitionist, Wendell Phillips, derisively referred to Lincoln as the "slave hound from Illinois" for his concessions to slavery in order to preserve the Union. The president-elect, he said, was an unwitting pawn of radical abolitionists:

> Not an Abolitionist, hardly an antislavery man, Mr. Lincoln consents to represent an antislavery idea. A pawn on the political chessboard, his value is in his position; with fair effort, we may soon change him for knight, bishop, or queen, and sweep the board. . . . The Republican party have undertaken a problem, the solution of which will force them to our position. . . . Not Mr. Seward's 'Union and Liberty,' which he stole and poisoned from Webster's 'Liberty and Union.' No: their motto will soon be 'Liberty first,' 'Union afterwards.'

Phillips's substitution of "Liberty first" and "Union afterwards" for "Liberty and Union, one and inseparable" expresses rather concisely the moral idealism of the radical abolitionists. Phillips and Garrison were willing to risk the dissolution of the Union and the abandonment of the Constitution to achieve the abstract promise of equality. As political idealists who sought to transform society overnight without regard for expediency or the constraints of the rule of law and the limitations of sociopolitical circumstances, the abolitionists focused entirely upon their purity of abstract principle, leaving the "results to God." Their blatant disregard for the moral consequences of their actions would most likely have resulted in policies that were exactly the opposite of the ideals they were attempting to realize. In his reckless devotion to principle, Phillips never thought through the consequences of actually allowing the South to secede from the Union. It can be argued, as Frederick Douglass did when he broke with Garrison, that the plight of African Americans would have been far worse if the South formed an independent Confederacy. African Americans would be trapped indefinitely without the promise of hope of improvement, freed from the moral embrace of the Union and submerged under a Confederate regime dedicated to the ends of racial supremacy and human inequality. In sum, the utopian alternatives proposed by Phillips to end slavery were self-defeating. The immediate abolition of slavery would have lost the support of the border states and War Democrats, thereby guaranteeing victory to the South. The acquiescence to the Union's dissolution in the name of abstract moral principle would practically result in the same conclusion: the indefinite perpetuation of slavery in the South. Phillips's political immoderation, so reminiscent of French Jacobinism, alienated southern moderates, undermined moderate dialogue, and thereby hastened the Civil War. In fact, a member of the South Carolina state legislature quoted Phillips's speech "as one justification for his state's secession from the Union."[54]

Unfortunately, among conservative critics, Lincoln's antislavery views are still confounded with those of the radical abolitionists of his time. Though Lincoln opposed the extension of slavery and looked forward to its eventual abolition when circumstances permitted, he did not hold the Constitution in contempt and did not demand immediate and uncompensated emancipation. Lincoln was committed to a policy of containment under both moral and legal auspices, not forcible abolition based solely upon his own moral convictions. On the other side of the political spectrum, critics from the New Left cite Lincoln's letter to Horace Greeley on August 1862 as irrefutable proof that his devotion to the Union was purely pragmatic, devoid of any higher moral aspiration. In order to press Lincoln toward emancipation, Horace Greeley, editor of the *New York Tribune,* wrote an article addressed to the president, entitled "The Prayer of Twenty Millions," criticizing Lincoln for his reluctance to emancipate: "We think you are unduly influenced by the councils, the representations, the menaces, of certain fossil politicians hailing from the Border States." Mindful that his response would be scrutinized in papers throughout the nation, Lincoln cautiously but clearly stated the North's primary objective during the war:

> My paramount object in this struggle *is* to save the Union, and is *not* either to save or to destroy slavery. If I could save the Union without freeing *any* slave I would do it; and if I could save it by freeing some and leaving others alone I would also do that. What I do about slavery, and the colored race, I do because it helps to save the Union; and what I forebear, I forebear because I do *not* believe it would hope to save the Union. . . . I have stated my purpose according to my view of *official duty;* and I intend no modification of my oft expressed *personal* wish that all men everywhere could be free.[55]

Lincoln was unsure about his constitutional authority to emancipate the slaves. He had consistently and repeatedly pledged that he could not touch slavery where it existed in the states from his earliest statements on slavery until his presidency. As much as he hated slavery, he had sworn an oath to uphold the Constitution, and that meant upholding its concessions to slavery as well. Before the Thirteenth Amendment, the federal division of power prohibited interference with slavery where it already existed at the time of the Constitution. Indeed, a House Resolution in 1790 explicitly prohibited Congress from emancipating the slaves in the southern states. An Emancipation Proclamation in defiance of the Constitution would lack legitimacy and would confirm the suspicion of southerners and northern moderates alike that the Republican Party was composed of fanatics who had no respect for established legal procedure and the rule of law.[56]

Lincoln's primary political consideration was to maintain a fragile war coalition composed of radical and moderate Republicans who favored emancipation and of War Democrats, conservative Republicans, and the border states, who opposed emancipation. In particular, he had to maintain the political support of the border states that remained faithful to the Union despite the presence of slavery. The support of border states like Kentucky, Maryland, and Missouri was crucial to the Union's success. Alienating them would upset the balance of power in favor of the South. Lincoln once said, "to lose Kentucky is to lose the whole game." He correctly discerned that it was both illegal and inexpedient to abolish slavery in the border states without their consent. The needed support of War Democrats and the border states to win the war constrained Lincoln's political possibilities. To maintain a winning coalition he prudently equivocated on what preserving the Union meant in his reply to Greeley and elsewhere—to placate those who feared that the war would degenerate into an abolitionist crusade.

Given his commitment to an ordered liberty that balanced a legal obligation to the Constitution and a moral obligation to the Declaration, Lincoln believed that the Emancipation could only be legally justified as a war measure under the president's power in Article 2 as "Commander in Chief" of the armed forces. He maintained that it was a necessary and reasonable means (a war measure) taken by the nation's chief executive to impair the South's ability to make war: the act would encourage slaves laboring for the Confederacy to flee and support the advancing Union armies. In fact, this did happen, and the Union's war effort benefited greatly from it. The legal status of the emancipation as a war measure also explains why it did not apply to the border states that had slaves but remained within the Union.

The superficial interpretation that the Union's preservation excluded the ultimate goal of black freedom neglects Lincoln's many efforts toward compensated emancipation in the border states, disregards his commitment to the rule of law, and ignores his vision of a moral Union dedicated to the principles of the Declaration. In a word, it posits a false dichotomy between the twin goals of preserving the Union and ending slavery. It presumes that these two objectives were mutually exclusive. In fact, Lincoln envisioned the goals of preserving the Union and freeing the slaves to be related. David Herbert Donald explains this relationship, noting: "In Lincoln's mind there was no necessary disjunction between a war for the Union and a war to end slavery. Like most Republicans, he had long held the belief that if slavery could be contained it would inevitably die; a war that kept the slave states within the Union would, therefore, bring about the ultimate extinction of slavery." Preserving the Union was Lincoln's "paramount object," but it was never his sole intention. In his reply to Greeley, for instance, the word "paramount" does not mean "sole" or "only" but rather "foremost" or "principal." That is to say, Lincoln's language makes clear that, although the preservation of the Union was a priority, it was not the only political objective. The preservation of the Union was merely the precondition to ending slavery and extending the principle of equality. This is entirely consistent with the apple of gold and picture of silver analogy. In order to maintain the support of a broad coalition of border states and War Democrats to win the war, Lincoln equivocated when he spoke of his paramount objective in the war. His objective was actually twofold: (1) defeating the enemy and restoring the territorial integrity of the Union; and (2) in the long term, applying the moral principles of the Declaration, which was dependent upon accomplishing the first goal.[57]

Lincoln's scrupulous attention to legal justification should not obscure the moral intention of the emancipation as an "act of justice." Indeed, the South recognized that Lincoln was a principled and implacable foe of slavery—that is why they seceded in the first place. They correctly understood that slavery was eventually doomed to extinction in a regime committed to the principles of the Declaration and to a leader who would contain the spread of the institution. Textual evidence confirms that Lincoln envisioned the inseparability of liberty and Union to imply the twin goals of preserving the Union and ending slavery. At Peoria, the preservation of the Union meant preserving the principles the Union stood for, including its promise of equality to all men. And in 1856, Lincoln noted in a speech at Bloomington that "the Union must be preserved in the purity of its principles as well as in the integrity of its territorial parts." He spoke of "The Great Republic and the principle it lives by." In Lincoln's mind, the consistent extension of the Declaration's principle of equality to blacks was linked to the success of America's mission to serve as an exemplar of democracy: "In giving freedom to the slave, we assure freedom to the free—honorable alike in what we give, and what we preserve. We shall nobly save, or meanly lose, the last, best hope on earth." While en route to his inauguration, Lincoln delivered a speech at Trenton, New Jersey, an important historical site of the Revolutionary War, in which he, "exceedingly anxious that this Union, the Constitution, and the liberties of the people shall be perpetuated in accordance with the original idea for which that struggle was made," vowed to uphold the founders' revolutionary legacy of freedom. After the border state of Maryland had pledged to abolish slavery, Lincoln exclaimed: "Maryland is secure to Liberty and Union for all the future." And he stated that "a proclamation of general emancipation, 'giving Liberty and Union' as the national watch-word, would rouse the people and rally them to his support beyond any thing yet witnessed—appealing alike to conscience, sentiment and hope." Because he saw the Union as dedicated to higher moral ends than mere self-preservation, Lincoln warned the border states that slavery would eventually become a casualty of the war: "If the war continue long, as it must, if the object be not sooner attained, the institution in your states will be extinguished by mere friction and abrasion—by the mere incident of the war." In a letter to August Belmont, Lincoln explained that "Broken eggs cannot be mended," implying that the shell of slavery was doomed to inevitable destruction by the war. These utterances testify to the inseparable connection between preserving the Union and extending liberty in Lincoln's mind.[58]

Lincoln's commitment to liberty and Union was also shown by his efforts toward black suffrage. Before the Fifteenth Amendment, suffrage was left to the discretion of the states and was beyond the authority of the national government to regulate. Louisiana was the first reconstructed state, and it would serve as a model for subsequent states' readmission to the Union. In a letter to Governor Hahn of Louisiana, Lincoln recommended that blacks be given the right to vote in the newly reconstructed state. Lincoln's letter conveyed a personal aspiration to the governor: "I barely suggest for your private consideration, whether some of the colored people may not be let in—as, for instance, the very intelligent, and especially those who have fought gallantly in our ranks. They would probably help, in some trying time to come, to keep the jewel of liberty within the family of freedom."[59]

The great themes of Lincoln's biblical republicanism—his opposition to slavery, his defense of democracy, his interpretation of the Declaration as the nation's Decalogue, and his vision of an inclusive, moral Union—are all linked by the "central idea" of equality that he considered to be "the father of all moral principle." In turn, the axiomatic principle of equal consent was itself predicated upon a biblical understanding of human nature, one that appreciated both human dignity and depravity.

THE CULMINATION OF
LINCOLN'S POLITICAL FAITH

The development of Lincoln's civil theology, from his youthful call for a "political religion" in the Lyceum Address to his more mature reflections in the Peoria Address, culminates with the Second Inaugural Address–the crowning achievement and ultimate expression of his political faith. Delivered in the context of the North's imminent victory and the public outcry for revenge against a defeated South, the speech encapsulates many of the themes of biblical republicanism.[1]

The design of the Second Inaugural advances "from historical to political to theological explanation." It progresses from the past, to the present, to the future. The speech begins with a mere statement of fact, his reelection. Characteristically, Lincoln then provided an overview of the past, furnishing a wider historical perspective for understanding events in the present. It is remarkable that there is not even a hint of self-congratulation in the speech, especially in view of the fact that Lincoln had triumphed after a bitter contest to become the first president since Andrew Jackson to be reelected, a span of more than thirty years. Throughout the summer of 1864 and before Sherman's capture of Atlanta in the first days of September, the Democratic opposition was poised to win the election. The nation was exhausted by war; many were outraged by the immense death toll from four years of bloody conflict. Democrats excoriated Lincoln for his war policies and for his restriction of civil liberties throughout the North. The growth of a "substantial peace movement" clamored for an end to the war and a restoration of the status quo antebellum, a policy that would have reversed all strides made toward black freedom during the war. Things sank so low that in August 1864 the chairman of the Republican National Committee, Henry J. Raymond, informed Lincoln that his prospects for reelection were bleak, principally on account of "the want of military success, and the impression in some minds, the fear and suspicion in others, that we are not to have peace in any event under this administration until Slavery is abandoned."[2]

Without Lincoln's insistence that the end of slavery serve as a precondition for peace and readmission to the Union, it was quite possible that the institution would have lingered despite the North's military victory. On August 23, Lincoln wrote a private memorandum conceding defeat to the Democrats. During this nadir in the summer of 1864, two deeds in particular speak to Lincoln's moral integrity and confirm that his ambition was bounded by a dedication to a higher moral authority. The first was his principled commitment to constitutionalism and the nation's democratic process that prevented him from suspending an election during wartime when it may have been politically expedient, from the standpoint of serving his own naked ambition, to do so. If Lincoln were truly the "towering genius" of the Lyceum Address who would either "free the slaves or enslave free men" to advance his personal ambition, then surely he would have suspended the election rather than risk defeat. It is difficult to imagine that a Napoleon, an Alexander, or a Caesar would have consented to an election in a similar time of crisis, thereby resisting the temptation to seize power under the pretext of public security. Instead, Lincoln had accepted and prepared for the possibility of defeat, putting the good of the nation and its republican institutions ahead of his own self-interest. The second deed was Lincoln's decision to uphold the Emancipation Proclamation despite public opposition. Lincoln's unwillingness to retract it in order to gain public standing in the election testifies to his moral integrity as a leader. If Lincoln were truly a racist, the unscrupulous and cunning politician characterized by his critics, then he surely would have revoked the proclamation rather than risk losing the election. Once the war had progressed and circumstances made it legally and politically possible, Lincoln was inflexible in his prudent determination to rid the Union of the blight of slavery. As seen in chapter 1, his decision to sustain the emancipation in the face of relentless public and political criticism was made in consideration of a higher moral obligation to God that transcended his personal ambitions. Defending his decision to authorize the use of black soldiers in the Union army, he stated, "I am responsible for it to the American people, to the christian world, to history, and on my final account to God." Indeed, an examination of conscience prevented Lincoln from the treachery of breaking his "solemn vow" to God and to his black neighbors. Not he, but someone else, would have to be the people's "instrument" in executing the perfidious act of returning African Americans to slavery after they had been promised their freedom.[3]

Thus, in light of events during the tumultuous summer of 1864, there were good reasons to expect a strong statement of personal vindication from Lincoln against members of his own Republican Party like Salmon P. Chase who sought to replace him as a candidate, against the Democratic opposition who vehemently criticized his war policies (especially the Emancipation Proclamation), against northern copperheads who opposed the war altogether and sought peace at any price, and against the South who was now prostrate after Sherman's capture of Atlanta. Yet, rather than claiming a mandate from his overwhelming margin in the electoral college of 212–21, Lincoln provided a mere statement of fact declaring his reelection: "At this second appearing, to take the oath of presidential office, there is less occasion for an extended address than there was at the first." Instead of predicting a glorious consummation in which the enemies of the state would soon be vanquished and dragged before the victors in a triumphal procession, he simply declared, "With high hope for the future, no prediction in regard to it is ventured." These restrained statements are indicative of Lincoln's humility in contrasting human actions and strivings with God's grand design.[4]

The Second Inaugural reveals what public theologians Reinhold Niebuhr and Martin Marty have described as an "ironic perspective." This outlook acknowledges the distance between human intention and divine will. Niebuhr explains, "It was Lincoln's achievement to embrace a paradox which lies at the center of the spirituality of all western culture; namely, the affirmation of a meaningful history and the religious reservation about the partiality and bias which the human actors and agents betray in the definition of meaning." The ironic perspective stems from the human agent's humble recognition that the unintended consequences of man's folly are directed by God toward some benevolent end neither side anticipates or desires: "Neither party expected for the war, the magnitude, or the duration, which it has already attained. Neither anticipated that the *cause* of the conflict might cease with, or even before, the conflict itself should cease. Each looked for an easier triumph, and a result less fundamental and astounding." Indeed, each side's early prediction of a swift victory had been proved wrong by four years of carnage. No one but God could have predicted the magnitude and duration of the war.[5]

After describing events leading up to the conflict, Lincoln concluded his second paragraph with another factual, declarative statement, "And the war came." With this sentence, the subject of the Second Inaugural moved from events leading up to the war to the war itself. The shift conveyed to the listener a sense that the war had taken on a life of its own beyond the control of any human agency. It gave the impression that human beings were not fully in control of events, that there was a higher power superintending the course of history.[6]

The body of the speech then advanced toward a theological reflection on the ultimate meaning of the war in reference to God's providence. Noting the religious character of the struggle, Lincoln pointed to the supreme irony of each side claiming to be divinely sanctioned in its cause: "Both read the same Bible, and pray to the same God; and each invokes His aid against each other." The fact that both sides invoked the Bible against each other did not lead Lincoln to skepticism about the Bible's authoritativeness as guide for human life. In the next sentence he made clear that slavery was incompatible with divine justice, since it violated the moral precept of Genesis 3:19: "It may seem strange that any men should dare ask a just God's assistance in wringing their bread from the sweat of other men's faces [Genesis 3:19]; but let us judge not that we be not judged [Matthew 7:1]." Though Lincoln clearly believed that slavery was evil and that it violated the teachings of both natural reason and revelation, he tempered his condemnation by quoting Christ's injunction: "let us judge not that we be not judged." If slavery was, in fact, evil and incompatible with divine justice, then what did Lincoln mean by asking his fellow citizens to refrain from judgment? Surely, he did not believe that the biblical precept of Matthew 7:1 meant what Stephen A. Douglas interpreted it to mean—a moral relativism that rejected the authoritativeness of religious claims in public life. Rather, Lincoln's admonition not to judge his brethren was a warning against the sin of pride. It reminded his audience in the North that neither side of the conflict was pure in rectitude. Using biblical language civil theologically, he applied the moral precept of Matthew 7:1 to the nation as a whole, asking the participants to examine their own conscience before condemning others. In a Christian spirit of charity, he prompted his audience to distinguish between the sin of slavery of which the entire nation was somehow responsible and the sinner, those southerners who held slaves. The same spirit of charity imbued Lincoln's Temperance Address when he showed genuine sympathy for those suffering from alcohol addiction in contrast to the crusading reformers of the Washington Society who saw drunkards as beyond redemption:

> Surely no Christian will adhere to this objection. If they believe, as they profess, that Omnipotence condescended to take on himself the form of sinful man, and, as such, to die an ignominious death for their sakes, surely they will not refuse submission to the infinitely lesser condescension, for the temporal, and perhaps eternal salvation of a large, erring, and unfortunate class of their own fellow creatures.[7]

Lincoln cautioned against the sin of pride in his earlier strictures against judging the southern people, who to him were "just what we would be in their situation." "When southern people tell us they are no more responsible for the origin of slavery, than we; I acknowledge the fact," he announced at Peoria in 1854. "I surely will not blame them for not doing what I should not know how to do myself." Perhaps Lincoln's admonition to not judge others was also a subtle reminder to northerners of their own culpability. The border states who remained within the Union kept their slaves and had rejected Lincoln's myriad attempts at compensated emancipation only to abolish the institution reluctantly when it was clear that the president's support for the Thirteenth Amendment doomed slavery to final extinction. The North could not claim perfect rectitude given their complicity in American slavery, the reluctance of the border states to end slavery, and its own virulent racism (vividly manifested during the New York City Draft Riots when an angry mob burned down a black orphanage to express their opposition to black freedom). At the moment of triumph, Lincoln pierced the North's moral solace by declaring, "The prayers of both could not be answered; that of neither has been answered fully." The arrogance of southern proslavery theologians who justified the sin of slavery, the moral callousness of northerners who were indifferent to the plight of African Americans, and the self-righteousness of northern abolitionists who sought to wreak vengeance upon their southern brethren were all culpable before a just God. In sum, Lincoln's combined reading of the biblical precepts of Genesis 3:19 and Matthew 1:7 in the Second Inaugural provides an outstanding example of "how to make a strong moral argument without being moralistic."[8]

The next sentence in the paragraph involved another crucial transition in which God becomes the subject of the speech. Lincoln stated:

> The Almighty has his own purposes. "Woe unto the world because of offences! for it must needs be that offences come; but woe to that man by whom the offence cometh!" If we shall suppose that American Slavery is one of those offences which, in the providence of God, must needs come, but which, having continued through His appointed time, He now wills to remove, and that He gives to both North and South, this terrible war, as the woe due to those by whom the offence came, shall we discern therein any

departure from those divine attributes which the believers in a Living God always ascribe to Him?

By declaring that "The Almighty has his own purposes," Lincoln taught his fellow countrymen a needed lesson in humility, reminding them of the vast distance between human pretense and divine omniscience. If the war was what neither side wanted or expected, then what was its reason? Was it meaningless? Was it absurd? Was it random? Or did the struggle point to some higher end? Citing Matthew 18:7, Lincoln suggested that slavery was an offence against God and that the war was a just punishment merited by the nation as a whole. It would be incorrect, however, to say that Lincoln asserted this with the utmost certainty, as if God had revealed it to him directly through a special dispensation. A careful reading of the Second Inaugural shows that he used conditional language: "If we shall suppose that American slavery is one of those offences. . . ." Thus, it is more accurate to state that, if the war was indeed a punishment for the collective sin of slavery, then it must be accepted as part of God's providence.

It is highly significant that Lincoln characterized the sin or offense in general terms as "American Slavery" rather than southern slavery, more particularly. This suggested that the war was given to "both North and South" collectively "as the woe due to those by whom the offence came." Judging from a transcendent perspective, neither side was blameless. The theology of the Second Inaugural thus eschews a millenarian dualism that divides opposing sides into the children of light and children of darkness. Divine judgment transcends sectional divisions. Just as Lincoln referred to the entire nation "under God" in the Gettysburg Address, so in the Second Inaugural he placed the entire nation before the throne of divine judgment. His suggestion of collective responsibility to a benevolent God appealed to a shared sense of national destiny and mission to reunite the American people. Lincoln's political theology inveighs against a tribal God who favors a particular group or race simply because of outward manifestations of piety or burnt offerings; on the contrary, it affirms an inclusive God who is just in dispensing mercy and judgment to both sides alike.[9]

Contrary to those who allege that Lincoln was a fatalist who passively resigned to an impersonal force that shaped his destiny, the Second Inaugural Address reveals the sixteenth president's biblical faith in a living and personal God who can be reached through prayer, who intervenes in his Creation, and who aids his creatures through divine grace:

> Fondly do we hope—fervently do we pray—that this mighty scourge of war may speedily pass away. Yet, if God wills that it continue, until all the wealth piled by the bond-man's two hundred and fifty years of unrequited toil shall be sunk, and until every drop of blood drawn with the lash, shall be paid by another drawn with the sword, as was said three thousand years ago, so still it must be said "the judgments of the Lord, are true and righteous altogether."

Despite the ultimate inscrutability of the divine will, Lincoln preached faith in God's superabundant justice. His national prayer invoked the mercy of a loving and living God to end the nation's suffering: "Fondly do we hope—fervently do we pray—that this mighty scourge of war may speedily pass away." Exhorting the American people to continue to trust in the ultimate justice of God, Lincoln appealed to Psalm 19—"the judgments of the Lord, are true and righteous altogether." Those who truly believe in God must trust that the national ordeal was not without purpose; it may have been used by God to bring about some greater good unknown to either side, perhaps the end of slavery and a "new birth of freedom." Romans 8:28 provides a parallel expression of this biblical faith: "And we know that all things work together for good to them that love God, to them who are called according to his purpose." Nonetheless, if God allowed the "fiery trial" of the Civil War to continue "until every drop of blood drawn with the lash, shall be paid by another drawn with the rod," then those who believe in him must still trust that it is to achieve some higher purpose. The metaphor of blood drawn by the whip being repaid with blood drawn from the sword conveyed the gravity of slavery as an offence against both God and man. The monstrous injustice of American slavery merited a just punishment. Yet if the suffering should continue, Lincoln asked, "shall we discern therein any departure from those divine attributes which the believers in a Living God always ascribe to Him?"[10]

Lincoln's invocation of a "Living God" with the attributes of justice and mercy acknowledges the existence of a personal God revealed by the Judeo-Christian faith, not an impersonal fate. More cynical scholars have suggested that Lincoln exempted himself from the class of believers in a living God by using the third person. As Ronald C. White, Jr., has shown, however, Lincoln's use of the third person in the Second Inaugural was stylistic, not esoteric. It was wholly in keeping with the form and style of other speeches. By asking the question in the third person, Lincoln prompted the entire nation to practice the Christianity that it preached, exhorting his fellow countrymen to trust in a benevolent God who will bring good out of the national suffering and to love thy neighbor. The use of the third person allowed Lincoln to avoid the suggestion of his own self-righteousness in contrast with the nation's hypocrisy.[11]

Toward the end of the speech, Lincoln appealed to the Christian teaching of charity as a means to reconcile former friends and to heal the nation's suffering: "With malice toward none; with charity for all; with firmness in the right, as God gives us to see the right, let us strive on to finish the work we are in; to bind up the nation's wounds; to care for him who shall have borne the battle, and for his widow, and his orphan—to do all which may achieve and cherish a just, and a lasting peace among ourselves, and with all nations." Lincoln's appeal to charity demonstrated the extent to which Christianity imbued his moral and political outlook. In the Second Inaugural, charity is contrasted to its opposite, malice—a deliberate, vindictive action against one's fellows. By adopting the Christian rule of charity, Lincoln exhorted his audience to love their enemies as well as their neighbors. Practically speaking, that meant forgiving the South for the war, extending mercy to the defeated, and taking all due measures to readmit the southern brethren back into the Union, just as the father had welcomed back his prodigal son. Lincoln's actions contrasted starkly with those who wanted to treat the southern states as conquered provinces, to hang all the leaders of the Confederacy, and to confiscate their property: to the victors go the spoils. Contrary to this pagan ethic, Lincoln manifested a Christian compassion in his treatment of the defeated South: "I shall do all I can to save the government, which is my sworn duty as well as my personal inclination. I shall do nothing in malice. What I deal with is too vast for malicious dealing." When Radical Republicans demanded an "ironclad oath" of both future loyalty and past purity before readmitting southern citizens to the Union, Lincoln responded: "On principle I dislike an oath which requires a man to swear he has not done wrong. It rejects the Christian principle of forgiveness on terms of repentance. I think it is enough if the man does no wrong hereafter." Only the superabundant love and healing of a living God was powerful enough to overcome the devastation caused by the war. According to Lincoln, the human striving for peace, charity, and justice was aided by divine illumination: "with firmness in the right, as God gives us to see the right." Lincoln's compassion toward the vanquished and his courage in resisting the temptation to manipulate the base emotions of hatred and revenge for the sake of bolstering his immediate popularity with a vindictive public further testify to his biblical magnanimity.[12]

Indeed, there is a stunning contrast between Lincoln's humility and charity in the Second Inaugural Address and the pride and malice of northern theologians bent on punishing the South. Around the same time of the Second Inaugural, the renowned preacher Henry Ward Beecher delivered a speech at Fort Sumter that cast eternal damnation upon his enemies:

> I charge the whole guilt of this war upon the ambitious, educated, plotting, political leaders of the South. They have shed this ocean of blood. . . . A day will come when God will reveal judgment, and arraign at his bar these mighty miscreants. . . . And from a thousand battle-fields shall rise up armies of airy witnesses, who, with the memory of their awful sufferings, shall confront these miscreants with shrieks of fierce accusation; and every pale and starved prisoner shall raise his skinny hand in judgment. Blood shall cry out for vengeance, and tears shall plead for justice, and grief shall silently beckon, and love, heart-smitten, shall wail for justice. . . . And, then, these guiltiest and most remorseless traitors . . . these most accursed and detested of criminals, that have drenched in needless blood, and moved the foundations of their times with hideous crimes and cruelty, caught up in black clouds full of voices of vengeance and lurid with punishment, shall be whirled aloft and plunged downward forever and forever in an endless retribution; while God shall say, "Thus shall it be to all who betray their country"; and all in heaven and upon the earth will say, "Amen!"

Comparing the expression of biblical faith in the Second Inaugural Address to Lincoln's contemporaries, Niebuhr concluded that "Lincoln's religious convictions were superior in depth and purity to those, not only of the political leaders of his day, but of the religious leaders of his era." Niebuhr claimed his view was the objective "judgment of sober history, uninfluenced by the usual hagiography of nations and their heroes."[13]

Because the Second Inaugural Address affirmed the inscrutability of God's will, assigned culpability to both sides of the conflict, and endorsed a spirit of charity and magnanimity toward the vanquished, it was not received well by radicals who demanded a triumphal assertion of the North's righteousness. In response to these critics, Lincoln explained to Thurlow Weed:

> I believe it [the Second Inaugural] is not immediately popular. Men are not flattered by being shown that there has been a difference in purpose between the Almighty and them. To deny it, however, in this case, is to deny that there is a God governing the world. It is a truth which I thought needed to be told; and as whatever humiliation there is in it, falls most directly on myself, I thought others might afford for me to tell it.[14]

To be sure, the public expression of biblical faith in the Second Inaugural in 1864 is remarkably consistent with Lincoln's earlier private expression in his Meditation on the Divine Will in 1862, his correspondence with Mrs. Gurney in 1862, and his youthful letters to Joshua Speed twenty years earlier in 1842. It is likely that Lincoln's vision of God's providence in the Second Inaugural Address was also inspired by the preaching of Phineas Gurley, whose New York Avenue church he attended during his presidency and whose Presbyterian theology was parallel to Lincoln's own understanding of the divine will. Given the coherence between his private and public religious outlook, the Second Inaugural has been characterized as a public "expression of Lincoln's living faith." All of these religious utterances, from his youthful correspondence with Joshua Speed to mature faith in the Second Inaugural Address, share a common preoccupation with the meaning of suffering and with the need to nevertheless trust in the ultimate benevolence of God. To say that Lincoln's expression of biblical faith was consistent, however, does not exclude the possibility that as a young man he had reservations about a literal interpretation of the Bible or that, in his maturity, especially after the death of his son Willie in 1862, his faith deepened. Though Lincoln did not confess fully the interior acts of his heart and the spiritual journey of his soul, a careful study of these sources nonetheless indicates that his private and public articulation of religious experience consistently affirmed the core elements of what has been described in this book as "biblical faith."[15]

Lincoln's letter to Albert Hodges written about a year before the Second Inaugural further demonstrates the consistency between his public and private articulation of biblical faith. Hodges was a newspaper editor and a War Democrat from Kentucky who expressed concerns about emancipation and the administration's war policies. In his response, Lincoln placed the struggle in the hands of God and, as he would in the Second Inaugural, pointed to the North's culpability in the conflict:

> I claim not to have controlled events, but confess plainly that events have controlled me. Now, at the end of three years struggle the nation's condition is not what either party, or any man devised, or expected. God alone can claim it.

Whither it is tending seems plain. If God now wills the removal of a great wrong, and wills also that we of the North as well as you of the South, shall pay fairly for our complicity in that wrong, impartial history will find therein new cause to attest and revere the justice and goodness of God.[16]

In his letter to Albert Hodges and the Second Inaugural alike, Lincoln announced, to the dismay of northern radicals, the guilt of both sides before God. In the former he spoke of the North's "complicity" in the "great wrong" of slavery. In the latter, he suggested that God "gives to both North and South, this terrible war, as the woe due to those by whom the offence [of slavery] came." In both utterances, he revealed the vast distance between God's intention and human pretensions. In the letter to Hodges, he explained that "the nation's condition is not what either party or any man devised, or expected." In the Second Inaugural he remarked: "The prayers of both could not be answered; that of neither has been answered fully." In both speeches, he humbly acknowledged the ultimate inscrutability of the divine will. In the former, he emphasized that "God alone can claim it," that is, claim to have moved events. In the latter, he stated: "The Almighty has his own purpose." Finally, in both he testified to the ultimate goodness, justice, and mercy of God in the face of suffering. In the former, he declared that "history will find therein new cause to attest and revere the justice and goodness of God." In the Second Inaugural he cited Psalm 19:9—"the judgments of the Lord, are true and righteous altogether." Contrary to critics who allege that Lincoln's civil theology was millenarian, his biblical republicanism led him to oppose the moral absolutism and self-righteousness of the radical abolitionists who claimed to know God's will and were called to execute it upon the South with a terrible vengeance.[17]

In conclusion, Lincoln's moral allegiance to the American regime was qualified by his commitment to higher standards of natural right. Like Jefferson, he believed that "an elective despotism was not the government" the United States fought for during the Revolution. The exercise of popular government is not absolute but is bounded by the moral law and the demands of virtue. Far from being a flatterer of American democracy, Lincoln was a friendly critic who prudently sought to bring his nation into conformity with universal standards of justice found in the Declaration. He sought to ennoble American democracy by challenging the nation to live up to its highest moral aspirations. Indeed, Lincoln's ironic designation of Americans as an "almost chosen people" invites a needed critical self-reflection on the meaning of our national Union and our destiny.[18]

Lincoln's example may serve as an inspiration to contemporary American leaders at all levels of community to reinvigorate the nation's "political faith." His leadership personifies the important reconciliation between consent and wisdom necessary to maintain the moral integrity of republican government. Indeed, his enduring teaching on democratic government exhorts today's "natural aristocracy" to preach the political creed of the regime against new forms of idolatry. Most notably, Martin Luther King, Jr., was a twentieth-century leader who articulated a version of biblical republicanism in his struggle for civil rights. It was no accident that King's celebrated "I Have A Dream" speech on August 28, 1963, was delivered at the site of the Lincoln Memorial, one hundred years after the Emancipation Proclamation. The beginning of King's speech established moral and political continuity with Lincoln and the Gettysburg Address: "Five score years ago, a great American, in whose symbolic shadow we stand, signed the Emancipation Proclamation." Like Lincoln, King did not undertake a new founding of the nation but sought to extend the principles of the founding more consistently. "It is a dream deeply rooted in the American dream." Like Lincoln, King was gifted in the use of principled rhetoric to express the nation's moral obligations:

> In a sense we have come to our nation's Capitol to cash a check. When the architects of our republic wrote the magnificent words of the Constitution and the Declaration of Independence, they were signing a promissory note to which every American was to fall heir. This note was the promise that all men would be guaranteed the unalienable rights of life, liberty, and the pursuit of happiness. It is obvious today that America has defaulted on this promissory note insofar as her citizens of color are concerned.

Both Lincoln and King characterized the founding principles of the nation in civil theological terms as a political creed: "I have a dream that one day this nation will rise up and live out the true meaning of its creed: 'We hold these truths to be self-evident; that all men are created equal.'" Both Lincoln and King saw American republicanism as grounded upon an ultimate moral foundation that bound the nation to a transcendent standard. Significantly, both leaders ultimately affirmed the unity of humanity and saw the destiny of black and white Americans inseparably linked through the promise and reality of the American dream. In the spirit of biblical magnanimity, neither man demonized his enemies or manipulated the base passions of fear, hatred, or revenge to elevate his own position. Both challenged the American people to live up to what was highest in themselves and in their tradition—"the better angels of our nature."

Lincoln's vision of a more perfect Union must remain inclusive, one that extends the founders' legacy of freedom to the entire human family. Indeed, there is strength in pluralism. America should continue to be a haven for those seeking civil and religious freedom. Without a shared consensus, however, amoral pluralism may lead to anarchy and balkanization. Lincoln also reminds us that the nation's motto, E Pluribus Unum, conveys a balanced relationship between the whole and the parts. The many are made one through fidelity to the common political faith.

Finally, Lincoln's biblical republicanism may provide future leaders with a model to vindicate the integrity of our humanity from the perennial temptation to play God or to dehumanize our fellows. As Lincoln noted in his Peoria Address nearly one hundred and fifty years ago, the American people must strive continually to make their Union "worthy of saving" by living up to the sacred obligations imposed upon them by God and their political faith in the Declaration.

NOTES

CHAPTER 1

1. Roy P. Basler, ed., *The Collected Works of Abraham Lincoln*, 8 vols. (New Brunswick, N.J.: Rutgers University Press, 1953–1955), 7:301–2.

2. Sydney E. Ahlstrom, *A Religious History of the American People* (New Haven, Conn.: Yale University Press, 1972), 672; Basler, *Collected Works*, 8:332–33.

3. Ronald C. White, Jr., *Lincoln's Greatest Speech: The Second Inaugural* (New York: Simon & Schuster, 2002), 192.

4. Robert Bellah, "Civil Religion in America," in Russell E. Richey and Donald G. Jones, eds., *Civil Religion in America* (New York: Harper & Row, 1974), 24. Also see Robert Bellah, "Religion and the Legitimation of the American Republic," in Robert Bellah and Phillip Hammond, eds., *Varieties of Civil Religion* (San Francisco: Harper and Row, 1980). In appreciation of Lincoln's global role, Mario Cuomo and Harold Holzer prepared an anthology of his writings for the people of Poland when they were building their democracy after the fall of the Iron Curtain. Mario Cuomo and Harold Holzer, eds., *Lincoln on Democracy* (New York: Harper Collins, 1990).

5. Basler, *Collected Works*, 3:462, 2:240, 454, 1:112, 2:243, 272, 3:81, 2:266, 275.

6. Ibid., 2:245, 4:3, 9; Harry V. Jaffa, *A New Birth of Freedom* (Lanham, Md.: Rowman and Littlefield, 2000), 123, 509; Dickinson quoted in Michael Novak, *On Two Wings: Humble Faith and Common Sense at the American Founding* (San Francisco: Encounter Books, 2002), 76, 135–36. Also see Allen C. Guelzo, *Abraham Lincoln: Redeemer President* (Grand Rapids, Mich.: William B. Eerdmans, 1999), 188, 196.

7. Basler, *Collected Works*, 2:242.

8. Richard John Neuhaus, *The Naked Public Square: Religion and Democracy in America* (Grand Rapids, Mich.: William B. Eerdmans, 1984); Ellis Sandoz, *A Government of Laws: Political Theory, Religion, and the American Founding* (Baton Rouge: Louisiana State University Press, 1990), 51–82; Jurgen Gebhardt, *Americanism: Revolutionary Order and Societal Self-Interpretation in the American Republic*, trans. Ruth Hein (Baton Rouge: Louisiana State University Press, 1993).

9. Bellah observes that Lincoln was "our greatest, perhaps our only civil theologian," in Bellah and Hammond, *Varieties of Civil Religion*; Neuhaus maintains that "Abraham Lincoln . . . has rightly been celebrated as the foremost theologian of the American experiment," in *Naked Public Square*, 61; John P. Diggins celebrates Lincoln as the founder of "a new political theology," in *The Lost Soul of American Politics: Virtue, Self-Interest and the Foundations of Liberalism* (Chicago: University of Chicago Press, 1986), 304–5; Michael P. Zuckert turns "to Lincoln for his wisdom on the problem of

civil religion," in Michael P. Zuckert, "Lincoln and the Problem of Civil Religion," in John A. Murley, Robert L. Stone, and William T. Braithwaite, eds., *Law and Philosophy: The Practice of Theory: Essays in Honor of George Anastaplo,* vol. 2 (Athens: Ohio University Press, 1992), 720–21; Glen E. Thurow emphasizes "that Lincoln is the central figure of American political religion," in *Abraham Lincoln and American Political Religion* (Albany: State University of New York Press, 1976), 10; Gebhardt maintains, "In word and deed Abraham Lincoln was a unique exponent of the 'political faith' of his fathers," in Gebhardt, *Americanism,* 189; Sidney Mead understands Lincoln to be "the most profound and representative theologian" of American civil religion," in "The Nation with the Soul of a Church," in Russell E. Richey and Donald G. Jones, eds., *American Civil Theology* (New York: Harper & Row, 1974), 63; Marvin B. Endy, Jr., calls Lincoln the "preeminent prophet of American civil religion . . . the high priest of American civic piety," in "Abraham Lincoln and American Civil Religion: A Reinterpretation," *Church History* 44 (1975): 229; and Harry V. Jaffa explains that "Lincoln saw himself not only as the savior of the [nation's] political institutions, but by that fact the founder of a political religion," in *Crisis of the House Divided: An Interpretation of the Issues in the Lincoln-Douglas Debates* (Garden City, N.Y.: Doubleday, 1959), 245.

10. David Hein, "Lincoln's Theology and Political Ethics," in Kenneth W. Thompson, ed., *Essays on Lincoln's Faith and Politics* (Lanham, Md.: University Press of America, 1983), 160–85. David Hein concisely summarizes this civil theological view of public life:

> It is important to remember that Lincoln's political ethics were grounded in his faith. To state this is to say more than that he derived his fundamental political attitudes to such issues as slavery from the understandings of man and labor and corporate responsibility contained within the passages of biblical canon. It is to affirm that his actions as a statesman and his thinking about his duties as a leader were consistently carried out within the vistas opened up by an overall theological outlook. It is to point out that Lincoln's ethics were theocentric, God-centered; it is to note that his political ethics are incapable of being grasped apart from his theology.

11. John Courtney Murray, *We Hold These Truths: Catholic Reflections on the American Proposition* (Kansas City, Mo.: Sheed and Ward, 1960); Walter Lippman, *The Public Philosophy* (Chicago: University of Chicago Press).

12. Eric Voegelin, *Order and History,* vol. 1, *Israel and Revelation* (Baton Rouge: Louisiana State University Press, 1974); Christopher Lasch, *The Revolt of the Elites and the Betrayal of Democracy* (New York: W. W. Norton, 1995), 222.

13. Eric Voegelin, *The New Science of Politics: An Introduction* (Chicago: University of Chicago Press, 1952), 27–51.

14. Eric Voegelin analyzes the historical derailment of civil theology into ideology (ersatz religion) as well. See Eric Voegelin, *Science, Politics, and Gnosticism: Two Essays* (Chicago: Regnery, 1968), 80–81, 107–87.

15. This lineage might include the following: Plato's condemnation of "unseemly symbolizations of the gods" in the *Republic* (377b–94c); Varro's classification of three genera of theology—mythical, physical, and civil; Cicero's inquiry concerning the nature of the gods and divine providence; Augustine's critique of pagan religion and his transcendent distinction between the *civitas terrena* and the *civitas Dei;* Machiavelli's contempt for the Christian virtues and his celebration of the martial virtues fostered by pagan religion; Spinoza's tripartite classification of religion as *amor dei in-*

tellectualis, religio catholica, and *vana religio;* Hobbes's attempt to ground political authority on the basis of a secularized civil theology; and, finally, Rousseau's articulation
of a nonsectarian, civil religion in the *Social Contract.* These constitute only a few of
the more notable examples of civil theology. They have been mentioned not as an ex-
haustive list but as reference points to an inquiry concerning the proper relationship
between religion and politics. See Voegelin, *New Science of Politics,* 27–106, 152–61;
Eric Voegelin, *Order and History,* vol. 3, *Plato and Aristotle* (Baton Rouge: Louisiana
State University Press, 1987), 67–70; Plato, *The Republic,* ed. Allan Bloom (New York:
Basic Books, 1968), 55–72; Cicero, *The Nature of the Gods,* trans. Horace C. P. McGregor
(New York: Penguin, 1984), 152–90, 234–35; St. Augustine, *The City of God,* trans. Marcus Dods (New York: Modern Library, 1950), 182–206, 478–669; Niccolo Machiavelli,
The Discourses, ed. Bernard Crick and trans. Leslie J. Walker (New York: Penguin,
1987), 139–52, 244, 277–81, 288–90, 312–13, 369–72, 385–90, 467; Benedict de Spinoza, *A Theologico-Political Treatise,* trans. R. H. M. Elwes (New York: Dover, 1951),
182–89; Thomas Hobbes, *Leviathan,* ed. Richard Tuck (Cambridge: Cambridge University Press, 1991), 75, 79–85, 90–91, 148, 184–87, 486; Jean-Jacques Rousseau, *The Social Contract,* trans. Maurice Cranston (New York: Penguin, 1986), 176–87.

16. Diggins, *Lost Soul of American Politics,* 297. Ellis Sandoz in *Government of
Laws* traces the historical lineage of civil theology and then subsequently describes its
influence on the American founding. Like Voegelin, Jurgen Gebhardt views American
civil theology as a form of societal self-interpretation (*Americanism,* 206).

17. Bellah, "Civil Religion in America," 24–25.

18. Neuhaus, *Naked Public Square,* 60, 80–81. Neuhaus states:

> [A] religious evacuation of the public square cannot be sustained, either in concept or in
> practice. When religion in any traditional or recognizable form is excluded from the public
> square, it does not mean that the public square is in fact naked. This is the other side of
> the "naked public square" metaphor. When recognizable religion is excluded, the vacuum
> will be filled by *ersatz* religion, by religion bootlegged into public space under other names.
> Again, to paraphrase Spinoza: transcendence abhors a vacuum. The reason why the naked
> public square cannot, in fact remain naked is in the very nature of law and laws. If law and
> laws are not seen to be coherently related to basic presuppositions about right and wrong,
> good and evil, they will be condemned as illegitimate. After having excluded traditional
> religion, then, the legal and political trick is to address questions of right and wrong in a
> way that is not "contaminated" by the label "religious." This relatively new sleight-of-
> hand results in what many have called "civil religion." It places a burden upon the law to
> act religiously without being suspected of committing religion.

19. Brian Tierney, *Crisis of Church and State, 1050–1300: With Selected Documents*
(Toronto: University of Toronto Press, 1988).

20. See Voegelin, *Science, Politics, and Gnosticism,* 53–73; and Albert Camus, *The
Rebel* (New York: Vintage Books, 1956).

21. Leo Strauss, *What Is Political Philosophy? And Other Studies* (1959; rpt.,
Chicago: University of Chicago Press, 1988); Neuhaus, *Naked Public Square,* 80–81;
David Walsh, *After Ideology: Recovering the Spiritual Foundations of Freedom* (San Fran-
cisco: Harper Collins, 1990).

22. *Zorach* v. *Clauson* is cited from Lee Epstein and Thomas Walker, eds., *Constitutional Law for a Changing America* (Washington, D.C.: CQ Press, 2001), 313.

23. Jaffa, *New Birth of Freedom,* 140–42, 147–49, 153–59; Novak, *On Two Wings,*

140–41; Michael J. Malbin, *Religion and Politics: The Intentions of the Authors of the First Amendment* (Washington, D.C.: AEI, 1978), 12–28; James Reichley, *Religion in American Public Life* (Washington, D.C.: Brookings Institution, 1985), 112–13.

24. Reichley, *Religion in American Public Life,* 113; Rush cited in Novak, *On Two Wings,* 34–35; Adams cited in Neuhaus, *Naked Public Square,* 95, and in Gebhardt, *Americanism,* 13; Tocqueville cited in Reichley, *Religion in American Public Life,* 113.

25. Basler, *Collected Works,* 4:482, 6:497. Also see Lucas E. Morel, *Lincoln's Sacred Effort* (Lanham, Md.: Lexington Books, 2000), 85–125; Schuyler Colfax, in Memorial Address in Chicago, April 30, 1865, cited in William E. Barton, *The Soul of Abraham Lincoln* (New York: George H. Doran, 1920), 95.

26. Reichley, *Religion in American Public Life,* 102–3; Lewis Copeland and Lawrence W. Lamm, eds., *The World's Great Speeches,* 3d ed. (New York: Dover), 254–55. Also see Paul F. Boller, *George Washington and Religion* (Dallas: Southern Methodist University Press, 1963).

27. Richard Brookhiser, *Founding Father* (New York: Free Press, 1996), 144–56; Reichley, *Religion in American Public Life,* 103. Brookhiser states: "Lincoln is the premier American bender of the Bible to political purposes. He was a greater stylist than Washington, with the cadences of the King James Version in his lungs. But in this, as in so many other things, Lincoln followed where the founders led."

28. Basler, *Collected Works,* 4:9–10.

29. Ibid., 2:552–53. In addition, see 2:274, 385, 453, 465, 3:27, 80, 87, 89–90, 205, 232–34, 304, 311, 423–25, 443–45, 469, 4:1, 4–5, 9, 17, 19, 20, 432–33.

30. Ibid., 3:423–25.

31. Ibid., 4:17.

32. Ibid., 2:500, 3:205.

33. Ibid., 3:80.

34. Ibid., 2:552–53.

35. John Adams to John Taylor of Caroline, Apr. 15, 1814; Copeland and Lamm, *World's Greatest Speeches,* 255.

36. For instance, they may be conveyed in Holy Scripture (the Bible), in a speech (the Gettysburg address), in the plays of Shakespeare, in a founding document (the Declaration of Independence), in a formal treatise (Locke's *Second Treatise on Government*), in a mythical account (the *Iliad*), in music (consider the influence of Verdi's operas on Italian nationalism), in art and architecture (consider Michelangelo's David as a political inspiration to Florentines).

37. See David M. Potter, *The Impending Crisis: 1848–1861,* ed. Don E. Fehrenbacher (New York: Harper & Row, 1976). It would be difficult to understand Lincoln and the antebellum period without considering the influence of the following on public opinion at the time: Senator John Hammond's "Cotton is King" speech; Harriet Beecher Stowe's *Uncle Tom's Cabin;* Hinton Rowan Helper's *The Impending Crisis of the South;* George Fitzhugh's "mud-sill" critique of free labor; John C. Calhoun's doctrine of state sovereignty and nullification; Daniel Webster's vision of the Union; Stephen A. Douglas's doctrine of popular sovereignty; Frederick A. Ross's proslavery theology; William Seward's "Higher Law" and "Irrepressible Conflict" speeches; Wendell Phillips's and William Lloyd Garrison's radical abolitionism and their case for disunion; Charles Sumner's "The Crime against Kansas" phillipic; and Frederick Douglass's "Fourth of July Oration."

38. Yves René Marie Simon, *A General Theory of Authority* ([Notre Dame, Ind.]: University of Notre Dame Press, 1962), 119; Murray, *We Hold These Truths.*

39. Basler, *Collected Works*, 4:432–33. Lincoln's view of the southern cultural elite's influence on public opinion is corroborated by the Civil War–era historian Allan Nevins in *Ordeal of the Union*, 2 vols (New York: Scribner, 1947), 1:242–43. In 1857, Hinton Rowan Helper, a native son of Dixie from North Carolina, published his controversial and influential work, *The Impending Crisis of the South*. This work attributed the South's social, economic, and political decline to the corruption of its cultural elite, "the slaveocracy." Helper maintained that the vast socioeconomic differences between the elite Southern gentry who owned large plantations and the mass of small farmers who subsisted off small plots of land prevented any meaningful dissent in the political process. He warned his fellow southerners that the "slaveocracy" was leading Dixie down a suicidal path. It is quite possible that Lincoln's case against the southern elite was influenced, to some extent, by Helper's argument. In accordance with Helper's work, Lincoln maintained that the act of secession was prepared far in advance by the southern elite, whom he refers to as "the movers" of secession. Indeed, southern fire-eaters molded the climate of opinion that made secession both compelling and attractive.

40. Basler, *Collected Works*, 3:27, 424, 234, 2:242.

41. Ibid., 3:301–2. For a poignant recollection of Calhoun's responsibility for the Civil War, see "Calhoun's Real Monument" in Walt Whitman's *Specimen Days*.

42. Basler, *Collected Works*, 1:411–12.

43. Jaffa, *New Birth of Freedom*, 24–26.

44. Basler, *Collected Works*, 4:236.

45. Rogan Kersh, *Dreams of a More Perfect Union* (Ithaca, N.Y.: Cornell University Press, 2001); David F. Ericson, *The Shaping of American Liberalism: The Debates over Ratification, Nullification, and Slavery* (Chicago: University of Chicago Press, 1993), 92.

46. White, *Lincoln's Greatest Speech*, 103, 105; Miller, *Lincoln's Virtues*, 67. See James M. McPherson, *For Cause and Comrades: Why Men Fought in the Civil War* (New York: Oxford University Press, 1996).

47. White, *Lincoln's Greatest Speech*, 109; Guelzo, *Abraham Lincoln*, 36–37, 50–51, 80–81.

48. Sandoz, *Government of Laws*; Gebhardt, *Americanism*; Paul A. Rahe, *Republics Ancient and Modern* (Chapel Hill: University of North Carolina Press, 1994); Gordon S. Wood, *The Creation of the American Republic, 1776–1787* (Chapel Hill: University of North Carolina Press, 1969); Clinton Rossiter, *Seedtime of the Republic: The Origin of the American Tradition of Political Liberty* (New York: Harcourt Brace, 1953); Barry Alan Shain, *The Myth of American Individualism: The Protestant Origins of American Political Thought* (Princeton, N.J.: Princeton University Press, 1994); Hannah Arendt, *On Revolution* (New York: Penguin, 1987); Thomas L. Pangle, *The Spirit of Modern Republicanism: The Moral Vision of the American Founders and the Philosophy of Locke* (Chicago: University of Chicago Press, 1988); Ericson, *Shaping of American Liberalism*; Louis Hartz, *The Liberal Tradition in America: An Interpretation of American Political Thought since the Revolution* (New York: Harcourt Brace Jovanivich, 1955).

49. David Herbert Donald, "Abraham Lincoln: Whig in the White House," in *Lincoln Reconsidered: Essays on the Civil War Era*, 2d ed. (New York: Random House, 1961), 187–208; James H. Read, *Power versus Liberty: Madison, Hamilton, Wilson, and Jefferson* (Charlottesville: University Press of Virginia, 2000); Basler, *Collected Works*, 4:426.

50. Alexander Hamilton, James Madison, and John Jay, *The Federalist Papers*, ed. Clinton Rossiter (New York: Mentor Books, 1961), no. 9.

51. Basler, *Collected Works*, 4:268.

52. Reinhold Niebuhr, *Reinhold Niebuhr: Theologian of Public Life,* ed. Larry L. Rasmussen (Minneapolis: Fortress Press, 1991), 255–56. Niebuhr emphasizes the correspondence between the teachings of the Bible and the justification of democratic government: "[F]ree societies are the fortunate products of the confluence of Christian and secular forces. For a long time a debate has been waged between Christian and secular forces on the question of whether democracy is the product of Christian faith or a secular culture. The debate has been inconclusive because, as a matter of history, both Christian and secular forces were involved in establishing the political institutions of democracy; and the cultural resources of modern free societies are jointly furnished by both Christianity and modern secularism." For a readable, concise, and cogent account that documents the founders' views of the compatibility of faith and reason, see Novak, *On Two Wings;* also see a valuable collection of primary sources: Ellis Sandoz, ed., *Political Sermons of the American Founding Era, 1730–1805* (Indianapolis: Liberty Press, 1991).

53. Cited in Novak, *On Two Wings,* 35, 37; Adams quoted in David McCullough, *John Adams* (New York: Simon and Schuster, 2001), 619; Alexis de Tocqueville, *Democracy in America,* trans. George Lawrence and ed. J. P. Mayer (New York: Doubleday, 1969), 292–93.

54. Ahlstrom, *Religious History,* 68–83, 123–50. Also see Perry Miller, *Errand into the Wilderness* (Cambridge, Mass.: Harvard University Press, 1976); Conrad Cherry, ed., *God's New Israel: Religious Interpretations of American Destiny* (Englewood Cliffs, N.J.: Prentice-Hall, 1971).

55. Michael B. Levy, ed., *Political Thought in America: An Anthology* (Chicago: Dorsey Press, 1988), 6–12 (I have modernized the seventeenth-century spelling but followed Winthrop's punctuation); Bellah, "Civil Religion in America," 40.

56. Hamilton, Madison, and Jay, *Federalist Papers,* no. 1, 33.

57. Ibid., no. 11.

58. Ibid., no. 11, 91.

59. "Inauguration Address, March 4, 1801," in Adrienne Koch and William Peden, eds., *The Life and Selected Writings of Thomas Jefferson* (1944; rpt., New York: Modern Library, 1993), 299; Richard Hofstadter, *The Idea of a Party System: The Rise of Legitimate Opposition in the United States, 1780–1840* (Berkeley: University of California Press, 1969); Jaffa, *New Birth of Freedom.*

60. "The Constitution Not a Compact," in Charles M. Wiltse, ed., *The Papers of Daniel Webster: Speeches and Formal Writings,* vol. 1, *1800–1833,* (Hanover, N.H.: University Press of New England, 1986), 611, 618–19; White, *Lincoln's Greatest Speech,* 73.

61. Mark E. Neely, Jr., *The Last Best Hope of Earth: Abraham Lincoln and the Promise of America* (Cambridge, Mass.: Harvard University Press, 1993), 611, 618–19; Basler, *Collected Works,* 4:426, 439.

62. Basler, *Collected Works,* 2:222, 242.

63. Neely, *Last Best Hope;* Basler, *Collected Works,* 5:537.

64. Hein, "Lincoln's Theology and Political Ethics."

65. Basler, *Collected Works,* 4:236, 7:282. Lincoln once explained: "I claim not to have controlled events, but confess plainly that events have controlled me. Now, at the end of three years struggle the nation's condition is not what either party, or any man devised or expected. God alone can claim it. Whither it is tending seems plain. If God now wills the removal of a great wrong, and wills also that we of the North as well as you of the South, shall pay fairly for our complicity in that wrong, impartial justice will find therein new cause to attest and revere the justice and goodness of God."

66. Bellah, "Civil Religion in America," 31; Jaffa, *New Birth of Freedom*, 3–72; Basler, *Collected Works*, 3:375–76; Koch and Peden, *Writings of Jefferson*, 656–57; Basler, *Collected Works*, 4:240.

67. Koch and Peden, *Writings of Jefferson*, 641; cited in Allan Nevins, *The Emergence of Lincoln*, 2 vols. (New York: Scribner, 1950) 1:200; Basler, *Collected Works*, 3:375, 5:51–53.

68. Koch and Peden, *Writings of Jefferson*, 622; Basler, *Collected Works*, 4:438.

69. Koch and Peden, *Writings of Jefferson*, 299–300.

70. Ibid., 258, 659, 299–300.

71. Ibid., 579–80.

72. Jaffa, *New Birth of Freedom*, 20–26.

73. Koch and Peden, *Writings of Jefferson*, 257–58.

74. Basler, *Collected Works*, 3:410, 220.

75. Ibid., 3:227, 300.

76. Two fine complementary works on Lincoln's religion and politics are Hein, "Lincoln's Theology and Political Ethics," 105–79; and Lucas Morel's *Lincoln's Sacred Effort*.

Chapter 2

1. Basler, *Collected Works*, 7:542. William J. Wolf, a Protestant minister, stated in 1959 that "Lincoln's knowledge of the Bible far exceeded the content-grasp of most present-day clergymen," in *The Religion of Abraham Lincoln* (New York: Seabury, 1963) 39. Guelzo observes that Lincoln's "speeches and public documents were littered with biblical allusions from the 1830's onward" (*Abraham Lincoln*, 151). For Lincoln's reading of the Bible, also see William Lee Miller, *Lincoln's Virtues: An Ethical Biography* (New York: Alfred A. Knopf, 2002), 50.

2. White, *Lincoln's Greatest Speech*, 112; Morel, *Lincoln's Sacred Effort*; Basler, *Collected Works*, 4:3. For Lincoln's appeal to natural theology against slavery, see 2:222, 3:462–63, 479–80, 4:3, 9, 10:44–45.

3. The exchange between Speed and Lincoln is cited in Richard N. Current, *The Lincoln Nobody Knows* (New York: Hill and Wang, 1984), 64–65.

4. Basler, *Collected Works*, 5:419–20.

5. Ibid., 2:3–4.

6. Ibid., 3:541; Thomas Aquinas, *Summa Theologiae*, I–II, Q.95, a.3.

7. Basler, *Collected Works*, 5:403–4, 478, 7:535. Elton Trueblood states, "Even a cursory study of Lincoln's speaking style makes the sensitive reader aware of the numerous ways in which the Bible influenced his style, both spoken and written. . . . Biblical language was so deeply embedded in the great man's mind that it became his normal way of speaking" (*Abraham Lincoln: Theologian of American Anguish* [New York: Phoenix Press, 1986], 76–77).

8. Basler, *Collected Works*, 4:270–71. For some examples of how Lincoln used biblical language in a theological sense, see 4:51, 52, 160, 190–91, 199, 204, 207, 220–21, 226, 234, 236, 403–4, 478, 5:53, 212–13, 215–16, 279, 356, 404, 478, 518, 537, 7:535, 8:50–51, 332–33.

9. Ibid., 8:332–33.

10. Mark A. Noll, "'Both . . . Pray to the Same God': The Singularity of Lincoln's Faith in the Era of the Civil War," *Journal of the Abraham Lincoln Association* 18, no. 1 (1997): 4. Noll elegantly describes the theological depth of Lincoln's Second Inaugural:

"The simple truth is that none of America's great religious leaders—as defined by contemporaries or later critics—mustered the theological power so economically expressed in Lincoln's second inaugural. None probed so profoundly the ways of God or the response of humans to the divine constitution of the world. None penetrated as deeply into the nature of Providence. And none described the fate of humanity before God with the humility of sagacity of the President." The final chapter of this work will consider the Second Inaugural more fully as an expression of Lincoln's living faith in response to the millenarian political theologies of his own time.

11. Basler, *Collected Works*, 5:403–4.

12. John G. Nicolay and John Hay, *Abraham Lincoln: A History*, 10 vols. (New York: Century, 1890), 6:340–42.

13. Guelzo, *Abraham Lincoln*, 327.

14. Basler, *Collected Works*, 4:16–17. See chap. 3 for more on Lincoln and Fitzhugh.

15. Ibid., 3:376, 2:266.

16. George Anastaplo, *The Constitution of 1787: A Commentary* (Baltimore: Johns Hopkins University Press, 1989), 1. For some examples of how Lincoln used biblical language in a didactic sense, see Basler, *Collected Works*, 1:167, 273, 315, 347, 2:141, 275, 278, 318, 499, 501, 510–11, 461, 3:17, 436, 462.

17. Basler, *Collected Works*, 2:461.

18. Don E. Fehrenbacher, *Prelude to Greatness: Lincoln in the 1850's* (Stanford, Calif.: Stanford University Press, 1962), 70–95; Miller, *Lincoln's Virtues*, 332–33. See Guelzo, "Moral Principle is all that Unites us," in *Abraham Lincoln*.

19. Dwight G. Anderson, "Quest for Immortality: A Theory of Abraham Lincoln's Political Psychology," in Gabor S. Boritt and Norman O. Forness, eds., *The Historian's Lincoln: Pseudohistory, Psychohistory, and History* (Urbana: University of Illinois Press, 1988), 263–64; Charles B. Strozier, *Lincoln's Quest for Union: Public and Private Meanings* (New York: Basic Books, 1982). To Strozier, another psychohistorian, the metaphor reveals Lincoln's subconscious quest for inner harmony and order.

20. Basler, *Collected Works*, 3:436.

21. Diggins, *Lost Soul of American Politics*, 303; Guelzo, *Abraham Lincoln*, 38. For examples of Lincoln's use of biblical language in an evocative sense, see Basler, *Collected Works*, 1:115, 178, 204, 278–79, 2:132, 278, 318, 366, 404, 498–99, 3:95, 488.

22. Morel, *Lincoln's Sacred Effort*, 45; Jaffa, *New Birth of Freedom*.

23. Basler, *Collected Works*, 1:178–79.

24. Ibid., 1:439.

25. David Herbert Donald, *Lincoln* (New York: Simon & Schuster, 1995), 125; Basler, *Collected Works*, 1:472–73.

26. Guelzo, *Abraham Lincoln*; Basler, *Collected Works*, 3:344, 4:121; Novak, *On Two Wings* (Blackstone and Wilson quoted on 33 and 37).

27. Voegelin, *Order and History*, vol. 3, *Plato and Aristotle*, 28–39.

28. Relying only on partial statement by Herndon, Glen Thurow denies the relevance of whether Lincoln sincerely believed in what he stated publicly about religion:

> The questions of whether Lincoln had a private faith in God and if so, what his beliefs were, are unaswerable. Although these questions have stirred many men, both scholars and non-scholars, since Lincoln's law partner, William Herndon, tendentiously announced that the dead Lincoln had been an unbeliever, we have no reliable knowledge of Lincoln's private faith, if there was any. We have only the testimony of men like Herndon who

heard what they wished to hear. Our only trustworhty knowledge of Lincoln's "religion" appears in his public speeches and writings. These works reveal that Lincoln's thought was preoccupied with politics, to say the least. Except for a few expressions of sympathy, fom which little can be deduced, all of Lincoln's religious expressions appear as part of utterances that directly address political problems, that are given in a political context, or that intend to have political effects. Lincoln's religion, as we know it, is part of his political rhetoric and cannot be divorced from it. In this sense, Lincoln's religion is political religion. (Thurow, *Lincoln and American Political Religion*, xii.)

I further disagree with Thurow's assertion that "we have no reliable knowledge of Lincoln's private faith, if there was any." On the contrary, as has been shown throughout this chapter, there is ample evidence from the primary sources to confirm Lincoln's private belief in what has been characterized as biblical faith. In addition to neglecting the primary sources that express Lincoln's private faith, Thurow ignores the manifest coherence between Lincoln's private expression of this faith and his public articulation of it. See chap. 4 for a discussion of Thurow's Straussian interpretation of Lincoln's "political religion."

29. Donald, *Lincoln*, 566–67. Donald states: "He might have put his argument in terms of the doctrine of necessity, in which he had believed, but that was not a dogma accepted by most Americans. Addressing a devout, Bible reading public, Lincoln knew he would be understood when he invoked the familiar doctrine of exact retribution, the belief that the punishment for a violation of God's law would equal the offense itself." See White's cogent response to the utility argument in *Lincoln's Greatest Speech*, 123–27.

30. J. G. Randall and R. N. Current, *Lincoln, the President*, vol. 4, *The Last Full Measure* (New York: Dodd, Mead, 1955), 375; Lincoln quoted in William Eleroy Curtis, *The True Abraham Lincoln* (Philadelphia: J. B. Lippincott, 1903), 383.

31. Thurow, *Lincoln and American Political Religion*, xii (see n. 24 above); Herndon to J. E. Remsburg, Sept. 10, 1887, is cited in Barton, *Soul of Abraham Lincoln*, 142; David Herbert Donald, *Lincoln's Herndon* (1948; rpt., New York: Da Capo, 1989), 214.

32. William H. Herndon and Jesse W. Weik, *Herndon's Life of Lincoln* (1942; rpt., New York: Da Capo Press, 1983), 360; Basler, *Collected Works*, 2:96–97.

33. Herndon quoted in Barton, *Soul of Abraham Lincoln*, 77–78.

34. Randall and Current, *Lincoln, the President*, vol. 4, *The Last Full Measure*, 373–74. Randall and Current explain:

If Lincoln was no professing Christian, neither was he in any sense an atheist. Indeed, even Herndon did not really think he was. Herndon was driven to overstatement by his zeal against the cant of pious moralizers, yet he sometimes qualified his statements and contradicted himself. "I affirm that Mr. Lincoln died an unbeliever—was not an evangelical Christian," he said in a rebuttal against the Rev. James A. Reed. On another occasion Herndon declared that Lincoln "was in short an infidel—was a universalist—was a Unitarian— a Theist. He did not believe that Jesus was God nor the son of God etc." Of course, a theist is not an atheist and, except by fundamentalist standards, a universalist or unitarian is hardly an infidel. Nor is a person necessarily an unbeliever simply because he is not an "evangelical" Christian.

35. Donald, *Lincoln's Herndon*, 359.
36. Guelzo, *Abraham Lincoln*, 34–35, 20; Barton, *Soul of Abraham Lincoln*, 271–72.

37. Barton, *Soul of Abraham Lincoln,* 152–53.

38. Ibid., 153.

39. Basler, *Collected Works,* 1:320; Herndon and Weik, *Herndon's Life of Lincoln,* 359–60.

40. Barton, *Soul of Abraham Lincoln,* 33, 64–65; Basler, *Collected Works,* 1:382–83.

41. Basler, *Collected Works,* 1:383.

42. James Smith, *The Christian's Defence, Containing a Fair Statement and Impartial Examination of the Leading Objections Urged by Infidels, against the Antiquity, Genuineness, Credibility, and Inspiration of the Holy Scripture* (Cincinnati: J. A. James, 1843); Ninian Edwards quoted in White, *Lincoln's Greatest Speech,* 131; Guelzo, *Abraham Lincoln,* 149–53. Edward's testimony may be found in "A Lecture on the Religion of Abraham Lincoln," in *Scribner's Monthly,* published by Pastor James A. Reed of the First Presbyterian Church of Springfield, Ill.

43. White, *Lincoln's Greatest Speech,* 129–44.

44. Ibid., 138; Noah Brooks to James A. Reed, Dec. 31, 1872, originally cited in Reed, "The Later Life and Religious Sentiments of Abraham Lincoln," *Scribner's Monthly* 6 (July 1873): 340; Taft and Pomoroy cited in White, *Lincoln's Greatest Speech,* 111 (Pomoroy originally cited in Rebecca R. Pomoroy, "What His Nurse Knew," *Magazine of History* 32, no. 1 [1926]: 47).

45. White, *Lincoln's Greatest Speech,* 136–37. "Though Lincoln's fatalism grew and developed while he was in the White House, it was in itself nothing new with him, not a product of the Presidential Years. . . . Whatever the source of Lincoln's religious feeling, it became a vibrant force in his thought and action as President" (Randall and Current, *Last Full Measure,* 370, 376–77). Other historians to use the term "fatalism" include Donald, *Lincoln,* 15; Stephen B. Oates, *With Malice toward None: The Life of Abraham Lincoln* (New York: Mentor, 1978), 29, 70–71, 292–93. For a defense of Lincoln's belief in free will, see Miller, *Lincoln's Virtues,* 89–91.

46. Basler, *Collected Works,* 1:267. Speed's testimony is cited in Current, *The Lincoln Nobody Knows,* 64–65.

47. Basler, *Collected Works,* 1:289.

48. Ibid., 7:301–2.

49. Ibid., 6:535–36.

50. Ibid., 4:226; Nevins, *Emergence,* 2:99.

51. Basler, *Collected Works,* 5:478.

52. See Hein, "Lincoln's Theology and Political Ethics"; Oates, *Malice toward None,* 413.

53. Basler, *Collected Works,* 6:535–36; C. S. Lewis, *The Problem of Pain* (New York: MacMillan Publishing Company, 1962).

54. Ibid., 7:535.

55. Howard K. Beale, ed., *The Diary of Gideon Welles: Secretary of the Navy under Lincoln and Johnson,* 3 vols. (New York: W. W. Norton, 1960), 1:142–43.

56. Robert B. Warden, *An Account of the Private Life and Public Services of Salmon Portland Chase* (Cincinnati: Wilstach, Baldwin, 1874), 481–82 (also quoted in Nicolay and Hay, *Abraham Lincoln,* 6:159–60); F. B. Carpenter, *Six Months in the White House with Abraham Lincoln: The Story of a Picture* (New York: Hurd and Houghton, 1866), 89, 90.

57. David E. Long, *The Jewel of Liberty: Abraham Lincoln's Re-election and the End of Slavery* (Mechanicsburg, Pa.: Stackpole, 1994); Basler, *Collected Works,* 7:500, 507, 302.

58. Rusling and Sickles quoted in Barton, *Soul of Abraham Lincoln,* 198–202.

59. Keckley quoted in Barton, *Soul of Abraham Lincoln,* 203–4.

60. See J. David Greenstone, *The Lincoln Persuasion: Remaking American Liberalism* (Princeton, N.J.: Princeton University Press, 1993).

CHAPTER 3

1. Basler, *Collected Works*, 3:205; Alexander H. Stephens, *Public and Private Letters and Speeches* (Philadelphia: National Publishing, 1866), 721–22; Ahlstrom, *Religious History*, 673. See also Jaffa, *New Birth of Freedom*, 153–69.

2. Basler, *Collected Works*, 5:51–53; George Fitzhugh, *Cannibals All! or, Slaves without Masters*, ed. C. Vann Woodward (Cambridge, Mass.: Harvard University Press, Belknap Press, 1988), 243–44; Basler, *Collected Works*, 2:275, 283, 3:205, 301, 4:115; J. H. Hammond, "Slavery in the Light of Political Science," in E. N. Elliott, ed., *Cotton Is King, and Pro-slavery Arguments comprising the Writings of Hammond, Harper, Christy, Stringfellow, Hodge, Bledsoe, and Cartwright, on This Important Subject* (New York: Negro Universities Press, 1969), 637–38; Basler, *Collected Works*, 3:375.

3. "The War of the South Vindicated," *Southern Presbyterian Review* 15, no. 4 (1863): 497–98.

4. Fitzhugh, *Cannibals All!* 7; Guelzo, *Abraham Lincoln*, 137; Herndon and Weik, *Herndon's Life of Lincoln*, 293; Gebhardt, *Americanism*, 188; George Fitzhugh, *Sociology for the South; or, The Failure of Free Society* (1854; rpt., New York: B. Franklin, 1965), 94. In *Americanism*, Jurgen Gebhardt correctly emphasizes the extent to which Lincoln's political thought was developed as a dialectical response to Fitzhugh: "Lincoln perceived the conflict of two types of transcendental truths in American society, though they could represent only one truth—that is, the truth of the fathers. Lincoln consciously and emphatically accepted the claim of Fitzhugh's 'Sociology of the South': American society can be based on but *one* principle. . . . Lincoln transformed a theoretical insight into a plausible symbolic formulation by taking Fitzhugh's argument seriously and turning it against him. It is a matter of slavery as a principle of social order, not of the particular institution in the South."

5. Frederick A. Ross, *Slavery Ordained of God* (1857; rpt., Miami, Fla.: Mnemosyne, 1969), 36–37. For the historical context that steadily disposed the southern climate of public opinion to accept slavery as a positive good and a social political blessing for master and slave alike, see Donald, *Lincoln*, 187. Likewise, the historian Allan Nevins relates the influence of Fitzhugh on southern public opinion: "While [Fitzhugh's dream] was both absurd and vicious, the writer's explicit criticism of the capitalist recklessness and laissez faire toleration of poverty had a trenchancy which gave it wide influence in the South. . . . Altogether, his books and his articles in De Bow's gave comfort to many Southerners who, facing the rising storm of world disapproval of slavery, wanted some answer, however flimsy, to the increasingly searching attacks made upon their system by able Northern and British writers" (Nevins, *Ordeal*, 1:94).

6. Basler, *Collected Works*, 3:204–5.

7. Nevins, *Ordeal*, 1:94; Eugene D. Genovese, *The Slaveholders' Dilemma: Freedom and Progress in Southern Conservative Thought, 1820–1860* (Columbia: South Carolina University Press, 1992), 1; Eugene D. Genovese, *The Southern Tradition: The Achievement and Limitations of an American Conservatism* (Cambridge, Mass.: Harvard University Press, 1994), 32–33.

8. Guelzo, *Abraham Lincoln*, 134–35.

9. Genovese, *Southern Tradition*, 33.

10. Basler, *Collected Works,* 3:462–63.

11. Fitzhugh, *Cannibals All!* 218–19; Basler, *Collected Works,* 2:222.

12. Basler, *Collected Works,* 7:368; Ahlstrom, *Religious History,* 671–72; Reichley, *Religion in American Public Life,* 197.

13. Novak, *On Two Wings,* 39.

14. Basler, *Collected Works,* 8:155, 4:19.

15. Samuel Seabury, *American Slavery Distinguished from the Slavery of English Theorists and Justified by the Law of Nature* (New York: Mason Brothers, 1861); Elliott, *Cotton Is King,* x.

16. Joseph R. Fornieri, "Biblical Republicanism: Abraham Lincoln's Civil Theology" (Ph.D. diss., Catholic University of America, 1996); Jaffa notes this as well (*New Birth of Freedom,* 153–69).

17. Thornton Stringfellow, "The Bible Argument; or, Slavery in the Light of Divine Revelation," in Elliot, *Cotton Is King,* 463.

18. Davis quoted in Jaffa, *New Birth of Freedom,* 156.

19. Albert Taylor Bledsoe, "Liberty and Slavery; or, Slavery in the Light of Moral and Political Philosophy," in Elliot, *Cotton Is King,* 337.

20. Philip S. Foner, ed., *Frederick Douglass: Selected Speeches and Writings* (Chicago: Lawrence Hill Books, 1999), 196. In his celebrated speech, "The Meaning of July Fourth for the Negro" at Rochester on July 5, 1852, Douglass provides a version of biblical republicanism against slavery comparable to Lincoln's.

21. Basler, *Collected Works,* 3:204.

22. Ibid., 2:278, 3:315, 2:500. On proslavery theology and divine right, see 2:278, 318, 323, 500, 3:315, 452, 5:51–53.

23. Ibid., 2:318.

24. Ibid., 2:255, 3:9–10. See Miller, *Lincoln's Virtues,* 340–74.

25. Basler, *Collected Works,* 4:271, 2:501 (also quoted in Miller, *Lincoln's Virtues,* 344).

26. Ibid., 3:311.

27. Ibid., 3:275.

28. Ibid., 2:278.

29. Ibid., 3:445.

30. *Memphis Daily Avalanche,* Nov. 30, 1858; Basler, *Collected Works,* 3:443, 368–69, 430, 503, 4:4, 10, 18, 19.

31. Timothy L. Smith, *Revivalism and Social Reform: American Protestantism on the Eve of the Civil War* (New York: Harper Torchbooks, 1965), 180.

CHAPTER 4

1. Thomas F. Schwartz, "The Springfield Lyceums and Lincoln's 1838 Speech," *Illinois Historical Journal* 83, no. 1 (1990): 45.

2. Neely, *Last Best Hope.* Most recently, William Lee Miller has provided an outstanding analysis of Lincoln's Springfield Address, a shorter speech, upon which much of Lincoln's Peoria Address was based. Although Miller's analysis focuses upon the ethical dimensions of the Springfield Address, this work focuses upon Lincoln's civil theological outlook in the more extended Peoria Address, which constitutes a model of biblical republicanism (*Lincoln's Virtues,* 252–69).

3. Basler, *Collected Works,* 1:112.

4. Edmund Wilson, *Patriotic Gore: Studies in the Literature of the American Civil War* (New York: Oxford University Press, 1962), 108; George B. Forgie, "Lincoln's

Tyrants," in Boritt and Forness, *Historian's Lincoln,* 296; Anderson, "Quest for Immortality," 260, 265. Garry Wills correctly observes that these scholars "make the Lyceum speech a key not only to Lincoln's personal life but to his political ideals and significance" (*Lincoln at Gettysburg: The Words That Remade America* [New York: Simon & Schuster, 1992], 81, 89).

5. Forgie, "Lincoln's Tyrants," 297–98; Strozier, *Lincoln's Quest for Union,* 61. Forgie maintains that the Lyceum Address reveals the "problem of ambition in a post heroic age."

6. Jaffa, *Crisis of the House Divided,* 183; Laurence Berns, "Lincoln's Perpetuation Speech," in Leo Paul S. de Alvarez, ed., *Abraham Lincoln: The Gettysburg Address and American Constitutionalism* (Irving, Tex.: University of Dallas Press, 1976), 12; Zuckert, "Lincoln and the Problem of Civil Religion," 721. The eminent historian Mark Neely criticizes the Straussian's overreliance upon the Lyceum Address as the key to understanding Lincoln's "political religion," a trend he traces back to "the prominence given the Lyceum speech and Wilson's interpretation of it in Harry V. Jaffa's *Crisis of the House Divided*" ("Lincoln's Lyceum Speech and the Origins of a Modern Myth," *Lincoln Lore,* no. 1776 [1987]: 3). For an important and provocative exposition of the Straussian view of Lincoln's ambition as it relates to his "political religion," see William Corlett, "The Availability of Lincoln's Political Religion," *Political Theory* 10 (1982): 520–40. Although I do not reach the same conclusion as Corlett about Lincoln's political motivation, his description of the Straussian perspective on the subject is essentially correct and deserves much greater attention than it has received by scholars.

7. Spinoza's *religio catholica* constitutes the theoretical source of the Straussian view of Lincoln's "political religion" (cf. Leo Strauss, *Spinoza's Critique of Religion* [New York: Shocken Books, 1965], 245–50, and the early Jaffa's interpretation of political religion). The comparison between *religio catholica* and "political religion" is both philosophically and textually verifiable (e.g., Jaffa, *Crisis of the House Divided,* 251–52). Jaffa identifies Lincoln as a "secular political rationalist" comparable to Spinoza. He states, "Lincoln, far from attacking rationalism, is in fact basing his whole case upon it." See Jaffa, *Crisis of the House Divided,* 238–39, 245, 249, 251–52, 265, 418–19, esp. nn. 16 and 21 to chap. 10. For a lucid explanation of Spinoza's *religio catholica* that helps to illuminate further the Straussian conception of Lincoln's "political religion," see Yirmiyahu Yovel, *Spinoza and Other Heretics,* vol. 2, *The Adventures of Immanence* (Princeton, N.J.: Princeton University Press, 1989).

8. Jaffa, *Crisis of the House Divided,* 245. Jaffa's teaching on the ontological status of natural law and right remains cryptic. In his most recent work, *A New Birth of Freedom,* Jaffa *seems* to have modified his earlier position and come closer to a Thomistic understanding of natural law. See *New Birth of Freedom,* 121–28, 509, and all of chap. 2. He states:

> In this, the perspective of the Declaration is in agreement with Thomas Aquinas's conception of the rational creature's participation in the eternal law, the law by which God governs the universe. The Declaration also assumes the existence of an eternal law when it speaks of an appeal to "the supreme judge of the world" and of "the protection of divine Providence." The voice of right reason in the natural law, therefore is as much the voice of God as is divine revelation. Also, since every member of the human species has the potentiality to participate in the natural law, in this decisive respect, all men are created equal. (*New Birth of Freedom,* 509.)

Jaffa seems, however, to qualify these remarks to the *careful reader*. After he discusses Thomas Aquinas, he includes a cryptic footnote referring to Winston Churchill's "Consistency in Politics," which states that "the truth may require a bodyguard of lies." In chap. 2 of *New Birth of Freedom,* after discussing the natural law, Jaffa then digresses into a *seemingly incongruous* discussion of this dictum by Churchill that raises questions about whether Jaffa's own teaching on natural right should be taken *exoterically or esoterically.* See also Jaffa, *New Birth of Freedom,* 121–28.

9. For Strauss's hermeneutical distinction between esoteric and exoteric teaching, see Leo Strauss, *Persecution and the Art of Writing* (1952; rpt., Chicago: University of Chicago Press, 1988). See also Strauss, "A Forgotten Kind of Writing," in *What Is Political Philosophy,* 221–32. Jaffa compares Lincoln's and Jefferson's religious heterodoxy in *Crisis of the House Divided,* 240. According to Jaffa, both Lincoln and Jefferson shared a mutual contempt "for the older religious tradition"; they differed in that "Lincoln, however, would never have expressed as openly, or rather as irascibly, as Jefferson does his contempt for the older religious tradition, which sees eternal salvation as something to which the powers of government might contribute positively."

10. Jaffa, *Crisis of the House Divided,* 419. See Strauss's crucial distinction between Aquinas's natural law and the Latin Averroist conception of natural right in Leo Strauss, *Natural Right and History* (Chicago: University of Chicago Press, 1953), 157–58. For one familiar with the medieval debate, Strauss makes clear his rejection of the Thomistic conception in favor of the Averroist view. It is no coincidence that this reference occurs almost exactly in the middle of *Natural Right and History.*

11. Zuckert, "Lincoln and the Problem of Civil Religion," 721; Jaffa, *Crisis of the House Divided,* 249; Thurow, *Lincoln and American Political Religion,* 80, xii; Basler, *Collected Works,* 1:115. In the preface of *Lincoln and American Political Religion,* Thurow states: "The problem of this book is the problem of political religion as it appears in Abraham Lincoln." And, significantly, Michael P. Zuckert's article on the subject is entitled "Lincoln and the Problem of Civil Religion." For an analysis of Spinoza's dualism, see Yovel, *Spinoza and Other Heretics,* vol. 2, *The Adventures of Immanence,* 12.

12. Berns, "Lincoln's Perpetuation Speech," 10.

13. Jaffa, *Crisis of the House Divided,* 229; Leo Paul S. de Alvarez, "Reflections on Lincoln's Political Religion," in de Alvarez, *Abraham Lincoln,* 172–73; George Anastaplo, "American Constitutionalism and the Virtue Of Prudence: Philadelphia, Paris, Washington, Gettysburg," in de Alvarez, *Abraham Lincoln,* 124; George Anastaplo, *Abraham Lincoln: A Consitutional Biography* (Lanham, Md.: Rowman and Littlefield, 1999), 326–27, 341–43, 347–50, esp. nn. 466, 489, 492, 494. Jaffa's comparison between Washington's use of religion and Lincoln's creation of a "political religion" in *Crisis of the House Divided* is entirely consistent with Spinoza's view of how the *religio catholica* transforms the secular into the sacred at an imaginary level for those who do not possess "superior minds with a superior education" (238–39).

14. M. E. Bradford, *A Better Guide than Reason: Studies in the American Revolution* (La Salle, Ill.: Sherwood Sugden, 1979), 42–55.

15. Basler, *Collected Works,* 6:34, 7:223. Also see Morel, *Lincoln's Sacred Effort,* 104–7.

16. Robert V. Bruce, "Commentary on 'Quest for Immortality,'" in Boritt and Forness, *Historian's Lincoln,* 276; Basler, *Collected Works,* 1:113.

17. Basler, *Collected Works,* 1:111; Jaffa, *Crisis of the House Divided.*

18. Guelzo, *Abraham Lincoln;* Basler, *Collected Works,* 1:112.

19. George M. Fredrickson "The Search for Order and Community," in Cullom

Davis et al., eds., *The Public and Private Lincoln: Contemporary Perspectives* (Carbondale: Southern Illinois University Press, 1979), 90–91; Basler, *Collected Works*, 1:65, 69; Bruce, "Commentary," 276; Wills, *Lincoln at Gettysburg*, 82.

20. Schwartz, "Springfield Lyceums," 45, 49; White, *Lincoln's Greatest Speech*, 71. Also see Edward G. Parker, *The Golden Age of Oratory* (Boston: Whittemore, Niles, Hall, 1857).

21. Diggins, *Lost Soul of American Politics*, 305; Joseph R. Fornieri, "Parallel Covenants of Republicanism: Washington's Farewell Address and Lincoln's Lyceum Address," paper delivered at American Studies Deep South Presidential Conference, Shreveport, La., Sept. 17–18, 1998.

22. Guelzo, *Abraham Lincoln*, 34; Basler, *Collected Works*, 4:235, 1:115; Miller, *Lincoln's Virtues*, 141; Basler, *Collected Works*, 1:279, 2:283, 3:550, 4:190–91. Dwight Anderson states: "For George Washington, it can be shown, provided Lincoln with an imaginary father whom he both emulated and defied, and finally, by ceremonial apotheosis, elevated to divine rank. . . . At first he sought political success by upholding Washington's advice and example; failing there, he seized upon the alternative, eventually presiding over the destruction of Washington's Union, and becoming the very tyrant against whom Washington had warned. Sublimating guilt into political authority, Lincoln took Washington's place as the father of his country" ("Quest for Immortality," 254).

23. Joseph R. Fornieri, "Lincoln and the Emancipation Proclamation: A Model of Prudent Leadership," in Ethan Fishman, ed., *Tempered Strength: Studies in the Nature and Scope of Prudential Leadership* (Lanham, Md.: Lexington Books, 2002), 125–49; T. Harry Williams, "Abraham Lincoln—Principle and Pragmatism in Politics: A Review Article," *Mississippi Valley Historical Review* 40 (1953): 89–106; Ethan Fishman, "Under the Circumstances: Abraham Lincoln and Classical Prudence," in Frank J. Williams, William D. Pederson, and Vincent J. Marsala, eds., *Abraham Lincoln: Sources and Styles of Leadership* (Wesport, Conn.: Greenwood Press, 1994), 3–16; Don E. Fehrenbacher, "Lincoln and the Weight of Responsibility," in *Journal of the Illinois State Historical Society* 68 (1975).

24. Ralph Lerner, "Lincoln's Revolution," in *Revolutions Revisited: Two Faces of the Politics of the Enlightenment* (Chapel Hill: University of North Carolina Press, 1994), 102; Miller, *Lincoln's Virtues*, 233; William E. Gienapp, *This Fiery Trial: The Speeches and Writings of Abraham Lincoln* (New York: Oxford University Press, 2002), 28..

25. Basler, *Collected Works*, 3:512.

26. Donald, *Lincoln's Herndon;* Basler, *Collected Works*, 1:8; Miller, *Lincoln's Virtues*, 339; Basler, *Collected Works*, 2:547.

27. Miller, *Lincoln's Virtues*, 339.

28. Kenneth L. Deutsch, "Thomas Aquinas on Magnanimous and Prudent Statesmanship," in Fishman, *Tempered Strength*, 33–52.

29. Basler, *Collected Works*, 3:334; Miller, *Lincoln's Virtues*, 147–53, 223, 322, 327, 335–39; Noll, "'Both . . . Pray to the Same God,'" 3–26; Basler, *Collected Works*, 2:266, 1:378, 2:90.

30. Basler, *Collected Works*, 2:266, 272, 275–76.

31. Ibid., 2:248

32. Jeanne Bethke Elshtain, *Augustine and the Limits of Politics* (Notre Dame, Ind.: University of Notre Dame Press, 1995). See the following for a treatment of Lincoln's racial views: Don E. Fehrenbacher, "Only His Stepchildren: Lincoln and the Negro," *Civil War History* 20 (December 1974); Lerone Bennett, Jr., "Was Abe Lincoln a

White Supremacist?" *Ebony* 23 (February 1968); Robert F. Durden, "Abraham Lincoln, Honkey or Equalitarian?" in *South Atlantic Quarterly* 71 (summer 1972); George Fredrickson, "A Man but Not a Brother: Abraham Lincoln and Racial Equality," *Journal of Southern History* 41 (1975): 39–58; LaWanda Cox, *Lincoln and Black Freedom: A Study in Presidential Leadership* (Columbia: University of South Carolina Press, 1994).

33. White, *Lincoln's Greatest Speech*, 64; Basler, *Collected Works*, 2:248.

34. See Article 6 of Northwest Ordinance; Anastaplo, *Abraham Lincoln*, 39–50; Basler, *Collected Works*, 3:522–50.

35. Basler, *Collected Works*, 2:249–50.

36. Ibid., 2:255.

37. Ibid., 2:272.

38. Guelzo, *Abraham Lincoln*, 53–57, 59, 66, 103, 145–46, 133; Basler, *Collected Works*, 2:121–32, 137–38, 3:77–80.

39. Jaffa, *New Birth of Freedom*; Basler, *Collected Works*, 2:252, 1:74–77.

40. Basler, *Collected Works*, 2:253–54, 259.

41. Ibid., 2:255.

42. Ibid.

43. Lerner, "Lincoln's Revolution," 88–111.

44. Basler, *Collected Works*, 2:256; Lerone Bennett, Jr., *Forced into Glory: Abraham Lincoln's White Dream* (Chicago: Johnson, 2000); Lerner, "Lincoln's Revolution," 82–111.

45. Jaffa, *Crisis of the House Divided*, 376–79.

46. Basler, *Collected Works*, 2:281–82.

47. Vernon J. Bourke, "The Synderesis Rule and Right Reason" *Monist* 66, no. 1 (1983): 72–81; Basler, *Collected Works*, 1:179, 2:228, 245, 264–65, 271, 281–82, 299, 322, 353, 385, 409, 498, 3:18, 80, 95, 323–24, 541–42, 4:238, 7:535.

48. Basler, *Collected Works*, 2:264–65. In *Lost Soul of American Politics*, Diggins correctly notes that Lincoln's political ethics were informed by a biblical view of conscience and humility: "In appealing to spiritual conscience Lincoln was not only exploiting the shame of a nation. He was also bringing ethics to the forefront of politics by demonstrating that moral judgment is embedded in the fabric of history. And Lincoln's concept of judgment was essentially Christian, for it was in reality self-judgment; Lincoln referred to 'we' the 'whole people', not they, the South" (330).

49. Eric Voegelin, "Reason the Classic Experience" in *Anamnesis* (Notre Dame, Ind.: University of Notre Dame Press, 1978), 89–116.

50. Basler, *Collected Works*, 2:271; Elshtain, *Augustine and the Limits of Politics*.

51. Vernon Bourke, in Lloyd P. Gerson, *Graceful Reason: Essays in Ancient and Medieval Philosophy* (Toronto: Pontifical Institute of Mediaeval Studies, 1983), 349–50; Basler, *Collected Works*, 7:281–83.

52. Basler, *Collected Works*, 2:265; Thomas J. DiLorenzo, *The Real Lincoln: A New Look at Abraham Lincoln, His Agenda, and an Unnecessary War* ([Roseville, Calif.]: Forum, 2002).

53. Basler, *Collected Works*, 2:265–66.

54. Ibid., 2:270–71.

55. Ibid., 273.

56. Ibid., 274.

57. Wills, *Lincoln at Gettysburg*.

58. Anastaplo, "American Constitutionalism," 77–170; George Anastaplo, "Slavery and the Constitution: Explorations," *Texas Tech Law Review* 20 (1989): 677–786;

Anastaplo, *Abraham Lincoln;* James Madison, Aug. 25, 1787; Roger Sherman, Aug. 25, 1787; George Mason, Aug. 22, 1787; Gouvernor Morris, Aug. 8, 1787; Luther Martin, Aug. 21, 1787.

59. Basler, *Collected Works,* 2:275, 7:243.

60. Ibid., 2:276.

61. Ibid., 2:278.

62. Ibid.

CHAPTER 5

1. Basler, *Collected Works,* 2:318.

2. Niebuhr, *Theologian of Public Life,* ed. Rasmussen, 250–62; Arthur Melzer, *The Natural Goodness of Man* (Chicago: University of Chicago Press, 1990); Basler, *Collected Works,* 5:373.

3. Niebuhr, *Theologian of Public Life,* ed. Rasmussen, 255.

4. I am grateful to David Walsh for emphasizing this as part of his teaching.

5. Jean Bethke Elshtain, *Public Man, Private Woman* (Princeton, N.J.: Princeton University Press) 19–55.

6. C. S. Lewis, *Present Concerns,* ed. Walter Hooper (New York: Harcourt Brace Jovanovich, 1986), 17. Related observations have been made by Neuhaus and Niebuhr. For Neuhaus, "democracy is the appropriate form of governance in a fallen creation in which no person or institution including the church, can infallibly speak for God. Democracy is the necessary expression of humility in which all persons are held accountable to transcendent purpose imperfectly discerned" (Neuhaus, *Naked Public Square,* 116); "The facts about human nature which make a monopoly of power dangerous and a balance of power desirable are best understood from the standpoint of the Christian faith" (Niebuhr, *Theologian of Public Life,* 255).

7. Basler, *Collected Works,* 2:532.

8. Ibid., 3:376.

9. Ibid., 1:273, 4:9.

10. David Herbert Donald, *Charles Sumner and the Coming of the Civil War* (Chicago: University of Chicago Press, 1981), 229–30; Niebuhr, *Theologian of Public Life,* 86.

11. Basler, *Collected Works,* 8:101, 3:121.

12. Ibid., 2:271, 3:310. "The prospect of owning slaves, [Lincoln] learned, was 'highly seductive to the thoughtless and giddy headed young men [of the South],' because slaves were 'most glittering ostentatious and displaying property in the world'" (Donald, *Lincoln,* 166).

13. Basler, *Collected Works,* 2:222, 498, 7:281, 2:353, 3:95, 2:281–82, 3:80, 18, 29.

14. Ibid., 4:3, 10:44–45. For Lincoln's appeal to natural theology against slavery, see 2:222, 3:462–63, 479–80, 4:9.

15. Ibid., 4:240, 253; Oates, *Malice toward None,* 32.

16. Jaffa, *Crisis of the House Divided,* 330–46; Basler, *Collected Works,* 1:488, 2:366, 475, 501, 3:334, 496, 6:428–29.

17. Jaffa, *Crisis of the House Divided,* 308–29; Basler, *Collected Works,* 3:222.

18. Harry V. Jaffa, *Equality and Liberty: Theory and Practice in American Politics* (New York: Oxford University Press, 1965), 177; Basler, *Collected Works,* 3:375.

19. Basler, *Collected Works,* 3:29.

20. Ibid., 2:406, 3:78, 80, 2:518; Jaffa, *Crisis of the House Divided,* 375–76.

21. See Guelzo, *Abraham Lincoln,* 197–99.

22. Basler, *Collected Works,* 2:385; Jaffa, *Crisis of the House Divided,* 347–62.

23. Basler, *Collected Works,* 2:501.

24. Ibid., 2:404.

25. Ibid., 2:385

26. Ibid.

27. Ibid., 3:424; Harry V. Jaffa, *The Conditions of Freedom: Essays in Political Philosophy* (Baltimore: Johns Hopkins University Press, 1975), 149–60.

28. Basler, *Collected Works,* 2:544–47.

29. Ibid., 3:425, 81, 2:264.

30. Ibid., 2:405–6.

31. Ibid., 3:462–63.

32. Ibid., 2:501.

33. Jaffa, "Equality as a Conservative Principle," in *How to Think about the American Revolution: A Bicentennial Cerebration* (Durham, N.C.: Carolina Academic Press, 1978), 13–48; Basler, *Collected Works,* 3:80.

34. Basler, *Collected Works,* 2:532, 266; Jaffa, *How to Think about the American Revolution,* 43.

35. Basler, *Collected Works,* 2:222–23. Notice how Kant borrows from the Golden Rule.

36. Ibid., 3:95.

37. Jaffa, *How to Think about the American Revolution,* 37. See Williams, Pederson, and Marsala, *Abraham Lincoln,* 17–70.

38. Nevins, *Emergence,* 2:254

39. Koch and Peden, *Writings of Jefferson,* 656–57.

40. Ibid., 641, 659, 665–66.

41. Marvin Meyers, ed., *The Mind of the Founder: Sources of the Political Thought of James Madison* (Hanover, N.H.: University Press of New England, 1973), 350.

42. Donald, *Lincoln,* 641; Wilson, *Eight Essays.*

43. Basler, *Collected Works,* 2:341, 4:236; Kersh, *Dreams of a More Perfect Union.*

44. Basler, *Collected Works,* 2:499–500.

45. Frank Williams, "Lincoln and Leadership: An International Perspective," in Williams, Pederson, and Marsala, *Abraham Lincoln,* 165–78; Francis Fukuyama, *The End of History and the Last Man* (New York: Avon Books, 1992); Basler, *Collected Works,* 1:438; Jaffa, *New Birth of Freedom,* 57, 280.

46. Donald, *Lincoln,* 412.

47. Gabor S. Boritt, *Abraham Lincoln and the Economics of the American Dream* (Urbana: University of Illinois Press, 1994). Jaffa, *Crisis of the House Divided;* Basler, *Collected Works,* 4:438.

48. Basler, *Collected Works,* 2:126, 4:438, 7:512.

49. Ibid., 2:323, 3:380.

50. Ibid., 4:440.

51. Ibid., 4:168–69.

52. Long, *Jewel of Liberty.*

53. William Lloyd Garrison, *Selections from the Writings and Speeches of William Lloyd Garrison* (1852; rpt., New York: Negro Universities Press), 116–19.

54. McPherson, *For Cause and Comrades,* 27–28; Miller, *Lincoln's Virtues,* 194–208.

55. Basler, *Collected Works,* 5:388–89.

56. Joseph J. Ellis, *Founding Brothers: The Revolutionary Generation* (New York: Alfred A. Knopf, 2000), 81–119.

57. Donald, *Lincoln,* 368. For Lincoln on emancipation in the border states, see Basler, *Collected Works,* 5:317–19, 29–31, 503–4, 7:49, 226–27, 251, 277, 8:41–42, 52–53, 84, 113–14.

58. Basler, *Collected Works,* 2:341, 5:537, 8:148, 5:350, 318.

59. Ibid., 7:243.

CONCLUSION

1. Ronald C. White, Jr., has aptly named his enriching study of the Second Inaugural Address *Lincoln's Greatest Speech.* My analysis of this speech is indebted to White's lucid and important study.

2. White, *Lincoln's Greatest Speech,* 86, 41–59 (Raymond is quoted on 46); Long, *Jewel of Liberty.*

3. Basler, *Collected Works,* 7:302.

4. White, *Lincoln's Greatest Speech,* 41–59.

5. Martin E. Marty, "Abraham Lincoln in War-time: An Ironic View of an Ironist," Fortenbaugh Lecture at Gettysburg College, Gettysburg, Pa., Nov. 19, 2000; Reinhold Niebuhr, "The Religion of Abraham Lincoln," in Allan Nevins, ed., *Lincoln and the Gettysburg Address: Commemmorative Papers* (Urbana: University of Illinois Press, 1964), 72–78.

6. White, *Lincoln's Greatest Speech,* 79.

7. Basler, *Collected Works,* 1:277; Miller, *Lincoln's Virtues,* 147–53.

8. Basler, *Collected Works,* 2:255; Miller, *Lincoln's Virtues,* 286–97.

9. White, *Lincoln's Greatest Speech,* 113.

10. Hein, "Lincoln's Theology and Political Ethics," 107.

11. White, *Lincoln's Greatest Speech,* 147.

12. Basler, *Collected Works,* 5:344–46, 7:169; White, *Lincoln's Greatest Speech,* 170–71.

13. Noll, "'Both . . . Pray to the Same God,'" 1–25; Niebuhr, "Religion of Abraham Lincoln", 72–78.

14. Basler, *Collected Works,* 8:356.

15. White, *Lincoln's Greatest Speech,* 127, 138–41; Niebuhr, "Religion of Abraham Lincoln," 72–78; Allen C. Guelzo, "Abraham Lincoln and the Doctrine of Necessity," *Journal of the Abraham Lincoln Association* 18, no. 1 (1997): 57–81. White demonstrates the remarkable consistency between the private faith in Lincoln's "Meditation on the Divine Will" and the public expression of this faith in the Second Inaugural Address by juxtaposing the language of the two speeches.

16. Basler, *Collected Works,* 7:282.

17. Niebuhr states: "But the chief evidence of the purity and profundity of Lincoln's sense of providence lies in his ability, though the responsible leader of a great nation, embattled with secessionist States and naturally tempted to do what all political leaders, indeed all men, have done through the ages, to avoid the error of identifying providence with the cause to which the agent is committed. He resisted this temptation. Among all the statesmen of ancient and modern periods, Lincoln alone had a

sense of historical meaning so high as to cast doubt on the intentions of both sides and to place the enemy into the same category of ambiguity as the nation to which his life was committed" ("Religion of Abraham Lincoln," 75).

18. Jaffa, *Crisis of the House Divided;* Jaffa, *New Birth of Freedom,* 10; "Interwar German-Speaking Emigres and American Political Thought: Strauss, Voegelin, and Arendt," *Political Science Reviewer* 29 (2000): 296–330.

SELECTED BIBLIOGRAPHY

Ahlstrom, Sydney E. *A Religious History of the American People.* New Haven, Conn.: Yale University Press, 1972.

Anastaplo, George. "American Constitutionalism and the Virtue of Prudence: Philadelphia, Paris, Washington, Gettysburg." In *Abraham Lincoln: The Gettysburg Address and American Constitutionalism,* edited by Leo Paul S. de Alvarez, 77–170. Irving, Tex.: University of Dallas Press, 1976.

——.*The Constitution of 1787: A Commentary.* Baltimore: Johns Hopkins University Press, 1989.

——. "Slavery and the Constitution: Explorations." *Texas Tech Law Review* 20 (1989): 677–786.

——. *Abraham Lincoln: A Constitutional Biography.* Lanham, Md.: Rowman and Littlefield, 1999.

Anderson, Dwight G. *Abraham Lincoln: The Quest for Immortality.* New York: Alfred A. Knopf, 1982.

——. "Quest for Immortality: A Theory of Abraham Lincoln's Political Psychology." In *The Historian's Lincoln: Pseudohistory, Psychohistory, and History,* edited by Gabor S. Boritt and Norman O. Forness, 253–74. Urbana: University of Illinois Press, 1988.

Arendt, Hannah. *On Revolution.* New York: Penguin, 1987.

Arkes, Hadley. *First Things: An Inquiry into the First Principles of Morals and Justice.* Princeton, N.J.: Princeton University Press, 1986.

Augustine, St. *The City of God.* Translated by Marcus Dods. New York: Modern Library, 1950.

Bailyn, Bernard. *The Ideological Origins of the American Revolution.* Enlarged ed. Cambridge, Mass.: Belknap, Harvard University Press, 1992.

Barton, William E. *The Soul of Abraham Lincoln.* New York: George H. Doran, 1920.

Basler, Roy P., ed. *The Collected Works of Abraham Lincoln.* 8 vols. New Brunswick, N.J.: Rutgers University Press, 1953–1955.

Beale, Howard K., ed. *The Diary of Gideon Welles: Secretary of the Navy under Lincoln and Johnson.* 3 vols. New York: W. W. Norton, 1960.

Becker, Carl L. *The Declaration of Independence: A Study in the History of Political Ideas.* New York: Vintage, 1970.

Bellah, Robert N. "Civil Religion in America." In *American Civil Religion,* edited by Russell E. Richey and Donald G. Jones, 21–44. New York: Harper & Row, 1974.

——. "Religion and the Legitimation of the American Republic." In *Varieties of Civil Religion,* edited by Robert Bellah and Phillip Hammond. San Francisco: Harper and Row, 1980.

————. *The Broken Covenant: American Civil Religion in Time of Trial.* Chicago: University of Chicago Press, 1992.

Berns, Laurence. "Lincoln's Perpetuation Speech." In *Abraham Lincoln: The Gettysburg Address and American Constitutionalism,* edited by Leo Paul S. de Alvarez, 7–13. Irving, Tex.: University of Dallas Press, 1976.

Boorstin, Daniel J. *The Genius of American Politics.* Chicago: University of Chicago Press, 1953.

————. *The Lost World of Thomas Jefferson.* Chicago: University of Chicago Press, 1981.

Boritt, Gabor S. *The Collected Works of Abraham Lincoln, Supplement, 1832–1865.* Westport, Conn.: Greenwood, 1974.

————. *Abraham Lincoln and the Economics of the American Dream.* Urbana: University of Illinois Press, 1994.

Boritt, Gabor S., and Norman O. Forness, eds. *The Historian's Lincoln: Pseudohistory, Psychohistory, and History.* Urbana: University of Illinois Press, 1988.

Bradford, M. E. *A Better Guide than Reason: Studies in the American Revolution.* La Salle, Ill.: Sherwood Sugden, 1979.

————. "The Lincoln Legacy: A Long View." *Modern Age* 24 (1980): 355–63.

Brooks, Phillips. "Abraham Lincoln." In *The Christ in Whom Christians Believe.* New York: Caldwell, 1900.

Brooks, William E. "Lincoln's Philosophy of History." *Christian Century* 57 (1940): 274–76.

Bruce, Robert V. "Commentary on 'Quest for Immortality.'" In *The Historian's Lincoln: Pseudohistory, Psychohistory, and History,* edited by Gabor S. Boritt and Norman O. Forness, 275–84. Urbana: University of Illinois Press, 1988.

Bullard, F. Lauriston. "The Religion of Abraham Lincoln." *Magazine of History* 34 (1921): 51–54.

Calhoun, John C. *The Essential Calhoun.* Edited by Clyde N. Wilson. New Brunswick, N.J.: Transaction Press, 1992.

Charnwood, Lord. *Abraham Lincoln.* New York: Pocket, 1917.

Cherry, Conrad, ed. *God's New Israel: Religious Interpretations of American Destiny.* Englewood Cliffs, N.J.: Prentice-Hall, 1971.

Cicero, Marcus Tullius. *The Nature of the Gods.* Translated by Horace C. P. McGregor. New York: Penguin, 1984.

————. *Cicero in Twenty-Eight Volumes.* Vol. 16, *De Re Publica, De Legibus.* Translated by C. W. Keyes. Cambridge, Mass.: Harvard University Press, Loeb Classical Library, 1988.

Copeland, Lewis, and Lawrence W. Lamm, eds. *The World's Great Speeches.* 3d ed. New York: Dover, 1973.

Corlett, William. "The Availability of Lincoln's Political Religion." *Political Theory* 10 (1982): 520–40.

Cox, LaWanda. *Lincoln and Black Freedom: A Study in Presidential Leadership.* Columbia: University of South Carolina Press, 1994.

Current, Richard Nelson. *Lincoln and the First Shot.* New York: J. B. Lippincott, 1963.

————. "Lincoln, the Civil War, and the American Mission." In *The Public and Private Lincoln,* edited by Cullom Davis et al., 137–46. Carbondale: Southern Illinois University Press, 1979.

————. *The Lincoln Nobody Knows.* New York: Hill and Wang, 1984.

Curtis, William Eleroy. *The True Abraham Lincoln.* Philadelphia: J. B. Lippincott, 1903.

De Alvarez, Leo Paul S., ed. *Abraham Lincoln: The Gettysburg Address and American Constitutionalism.* Irving, Tex.: University of Dallas Press, 1976.

Deutsch, Kenneth L. "Thomas Aquinas on Magnanimous and Prudent Statesmanship." In *Tempered Strength,* edited by Ethan Fishman, 33–52. Lanham, Md.: Lexington Books, 2002.

Diamond, Martin. *The Founding of the Democratic Republic.* Itasca, Ill.: F. E. Peacock, 1981.

———. *As Far as Republican Principles Will Admit: Essays by Martin Diamond.* Edited by William A. Schambra. Washington, D.C.: AEI Press, 1992.

Diggins, John P. *The Lost Soul of American Politics: Virtue, Self-Interest, and the Foundations of Liberalism.* New York: Basic Books, 1984.

Donald, David Herbert. *Lincoln Reconsidered: Essays on the Civil War Era.* 2d ed. New York: Random House, 1961.

———. *Charles Sumner and the Coming of the Civil War.* Chicago: University of Chicago Press, 1981.

———. *Lincoln's Herndon.* 1948. Reprint, New York: Da Capo, 1989.

———. *Lincoln.* New York: Simon & Schuster, 1995.

Elliott, E. N., ed., *Cotton Is King, and Pro-slavery Arguments comprising the Writings of Hammond, Harper, Christy, Stringfellow, Hodge, Bledsoe, and Cartwright, on This Important Subject.* 1860. Reprint, New York: Negro Universities Press.

Elshtain, Jean Bethke. *Public Man, Private Woman.* Princeton, N.J.: Princeton University Press, 1981.

———. *Augustine and the Limits of Politics.* Notre Dame, Ind.: University of Notre Dame Press, 1995.

———. *Democracy on Trial.* New York: Basic Books, 1995.

Endy, Melvin B., Jr. "Abraham Lincoln and American Civil Religion: A Reinterpretation." *Church History* 44 (1975): 229–41.

Ericson, David F. *The Shaping of American Liberalism: The Debates over Ratification, Nullification, and Slavery.* Chicago: University of Chicago Press, 1993.

Fehrenbacher, Don E. *Prelude to Greatness: Lincoln in the 1850's.* Stanford, Calif.: Stanford University Press, 1962.

———. "Only His Stepchildren: Lincoln and the Negro." *Civil War History* 20 (December 1974).

———. *The Dred Scott Case: Its Significance in American Law and Politics.* New York: Oxford University Press, 1978.

———. *Lincoln in Text and Context: Collected Essays.* Stanford, Calif.: Stanford University Press, 1987.

Fishman, Ethan. "Under the Circumstances: Abraham Lincoln and Classical Prudence." In *Abraham Lincoln: Sources and Style of Leadership,* edited by Frank J. Williams, William D. Pederson, and Vincent J. Marsala. Westport, Conn.: Greenwood Press, 1994.

Fitzhugh, George. *Cannibals All! or, Slaves Without Masters.* Edited by C. Vann Woodward. Cambridge, Mass.: Harvard University Press, Belknap Press, 1960.

———. *Sociology for the South; or, The Failure of Free Society.* 1854. Reprint, New York: B. Franklin, 1965.

Forgie, George B. *Patricide in the House Divided.* New York: W. W. Norton, 1979.

———. "Lincoln's Tyrants." In *The Historian's Lincoln: Pseudohistory, Psychohistory, and History,* edited by Gabor S. Boritt and Norman O. Forness, 285–301. Urbana: University of Illinois Press, 1988.

Fredrickson, George M. "A Man but Not a Brother: Abraham Lincoln and Racial Equality." *Journal of Southern History* 41 (1975): 39–58.

———. "The Search for Order and Community." In *The Public and Private Lincoln: Contemporary Perspectives,* edited by Cullom Davis et al., 86–98. Carbondale: Southern Illinois University Press, 1979.

Garrison, William Lloyd. *Selections from the Writings and Speeches of William LLoyd Garrison.* 1852. Reprint, New York: Negro Universities Press, 1968.

Gebhardt, Jurgen. *Americanism: Revolutionary Order and Societal Self-Interpretation in the American Republic.* Translated by Ruth Hein. Baton Rouge: Louisiana State University Press, 1993.

Genovese, Eugene D. *The Slaveholders' Dilemma: Freedom and Progress in Southern Conservative Thought, 1820–1860.* Columbia: University of South Carolina Press, 1992.

———. *The Southern Tradition: The Achievement and Limitations of an American Conservatism.* Cambridge, Mass.: Harvard University Press, 1994.

Greenstone, J. David. *The Lincoln Persuasion: Remaking American Liberalism.* Princeton, N.J.: Princeton University Press, 1993.

Grierson, Francis. *Abraham Lincoln: The Practical Mystic.* New York: John Lane, 1918.

Guelzo, Allen C. "Abraham Lincoln and the Doctrine of Necessity." *Journal of the Abraham Lincoln Association* 18, no. 1 (1997): 57–81.

———. *Abraham Lincoln: Redeemer President.* Grand Rapids, Mich.: William B. Eerdmans, 1999.

Hamilton, Alexander, James Madison, and John Jay. *The Federalist Papers.* Edited by Clinton Rossiter. New York: Mentor Books, 1961.

Hartz, Louis. *The Liberal Tradition in America: An Interpretation of American Political Thought since the Revolution.* New York: Harcourt Brace Jovanivich, 1955.

Hein, David. "Abraham Lincoln's Theological Outlook." Ph.D. diss., University of Virginia, 1982.

———. "Lincoln's Theology and Political Ethics." In *Essays on Lincoln's Faith and Politics,* edited by Kenneth W. Thompson, 105–79. Lanham, Md.: University Press of America, 1983.

———. "Lincoln's Faith: Commentary on 'Abraham Lincoln and American Political Religion.'" In *The Historian's Lincoln: Pseudohistory, Psychohistory, and History,* edited by Gabor S. Boritt and Norman O. Forness, 144–48. Urbana: University of Illinois Press, 1988.

Herndon, William H., and Jesse W. Weik. *Herndon's Life of Lincoln.* 1942. Reprint, New York: Da Capo Press, 1983.

Hill, John Wesley. *Abraham Lincoln, Man of God.* New York: G. P. Putnam's Sons, 1920.

Hofstadter, Richard. *The American Political Tradition and the Men Who Made It.* New York: A. A. Knopf, 1948.

Holland, J. G. *The Life of Abraham Lincoln.* Springfield, Mass.: Bill, 1866.

Horner, Harlan Hoyt. *The Growth of Lincoln's Faith.* New York: Abingdon, 1939.

Houser, M. L. *Some Religious Influences which Surrounded Lincoln.* Peoria, Ill.: Schriver, 1941.

Jaffa, Harry V. *Crisis of the House Divided: An Interpretation of the Issues in the Lincoln-Douglas Debates.* Garden City, N.Y.: Doubleday, 1959.

———. *Equality and Liberty: Theory and Practice in American Politics.* New York: Oxford University Press, 1965.

———. *The Conditions of Freedom: Essays in Political Philosophy.* Baltimore: Johns Hopkins University Press, 1975.

————. *How to Think about the American Revolution: A Bicentennial Cerebration.* Durham, N.C.: Carolina Academic Press, 1978.

————. *A New Birth of Freedom.* Lanham, Md.: Rowman and Littlefield, 2000.

Johnson, William J. *Abraham Lincoln: The Christian.* 1913. Reprint, Milford, Mich.: Mott Media, 1976.

Jonas, Hans. *The Gnostic Religion: The Message of the Alien God and the Beginnings of Christianity.* 2d ed. Boston: Beacon Press, 1963.

Jones, Edgar DeWitt. *Lincoln and the Preachers.* New York: Harper and Row, 1948.

Kendall, Wilmoore, and George Carey. *The Basic Symbols of the American Political Tradition.* Washington, D.C.: Catholic University Press, 1995.

Kersh, Rogan. *Dreams of a More Perfect Union.* Ithaca, N.Y.: Cornell University Press, 2001.

Kirk, Russell. *The Roots of American Order.* 3d ed. Washington, D.C.: Regnery Gateway, 1991.

Koch, Adrienne, and William Peden, eds. *The Life and Selected Writings of Thomas Jefferson.* 1944. Reprint, New York: Modern Library, 1993.

Lerner, Ralph. "Lincoln's Revolution." In *Revolutions Revisited: Two Faces of the Politics of Enlightenment.* Chapel Hill: University of North Carolina Press, 1994.

Lewis, Joseph. *Lincoln the Freethinker.* New York: Lincoln, 1924.

Long, David E. *The Jewel of Liberty: Abraham Lincoln's Re-election and the End of Slavery.* Mechanicsburg, Pa.: Stackpole, 1994.

Machiavelli, Niccolo. *The Discourses.* Edited by Bernard Crick and translated by Leslie J. Walker. New York: Penguin, 1987.

McKenna, George. "On Abortion: A Lincolnian Position." *Atlantic Monthly* 276, no. 3 (September 1995): 51–68.

McPherson, James M. *Battle Cry of Freedom: The Civil War Era.* New York: Oxford University Press, 1988.

————. *Abraham Lincoln and the Second American Revolution.* New York: Oxford University Press, 1991.

————. "A Passive President?" *Atlantic Monthly* 276, no. 5 (November 1995): 134–40.

————. *The Struggle for Equality: Abolitionists and the Negro in the Civil War and Reconstruction.* 2d ed. Princeton, N.J.: Princeton University Press, 1995.

————. *Drawn with the Sword: Reflections on the American Civil War.* New York: Oxford University Press, 1996.

McWilliams, Wilson Carey. "The Bible and the American Political Tradition." In *Religion and Politics,* edited by Myron J. Aronoff. New Brunswick, N.J.: Transaction, 1984.

Malbin, Michael J. *Religion and Politics: The Intentions of the Authors of the First Amendment.* Washington, D.C.: AEI, 1978.

Marty, Martin E. *Pilgrims in Their Own Land: 500 Years of Religion in America.* New York: Penguin, 1983.

————. "Abraham Lincoln in War-time: An Ironic View of an Ironist," Fortenbaugh Lecture at Gettysburg College, Gettysburg, Pa., Nov. 19, 2000.

Mead, Sidney. "The Nation with the Soul of a Church." In *American Civil Religion,* edited by Russell E. Richey and Donald G. Jones, 45–75. New York: Harper & Row, 1974.

Miller, Perry. *Errand into the Wilderness.* Cambridge, Mass.: Harvard University Press, 1956.

————. *The Life of the Mind in America from the Revolution to the Civil War.* New York: Harcourt Brace & World, 1965.

Miller, William Lee. *Lincoln's Virtues: An Ethical Biography.* New York: Alfred A. Knopf, 2002.

Morel, Lucas E. *Lincoln's Sacred Effort.* Lanham, Md.: Lexington Books, 2000.

Murray, John Courtney. *We Hold These Truths: Catholic Reflections on the American Proposition.* Kansas City, Mo.: Sheed and Ward, 1960.

Neal, Patrick. "Vulgar Liberalism." *Political Theory* 21, no. 4 (1993): 623–42.

Neely, Mark E., Jr. "Lincoln's Lyceum Speech and the Origins of a Modern Myth." *Lincoln Lore,* no. 1776 (1987): 1–3.

———. *The Last Best Hope of Earth: Abraham Lincoln and the Promise of America.* Cambridge, Mass.: Harvard University Press, 1993.

Neuhaus, Richard John. *The Naked Public Square: Religion and Democracy in America.* Grand Rapids, Mich.: William B. Eerdmans, 1984.

Nevins, Allan. *Ordeal of the Union.* 2 vols. New York: Scribner, 1947.

———. *The Emergence of Lincoln.* 2 vols. New York: Scribner, 1950.

Nicolay, John G., and John Hay. *Abraham Lincoln: A History.* 10 vols. New York: Century, 1890.

Niebuhr, Reinhold. *The Irony of American History.* New York: Scribner, 1962.

———. "The Religion of Abraham Lincoln." In *Lincoln and the Gettysburg Address: Commemorative Papers,* edited by Allan Nevins, 72–87. Urbana: University of Illinois Press, 1964.

———. *Reinhold Niebuhr: Theologian of Public Life.* Edited by Larry L. Rasmussen. Minneapolis: Fortress Press, 1991.

Noll, Mark A. "'Both . . . Pray to the Same God': The Singularity of Lincoln's Faith in the Era of the Civil War." *Journal of the Abraham Lincoln Association* 18, no. 1 (1997): 1–26.

Novak, Michael. *On Two Wings: Humble Faith and Common Sense at the American Founding.* San Francisco: Encounter Books, 2002.

Oates, Stephen B. *With Malice toward None: The Life of Abraham Lincoln.* New York: Harper & Row, 1978.

———. *Our Fiery Trial: Abraham Lincoln, John Brown, and the Civil War Era.* Amherst: University of Massachusetts Press, 1979.

Pangle, Thomas L. *The Spirit of Modern Republicanism: The Moral Vision of the American Founders and the Philosophy of Locke.* Chicago: University of Chicago Press, 1988.

———. *The Ennobling of Democracy: The Challenge of the Postmodern Age.* Baltimore: Johns Hopkins University Press, 1992.

Peterson, Merril D. *Adams and Jefferson: A Revolutionary Dialogue.* New York: Oxford University Press, 1978.

———. *Lincoln in American Memory.* New York: Oxford University Press, 1994.

Plato. *The Republic.* Edited by Allan Bloom. New York: Basic Books, 1968.

Potter, David M. *The Impending Crisis: 1848–1861.* Edited by Don E. Fehrenbacher. New York: Harper & Row, 1976.

Rahe, Paul A. *Republics Ancient and Modern: Classical Republicanism and the American Revolution.* Chapel Hill: University of North Carolina Press, 1992.

Randall, J. G., and R. N. Current. *Lincoln, the President.* Vol. 4, *The Last Full Measure.* New York: Dodd, Mead, 1955.

Rawls, John. "Justice as Fairness: Political not Metaphysical." *Philosophy and Public Affairs* 14 (summer 1985): 223–51.

———. "The Priority of Right and Ideas of the Good." *Philosophy and Public Affairs* 17 (fall 1988): 251–76.

Reichley, James. *Religion in American Public Life*. Washington, D.C.: Brookings Institution, 1985.

Ross, Frederick A. *Slavery Ordained of God*. 1857. Reprint, Miami, Fla.: Mnemosyne, 1969.

Rossiter, Clinton. *Seedtime of the Republic: The Origin of the American Tradition of Political Liberty*. New York: Harcourt Brace, 1953.

———. *1787: The Grand Convention*. New York: Macmillan, 1966.

Ryn, Claes G. *Democracy and the Ethical Life: A Philosophy of Politics and Community*. 2d ed. Washington, D.C.: Catholic University of America Press, 1990.

Sandburg, Carl. *Abraham Lincoln: The Prairie Years and the War Years. One-Volume Edition*. New York: Harcourt Brace, 1954.

Sandoz, Ellis. *A Government of Laws: Political Theory, Religion, and the American Founding*. Baton Rouge: Louisiana State University Press, 1990.

———, ed. *Political Sermons of the American Founding Era, 1730–1805*. Indianapolis: Liberty Press, 1991.

Schwartz, Thomas F. "The Springfield Lyceums and Lincoln's 1838 Speech." *Illinois Historical Journal* 83, no. 1 (1990): 45–49.

Seabury, Samuel. *American Slavery Distinguished from the Slavery of English Theorists, and Justified by the Law of Nature*. New York: Mason Brothers, 1861.

Settle, Raymond W. "Abraham Lincoln's Faith." *Christianity Today*, Feb. 3, 1958, 6–8.

Simon, Yves René Marie. *A General Theory of Authority*. [Notre Dame, Ind.]: University of Notre Dame Press, 1962.

Spinoza, Benedict de. *A Theologico-Political Treatise*. Translated by R. H. M. Elwes. New York: Dover, 1951.

———. *The Ethics and Selected Letters*. Translated by Samuel Shirley. Indianapolis: Hackett, 1982.

Stampp, Kenneth M., ed. *The Causes of the Civil War*. Rev. ed. New York: Englewood Cliffs, N.J.: Prentice-Hall, 1974.

———. "Commentary on 'Lincoln's Tyrants.'" In *The Historian's Lincoln: Pseudohistory, Psychohistory, and History*, edited by Gabor S. Boritt and Norman O. Forness, 302–7. Urbana: University of Illinois Press, 1988.

Storing, Herbert J. *What the Anti-Federalists Were For*. Chicago: University of Chicago Press, 1981.

Stowe, Harriet Beecher. *Uncle Tom's Cabin; or, Life among the Lowly*. 1852. Reprint, New York: Signet, 1981.

Strauss, Leo. *Natural Right and History*. Chicago: University of Chicago Press, 1953.

———. *Spinoza's Critique of Religion*. New York: Shocken, 1965.

———. *Persecution and the Art of Writing*. 1952. Reprint, Chicago: University of Chicago Press, 1988.

———. *What Is Political Philosophy? And Other Studies*. 1959. Reprint, Chicago: University of Chicago Press, 1988.

Strozier, Charles B. *Lincoln's Quest for Union: Public and Private Meanings*. New York: Basic Books, 1982.

———. "Lincoln's Quest for Union: Public and Private Meanings." In *The Historian's Lincoln: Pseudohistory, Psychohistory, and History*, edited by Gabor S. Boritt and Norman O. Forness, 211–41. Urbana: University of Illinois Press, 1988.

Thomas, Benjamin P. *Abraham Lincoln*. New York: Alfred A. Knopf, 1952.

Thomas, John L., "Antislavery and Utopia." In *The Antislavery Vanguard: New Essays on the Abolitionists*, edited by Martin Duberman. Princeton, N.J.: Princeton University Press, 1965.

Thurow, Glen E. *Abraham Lincoln and American Political Religion*. Albany: State University of New York Press, 1976.

———. "The Gettysburg Address and the Declaration of Independence." In *Abraham Lincoln: The Gettysburg Address and American Constitutionalism*, edited by Leo Paul S. de Alvarez, 55–75. Irving, Tex.: University of Dallas Press, 1976.

———. "Abraham Lincoln and American Political Religion." In *The Historian's Lincoln: Pseudohistory, Psychohistory, and History*, edited by Gabor S. Boritt and Norman O Forness, 125–43. Urbana: University of Illinois Press, 1988.

Trueblood, Elton. *Abraham Lincoln: Theologian of American Anguish*. New York: Phoenix Press, 1986.

Voegelin, Eric. *The New Science of Politics: An Introduction*. Chicago: University of Chicago Press, 1952.

———. *Science, Politics, and Gnosticism: Two Essays*. Chicago: Regnery, 1968.

———. *Order and History*. Vol. 1, *Israel and Revelation*. Baton Rouge: Louisiana State University Press, 1974.

———. *Anamnesis*. Notre Dame, Ind.: University of Notre Dame Press, 1978.

———. *Order and History*. Vol. 3, *Plato and Aristotle*. Baton Rouge: Louisiana State University Press, 1987.

Walsh, David. *After Ideology: Recovering the Spiritual Foundations of Freedom*. San Francisco: Harper Collins, 1990.

Weber, Max. *The Protestant Ethic and the Spirit of Capitalism*. Translated by Talcott Parsons. New York: Scribner, 1976.

Webster, Daniel. *Select Speeches of Daniel Webster, 1817–1845*. Boston: Heath, 1893.

White, Kermit Escus. "Abraham Lincoln and Christianity." Ph.D. diss., Boston University, 1954.

White, Ronald C., Jr. *Lincoln's Greatest Speech: The Second Inaugural*. New York: Simon & Schuster, 2002.

Williams, Frank J., William D. Pederson, and Vincent J. Marsala, eds. *Abraham Lincoln: Sources and Style of Leadership*. Westport, Conn.: Greenwood Press, 1994.

Williams, T. Harry. "Abraham Lincoln—Principle and Pragmatism in Politics: A Review Article." *Mississippi Valley Historical Review* 40 (1953): 89–106.

———. *Lincoln and the Radicals*. Madison: University of Wisconsin Press, 1972.

Wills, Garry. *Inventing America: Jefferson's Declaration of Independence*. Garden City, N.Y.: Doubleday, 1978.

———. *Lincoln at Gettysburg: The Words That Remade America*. New York: Simon & Schuster, 1992.

Wilson, Edmund. "Abraham Lincoln: The Union as Religious Mysticism." In *Eight Essays*. Garden City, N.Y.: Doubleday, 1954.

———. *Patriotic Gore: Studies in the Literature of the American Civil War*. New York: Oxford University Press, 1962.

Wish, Harvey, ed. *Ante-Bellum Writings of George Fitzhugh and Hinton Rowan Helper on Slavery*. New York: Capricorn Books, 1960.

Wolf, William J. *The Religion of Abraham Lincoln*. Published in 1959 as *The Almost Chosen People*. New York: Seabury, 1963.

———. "Lincoln and the Bible." *Presbyterian Life*, July 1, 1964, 6–13.

———. "Abraham Lincoln and Calvinism." In *Calvinism and the Political Order*, edited by George L. Hunt, 140–56. Philadelphia: Westminster, 1965.

———. *Freedom's Holy Light*. Wakefield, Mass.: Paramater, 1977.

Wood, Gordon S. *The Creation of the American Republic, 1776–1787.* Chapel Hill: University of North Carolina Press, 1969.

Zuckert, Michael. "Abraham Lincoln and the Problem of Civil Religion." In *Law and Philosophy: The Practice of Theory: Essays in Honor of George Anastaplo,* vol. 2, edited by John A. Murley, Robert L. Stone, and William T. Braithwaite, 720–43. Athens: Ohio University Press, 1992.

INDEX